SHIPWRECK_
———— OF THE ————
DEVON COAST

SHIPWRECKS
—— OF THE ——
DEVON COAST

Richard
Larn

COUNTRYSIDE BOOKS
NEWBURY, BERKSHIRE

First paperback edition 1996

© Richard Larn 1996

COUNTRYSIDE BOOKS
3 Catherine Road
Newbury, Berkshire

ISBN 1 85306 400 9

Cover illustration: *Shows the wreck of the Green Ranger,
driven onto rocks at Longpeak in November 1962*

Designed by Mon Mohan

Produced through MRM Associates Ltd, Reading
Typeset by Textype Typesetters, Cambridge
Printed by J.W. Arrowsmith Ltd, Bristol

CONTENTS

The Glen Strathallan being sunk off Bovisand, Plymouth Sound, 27 April 1970. See also page 42.

INTRODUCTION

In all of England, no counties other than Devon and Cornwall have coastlines that front two different sea areas, and this is not their only common feature. Indeed, a stranger could readily mistake one for the other, since they have equally bleak north coasts, with many miles of high unbroken and inhospitable cliffs and headlands, but a common softer coastline on the opposite side. Both north coasts are devoid of any major port or haven, whilst they abound on the south, and both counties have an exceptional record of shipping losses.

In Devon, devoid of any deep water harbours of refuge, the northern ports of Clovelly, Bideford, Barnstaple, Appledore or Ilfracombe were capable only of offering shelter to small craft, which alone has been the direct cause of many shipwrecks. The majority of the 600 wrecks on the North Devon coastline carried either Welsh coal, Cornish tin or copper, or were simply fishing and only the decline of these industries brought about an equal decline in the number of ship losses. Lundy Island, the great three-mile-long high granite platform off Hartland Point, in whose lee countless thousands of ships have sheltered in bad weather, has witnessed some 200 ship losses, but as elsewhere, many unrecorded vessels must have gone down at night due to collision or storm with all hands, passing into history in some distant Port Register as a simple hand written entry, 'reported missing'.

The south coasts of both Cornwall and Devon are far less severe, with more headlands, wide sweeping bays, lower cliffs and a number of major ports, Plymouth in particular being the second largest harbour and anchorage on the entire south coast of England. Some 800 vessels have been lost on the 150 miles of South Devon coast in direct contact with the sea, a much smaller proportion being in the coasting trade, with many more 'deep-sea' ships, including barques, liners and large steamships, motor-vessels, men o'war and modern warships, representative of the overall variety of international shipping which continues to use the English Channel.

This volume is a completely revised and updated edition of the original *Devon Shipwrecks* published by David & Charles in 1974, and has benefited from much additional research and correspondence with shipwreck enthusiasts, and remains the most comprehensive general work on Devon's shipwrecks to date. The Index of Ships contains every Devon shipwreck known to me, including many that were saved, and it is sub-divided for easy reference into South Devon, North Devon and Lundy Island. The sheer number of shipping incidents makes it impossible to detail each and every one in its respective chapter, but by cataloguing the name and date of every known loss, readers are provided with sufficient information to carry out their own additional research.

Richard and Bridget Larn
Charlestown, Cornwall
Autumn 1996

1

Plymouth Sound and the Eddystone

Described appropriately as 'the cradle of British seafarers', there was once a time when every leading town in Devon was a seaport of considerable standing. Certainly by the latter half of the 16th century, Devon was England's foremost seafaring county, its activities centred around Plymouth and Dartmouth. In the case of the former, the rivers Tamar, Tavy, Lynher and Plym, all of which flow into the sea, have combined to scour out the huge natural anchorage known today as Plymouth Sound, which has been a major contributory factor in the naval history of the British Isles.

Obviously, ships both large and small were being wrecked on the Devon coast from the earliest times. Of Plymouth itself, in 1794 it was said: 'wrecks often happen under Mount Batten and other eminences near the town', but records of shipwrecks in the area go back to 1362, when, for example, 'Hugo de Courteney and two other commissioners were appointed to hear and determine a case relating to spoil of wreck of a ship called the *Tarrit*. The offence was seizure of wreck at Plymouth belonging to the king.' Cross-Channel raids by the Bretons were frequent, and despite a chain boom across the harbour mouth, the crews of ships and the occupants of Sutton were forced to flee into the countryside on more than one occasion, leaving unattended vessels which were set on fire and lost. Even the Turks ventured as far as Plymouth looking for galley slaves, and in 1640 the bays of Wembury and Cawsand were strewn with abandoned ships, deliberately run ashore and wrecked rather than be allowed to fall into enemy hands.

The earliest wreck incident recorded in any detail was that of the *Lavinia*, a prize vessel captured from the French, which dragged her anchors until she went ashore on St Nicholas Isle in December 1603; whilst the first record of an entire fleet being endangered concerned the Duke of Buckingham, who had recently returned from Ile de Rhe. His

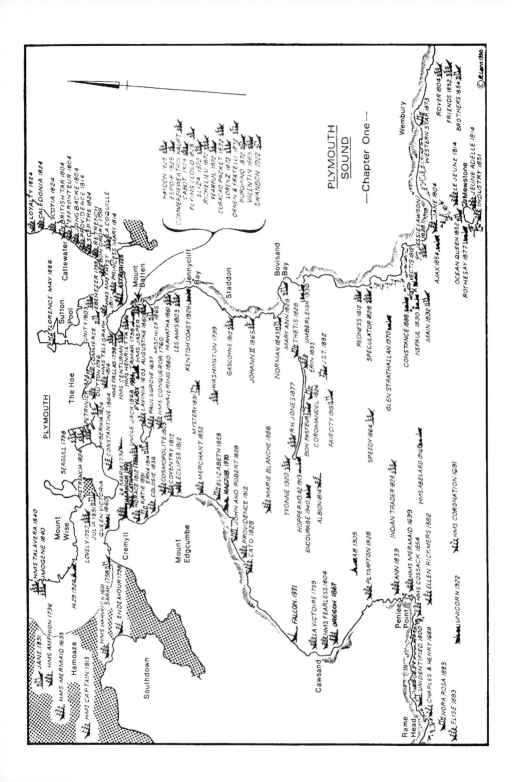

PLYMOUTH
SOUND
—Chapter One—

© R. Larn 1986

ships were caught at anchor during a severe gale on 26 November 1627, and by morning 15 of them were ashore in the Hamoaze and five in the Cattewater. How many of these, if any, were saved is not known, but iron cannon have frequently been dredged up from the mud. Several were raised during 1972, but could not be accurately dated apart from being of typical 16th century construction.

The closing months of 1689 saw a series of severe gales that played havoc with vessels both in and outside the Sound. A six gun fireship of 120 tons, the *Charles and Henry*, was lost somewhere close to Plymouth on 29 November, and on Christmas Day, the man o'war *Centurion*, 34 guns, 513 tons (bm), built by Pett & Ratcliffe in 1650, was lost on Mount Batten, along with the 62 gun *Henrietta*, launched in the Thames in 1654 as the *Langport*, only to be renamed in 1660. Of the many disasters concerning naval ships at Plymouth, the greatest loss of life occurred in the foundering of the 2nd rate *Coronation*, on 3 September 1691 during a gale, which also claimed the 60 gun, 3rd rate *Harwich*. The incident is best described in the words of Edward Barlow, who wrote:

'... and Admiral Russell being come up as far as Plymouth, and our coast being a lee shore to southerly winds, it then blowing hard and fearing bad weather, Admiral Russell bore up and sailed into Plymouth Sound. A great part of the fleet followed him, and running so hastily one upon another, caused many of them to run on board of one another. Some ran into the Cattewater, and in running into the Hamoaze, three or four ran ashore, one of them of 60 odd guns, named the *Harwich*, which was bilged and lost along with 420 men, the rest getting off much damaged. The *Coronation*, coming into the Sound and her anchor being let go, veered out cable to bring her up. She took a salley and sank down to rights in about 22 fathoms, having on board about 500 men, and not above 20 of them saved, and a ship of 90 guns, a very dreadful accident and a great loss, the cause of which is scarce known.'

The *Harwich*, of 993 tons (bm), built by Deane of Harwich in 1674, was in fact a 70 gun vessel and not 60 as suggested by Barlow, whilst the *Coronation*, of 1,346 tons (bm) had been launched at Portsmouth dockyard in 1685.

Following a long underwater search off Rame Head by a team of divers led by Peter McBride, which included the author, the upper deck remains of the *Coronation* were found in 1977, less than one mile off Penlee Point in 18 metres of water. The site, which contained three anchors and 15 iron guns, was identified from material which had fallen from her decks when she capsized, including the ship's bell, found intact, and a magnificent silver dish, bearing the crest of Captain Skelton. The main hull section of the *Coronation*, with her remaining guns, was located close inshore in Lady cove, in ten metres of water, and it is surprising that despite the close proximity of a naval dockyard with all the necessary lifting equipment even at that time, that her cannon and anchors had not been recovered. The *Harwich* had been run ashore under Mount Edgcumbe, where dockyard staff were able to remove all her guns, stores and rigging, after which the hull was sold to a Joseph Bingham on 20 February 1693 for breaking.

Following the loss of the *Harwich*, the Admiralty then buoyed the main channel leading into the Hamoaze, each bearing the name of some famous ship such as *Albermarle*, *Vanguard*, *Panther*, *Melampus* and *Asia*. There may be some truth that these names refer to vessels that actually struck reefs or went ashore in the vicinity, but this theory has not been substantiated. The reef known today as *Asia* was in fact, named *Africa* on charts prior to 1780.

Wrecks around the turn of the 18th century included two named *Mermaid*. The first of these, a 174 ton fireship, was accidentally burned on 25 February 1693, the other, a 5th rate, 32 gun frigate, foundered with all hands at the mouth of Plymouth Sound on 5 January 1699. Although not strictly wrecks in the accepted terms, the 36 gun prize *Saudadoes*, the 6th rate *Dunwich*, and the 4th rate *Moor*, were all deliberately sunk at Mount Batten as breakwaters, or foundations for breakwaters, between 1712 and 1716, to be joined by the *Vengeance* in October 1766.

The sloop *Lovely*, a victim of storm, drove from her moorings in 1757 to sink off the naval victualling yard, and in 1758 the *Sarah* struck a rock in coming down the Tamar after loading coal. She drifted off to sink in deep water near Cremyll passage, unlike the 70-gun *Conqueror*, only two years old when she went ashore on the south-east corner of St Nicholas Isle on 26 October 1760 to become a total wreck. At the court martial held aboard the *Barfleur*, the pilot was found to be 'highly blameable in getting the ship underway in such weather as prevailed at the time, and from his want of knowledge as a seaman, did not direct the proper sails to be set, by which neglect the *Conqueror* drove to leeward and was stranded'. The unfortunate pilot, Henry Harris, was confined in Marshalsea prison for 18 months.

Credit for the first successful submarine must go to the American, David Bushnell (1776), but there were many others experimenting and striving for the same goal, although the motives of some were doubtful. Amongst these was a Mr Day, who conducted two experiments at Plymouth, the latter regrettably proving fatal. It would appear that his talents were more mercenary than technical, since he was described as, '. . . a man, very illiterate and indigent in his circumstances. He was bred with no particular trade, but had been employed as a labourer amongst ships' carpenters at Yarmouth, his native place'. For reasons best known to himself, he had pursued his project for many years, and in fact conducted his first 'experiment' in the comparatively shallow Cattewater, where he remained underwater, inside a 'submarine vessel' for a full six hours of an ebb tide, followed by the flood, before unscrewing two pins that retained some ballast, thereby allowing the device to rise to the surface.

Mr Day approached a Charles Blake in 1774 with a scheme whereby wagers could be won, confident that he could remain underwater in 20 fathoms for six hours. Invited to London by his new sponsor, Day prepared a model of his device, then returned to Plymouth where a shipwright named Hunn accepted the task of converting a suitable vessel. That chosen was the 50 ton sloop *Maria*, purchased from a Mr Sparks for the sum of £350.

The experiment was conducted on 20 June 1774, when the refitted *Maria* was towed round to Millbay, where Day entered the chamber, taking with him, 'a hammock, watch, small wax taper, a bottle of water, and two ship's biscuits'. The hatch being sealed, the vessel was towed to a position given as, '150 fathoms offshore from Firestone Bay, due north of St Nicholas Isle.' Supervised by the sponsor, the flooding plugs were withdrawn, but she refused to sink, despite ten tons of ballast within the hull, and 20 tons hanging on the release bolts. A further 20 tons were added before finally she went under at 8 am, touching bottom in 30 metres of water. Moments later there was a violent ebullition of air and the surface boats expected a signal, but none came.

The appointed time for the vessel to return to the surface was 2 pm, and as the hour approached the Hoe became crowded with spectators, many of whom had wagers on the outcome. By late afternoon it was obvious that something had gone wrong, but a whole night was allowed to pass before the assistance of the Dockyard Superintendent, Lord Sandwich, was sought. Full use of the facilities was made available, and literally hundreds of men were employed sweeping for the wreck. At Mr Day's insistence, all projections and lifting attachments to aid salvage had been removed, leaving nothing on which grapnels could fasten. Finally located

On passage to the West Indies with troops, the English East Indiaman
Dutton *had been at sea seven weeks when she returned to Plymouth, to be
lost under the Hoe, 26 January 1796.*

in 22 fathoms, it was 3 August before ropes were swept beneath the vessel
and hauled taut.

The *Maria* was lifted on the tide and moved 90 metres to the south, only
to slip from her cradle and disappear again. Relocation and sweeping
wasted another month, and just as a second lift into shallow water
commenced on 21 October, a gale caused work to be abandoned. Mr Blake
then returned to London, unable to neglect his business any further, and
the wreck with its presumably drowned occupant was abandoned.

This minor tragedy was followed by a long succession of wrecks at the
Hoe, Mount Batten, St Nicholas Isle, and unspecified locations in the
Sound, but none of any great consequence until 1796, when two major
losses occurred, the East Indiaman *Dutton* and HMS *Amphion*. Bound for
the West Indies with part of the Queen's 2nd Regiment aboard, the *Dutton*
had already been at sea for seven weeks when her condition forced her
captain to turn back for Plymouth. Whilst making for the Cattewater,
since the open Sound offered little shelter, she struck Mount Batten shoal,

its warning buoy having gone adrift in a recent gale. Rudderless, the *Dutton* was swept helpless on to the rocks beneath the Hoe and within minutes all three masts fell, the entire wreck becoming a tangled mass of rigging and canvas. Panic broke out on board due to lack of leadership, the ship's officers having already abandoned their charge, leaving the remaining crew and passengers to their fate. Despite large numbers of spectators on the Hoe, not one of them made any attempt to effect a rescue, and it was not until Sir Edward Pellew, captain of the man o'war *Indefatigable*, appeared on the scene that anything was done. He risked his life by climbing aboard the *Dutton*, using the same rope by which her officers had escaped, but before leaving the shore he sent a message to his own ship calling for assistance, offering money to any local who would put a boat alongside the wreck.

In reaching the *Dutton*, Sir Edward injured his back when climbing round the fallen mainmast but, undaunted, assumed command and supervised her abandonment. Two boats from the *Indefatigable* arrived alongside, plus another from a schooner, and were instrumental in saving almost 600 lives, thanks to Sir Edward's intervention. The citizens of Plymouth showed their appreciation by awarding him the freedom of the city. The wreck of the *Dutton* made sufficient impression to inspire him to adopt a stranded ship in his crest when he was made a baronet the following year.

Until the end of the 18th century, warship losses continued to predominate in the Plymouth area, and whilst the *Coronation* was the most tragic in terms of lives lost, the most spectacular was that of the *Amphion*, in the Hamoaze. A 5th rate vessel of 680 tons (bm), carrying 32 guns, the *Amphion* had been launched at the royal Chatham yard on 21 December 1780. In September 1796 she was away cruising in the North Sea, on the lookout for signs of Napoleon's threatened invasion, when a gale sprang her foremast, forcing her to return to Plymouth.

The *Amphion* was brought into the Hamoaze on 14 September, placed alongside a sheer hulk, and work began on the removal of her bowsprit and damaged mast. The task was completed by the 21st of the month and orders came aboard for her to sail on the morning of the 23rd. As was the custom, a farewell party was held aboard and wives, children and sweethearts swarmed aboard the frigate, crowding her lower deck. Meanwhile, the ship's officers were dressing for the evening meal. A massive explosion occurred at 4.30 pm on 22 September, which was felt as a violent shock throughout Stonehouse and neighbouring Plymouth.

Even a considerable distance from the dockyard, the sky was seen to be bright red and people thronged the streets in a state of panic, thinking the town was under attack.

When the confusion had died down it was ascertained that the *Amphion* had blown up, fortunately without serious damage to nearby ships. Remarkably, the old receiving hulk *Yarmouth*, only yards away, survived the blast but was found to be well splattered with human remains. Amongst the few eye witnesses to the incident was the signal lieutenant aboard the flagship, moored a short distance downstream. At the inquiry he stated: 'she rose out of the water till part of her keel was visible, and the strangeness of the sight made me feel I was giddy. Almost as quick as the thought passed through my mind, she blew up.' So violent was the explosion that the entire forepart of the *Amphion* disintegrated, while the remainder fell back into the harbour and sank instantly in ten fathoms.

It was never established with any accuracy how many people were aboard at the time, but certainly there were not less than 100 visitors, in addition to her crew of some 215 officers and men. According to contemporary accounts, 300 out of the 312 aboard were killed, only ten men, one woman and a child surviving, some of whom received fearful injuries. The surface of the Hamoaze was strewn with broken timbers, spars and rigging, and 'the deck of the sheer hulk, to which the frigate was lashed, was red with blood and covered with mangled limbs and lifeless trunks, all blackened with powder'.

The accident was blamed on a gunner, said to be stealing gunpowder, who ignited some spilt explosive when drunk, so detonating the forward magazine. During salvage of the shattered forepart, a sack was recovered containing gunpowder concealed beneath a layer of ship's biscuit, which tended to support the allegation. Only a few of the ship's guns were recovered from the deep mud of the harbour and many weeks passed before the stern portion was dragged into the shallows alongside the dockyard wall, where the decomposed corpse of a female floated out from below decks.

On 10 December 1786, a strong gale from the south-west forced two ships to seek shelter in Plymouth Sound, the *Christian Hendrick* of Rotterdam, carrying wheat and cheese, and the Danish brigantine *Die Fraumetta Catharina von Flensburg* bound for Genoa, with a cargo of hemp and leather from St Petersburg. The Dutch vessel was the first to founder, the vessel being swept into Deadman's Bay where the crew scrambled ashore. The 53 ton Danish ship broke from her anchor, struck

St Nicholas Isle and went down under Raven's Cliff, on the west side of the Sound but without loss of life. The wreck site was located in 1973 when divers from the Plymouth Sound Sub-Aqua Club stumbled upon the ship's bell bearing her name, and the first of many hundreds of bales of hides, either reindeer or horse, which are currently being conserved and worked by a Cornish craftsman into a variety of leather goods.

Sheltered though Plymouth Sound might be from prevailing winds, it was open and unprotected from southerly gales and scarcely a month went by without some vessel beating her bottom out in the shallows. On 24 February 1798 a culm-laden schooner, the *Ebenezer*, was wrecked on Batten rocks, and less than two months later the 32 gun frigate *Pallas* was lost in exactly the same place. Commanded by the Hon H. Curzon, she parted her cables and went ashore, huge seas sweeping clean over the wreck. Despite the fact that the *Pallas* was on her beam ends, only one member of her crew lost his life. Three days later her already shattered timbers were joined by those of a large dockyard lighter, the *Tamar*, also put ashore by a gale. Bad weather brought the sloop *Seagull*, carrying coal from Liverpool, scurrying into Plymouth Sound for shelter, only to be driven into Millbay and lost on 17 September of that same year.

Before Christmas there was a repetition of the *Amphion* incident, fortunately with little loss of life, involving the French prize *La Coquille* for 44 guns, taken by Sir Warren off Ireland. One of many such prizes that filled the Cattewater, she blew up while at anchor at the foot of Millbrook Lake. The explosion destroyed her entire quarterdeck and sent the mizzen mast 90 metres into the air. Flames spread quickly to both remaining masts and in less than half an hour she had to be abandoned. Grapples were thrown aboard and the blazing vessel was then towed clear of the anchorage and run ashore on a mudbank north-east of Southdown, setting fire to the coal-laden brig *Endeavour* of Scarborough, on the way. Both vessels burned to the waterline and became total losses.

The gale of February 1799 was described by the *Gentleman's Magazine* as being, 'the most severe hurricane ever remembered at Plymouth'. The privateer *Bon Orde* was stranded and wrecked in the Cattewater, and the *La Victoire* went ashore and was lost in Cawsand Bay shortly after, in addition to others. In complete contrast, the Liverpool cotton ship *Washington* was lost by fire on 23 October, following the visit of a naval press gang. Her crew took to a specially prepared hiding-place deep down in the hold. Whilst in hiding, the cook dropped his knife and, in searching for it with a naked light, accidentally set some cotton alight. She burned all that day and half the night, and out of the 3,000 bales aboard valued at £30,000 only 350 were saved.

As storm after storm swept through the Sound, so they left behind an increasing trail of wrecked ships, drowned seamen, and impoverished owners. On Christmas Day 1803, a French prize named *Les Amis*, an unidentified brig, the privateer *Cosmopolite*, the *Unity* and several smaller craft were all wrecked. The larger of these, the 20 year old prize had been on passage from Martinique to Bordeaux with 178 hogsheads of sugar and 38 of coffee when she was captured by HMS *Malta*. After being blown ashore, her stern fell completely off and it became necessary to call on Col Longnead's battalion of Plymouth volunteers to mount guard over the cargo that lay scattered along the shore. A captain, two subalterns, and 40 rank and file remained on duty all night, during which time they fired several shots at water pirates who attempted to come in from seaward to plunder. The *Unity*, a brig carrying coal and pipe staves from Liverpool to Jersey, went down in Deadman's Bay with a sick member of her crew still in his bunk. By some remarkable act of providence, he floated up from the wreck long after she sank and was picked up alive.

Another gale on 19-20 January 1804 was particularly severe and ten vessels were lost in the area, including the brig o'war *Fearless* in Cawsand; the *British Tar*; *L'Effronteur*, a captured French privateer; the *Jong Backe*; and two fishing sloops, all of which sank in the Cattewater, whilst the *Jane* foundered close to the Mewstone. Still blowing hard, the wind swung from south-west to south-east on the 25th, causing many vessels to slip their cables and capsizing a large pinnace belonging to HMS *Prince* between St Nicholas Isle and Redding Point. Of the eleven men aboard, only one survived, the accident taking place in exactly the same place and in the same manner as that in which Capt Drew of HMS *Cerebus* and Capt Pulling of the *Kangaroo* had been drowned a few years earlier. Such accidents to store, liberty and prison boats amongst the fleet were commonplace. On 17 January 1805 a launch from the 110 gun *Hibernia* was upset and sunk on the Rennies, between the Shagstone and the mainland, with a midshipman and 23 seamen drowned. Several of the men in this particular incident were survivors from HMS *Venerable*, wrecked the previous year in Torbay.

In one respect, the first decade of the 19th century was dramatic and exciting for Plymouth, for during this period literally thousands of prize vessels were brought into the Sound, where they were either taken into the king's service or else stripped of their valuables and auctioned. These prizes brought wealth to just about everyone in some measure; the crews of the capturing ships enjoyed prize money; the monarch or government took any treasure aboard; the Navy acquired a number of additional ships; and the people of Plymouth welcomed the extra money that passed into their hands via traders.

Some of these captured vessels were exceptionally wealthy. On 17 January 1805 HMS *Phoenix*, of 44 guns, Capt Halsted, brought in the Spanish *El Mercurio*, whose hold contained 20,000 silver dollars, 300 ounces of gold dust, 80,000 animal horns, 140 barrels of tallow, 150 bales of wool, plus beef, copper, hides and cocoa. Later that month, the Spanish frigate *Santa Gertruda* was escorted in by the *Polyhemus*, and swelled the national coffers by over one and a half million silver dollars. It took seven carts, each drawn by four horses, to transfer the specie from the vessel to the Citadel, and later to London, but this was by no means the richest prize of them all. In March 1805, the 'Flying' *Pallas* as she was known, later wrecked on the east coast of Scotland, brought in a Spaniard with diamonds, gold and silver bullion, in addition to over £1m in coin.

The continuing stream of naval and merchant vessels wrecked annually in the vicinity of Plymouth were more than an embarrassment to those in authority, who really needed no reminder that something must be done to make Plymouth a safer anchorage. Several proposals for a breakwater were investigated and eventually a suitable design was chosen by the Master Attendants of the Woolwich and Plymouth dockyards, Joseph Whidby and Samuel Hemans respectively, in collaboration with John Rennie, who carried out the actual survey.

The decision to start work in August 1812 was accelerated by the wreck of the 38 gun frigate *Amethyst*. A 5th rate man o'war, built at Deptford in 1799, she drove from her anchorage in the Sound on 16 February 1811 in a west-southwesterly gale and went ashore shortly after midnight. Although her masts were cut down, she filled so quickly that her crew took to the boats immediately, all six of which were swamped within minutes and their occupants drowned. Various warships and transports sent boats to assist, but these too, capsized and were lost. The exact number of men who died that night is uncertain, since many pressed seamen from the *Amethyst* are known to have reached shore and promptly deserted. Contemporary accounts of the incident suggest that some 300 corpses were buried locally.

Naturally, progress on such a vast undertaking as this new breakwater was slow, its centre section alone being over 1,000 metres long, which did not include the canted arms at each end, roughly 110 metres each, so that when a particularly severe gale struck Plymouth on 18 October 1812, it offered no protection whatsoever. By morning, the new West Indiaman *Coventry* was found ashore and wrecked, along with the *Eclipse*, *Gascoyne*, *Horrace*, *Providence* and *Redness*, plus the *General Gates*, a detained American ship. By the end of 1813 the breakwater showed above the surface at low tide over its entire length, and there were official prophecies that no more wrecks would occur in the Sound, but that year, and for many more to come, there was no significant reduction in the annual total.

On 23 March of that same year HMS *Captain*, previously a 3rd rate, 74 gun ship converted to a hulk, caught fire in the Hamoaze and was completely destroyed. Over 200 cannon shots were fired into her waterline by guns hastily removed from the decks of other ships and mounted in launches, but it took three hours to send her to the bottom, by which time there was very little of value remaining. A Fowey-owned lighter, carrying sand for use on the breakwater, sank when overwhelmed by rough seas on 3 September, and a Portsmouth hoy went down on 1 December after striking the Shagstone. She left Plymouth with 52 people aboard, under the command of Capt John Davis. The apprentice was at the helm when, mistaking the outline of the Shagstone for a sail, he luffed up and caused the vessel to strike the rock. Those below decks were drowned in their bunks, and the few that managed to climb into the shrouds were thrown into the sea when she fell over on her starboard side. Thirty-six lives were lost, including ten marines, 16 women, three children and a number of Cornish miners.

A sharp fall in barometric pressure on 12 December 1814 forecast bad weather, and during the subsequent gale the *Providence* went ashore in the Cattewater, the *Jeune Adelle* became a total wreck on the Mewstone, and many other vessels suffered damage or lost their anchors. But this was minor compared with the storm of 18 January 1817 which, coinciding with exceptionally high tides, caused damage that was nothing short of appalling. As if intent on wreaking as much havoc as possible among shipping in the Sound, the strong wind from the south-east swung round to south-west and continued to oscillate between these points, steadily increasing in strength until by 4 pm it had reached hurricane force. Late that afternoon, three vessels were wrecked in close proximity to each other at Batten, and 180 metres of the still unfinished structure across the mouth of the Sound was torn up by the sea. Individual granite blocks, weighing five tons and over, were thrown completely over the breakwater, and a survey showed that at least 1,000 tons of stonework had been disturbed. HMS *Jasper*, a brig o'war carrying 67 persons, of whom 15 were females, was wrecked on Bears Head, Mount Batten, and all but two lost their lives. One of the survivors, able seaman John Bere, was on the forecastle when she struck. He grasped a rope hanging from the main yard and swung himself outboard, intending to drop into the sea and swim ashore. To his astonishment, he landed squarely in a small boat adrift in the Sound, which was then washed on to some rocks from which he was able to wade to safety.

Another warship, HMS *Telegraph*, previously the American privateer *Vengeance*, dragged three anchors clean across the Sound, finally going beam-on to the rocks under the eastern Hoe. William Kells was the only member of her crew to lose his life, being crushed to death between decks while trying to recover some personal property. Mr Dick, the ship's surgeon, despite a fractured leg, not only saved his wife from drowning but managed to get a line ashore, by which means the crew were saved.

Another victim of this storm was the packet ship *Princess Mary*, from Jamaica. She went down in Deadman's Bay with the loss of her master, Capt Gidley, his wife and son, brother-in-law, and two crew. The Gidleys had been married shortly before the vessel left England, and on its return, learning that it had overshot Falmouth and entered Plymouth, Mrs Gidley, her newborn son and brother, journeyed by road from Cornwall and embarked for the short passage back to Penryn. All six bodies were later recovered from the sea and laid side by side in the back room of the King's Arms before burial in a common grave. The *Western Daily Mercury* gave a graphic insight into what followed: 'The three wrecks filled the lower classes of the port with rejoicing, their sole object being pillage. Hundreds, if not thousands of them are to be viewed in all directions, bearing off portions of the wrecks not merely by hand, but in buckets, barrows, by hand carts, and all are heard to be congratulating each other on what they jocularly call Godsends.'

Further damage to the seaward face of the breakwater occurred in 1824, on 23 November, when something like 22 vessels went down in the Cattewater. A total of 730 metres of stonework was thrown out of position, most of it rolling over to the northern side and reducing the gradient of the seaward slope from three to five-in-one. For some time Rennie had recommended that the authorities take a lesson from nature and let the sea dictate the best slope. Although he never lived to see the

The South Shields registered barque Oregon, *which drove ashore under Fort Picklecombe, 4 March 1833 and became a total loss.*

change, the 1824 hurricane convinced the government and brought about a permanent alteration in the breakwater's seaward gradient.

The most remarkable incident that night concerned the ketch *Coromandel*. Bound from Portugal to the Downs with cork, for orders, the *Coromandel* was capsized by heavy seas when close to the Eddystone. Only two of her crew were on deck at the time, the helmsman and lookout, both of whom disappeared and presumably drowned, leaving Capt Renton, the two remaining crew, and a passenger in the unenviable position of being trapped in the cabin of an inverted vessel. In complete darkness, with the water level rising by the minute, the four terrified men crept inside part of the bilge used to store coal, remaining there with water up to their chins for over six hours. Fortunately, the ketch drifted towards Plymouth instead of out to sea and eventually impaled itself on a sunken projection on the breakwater, allowing the trapped men to escape at low tide.

What part, if any, the Plymouth lifeboat played in all this drama is uncertain, since no mention of it can be found in local newspapers or lifeboat reports. That one existed is in no doubt, since a Greathead boat, built at South Shields, had been installed since 20 July 1803, but appears to have simply rotted away in its boathouse. A second lifeboat appeared in service here in April 1826, but this, too, seems to have remained unused and was eventually transferred to the Isles of Scilly.

As the 19th century progressed, so the annual total of wreck incidents around the Plymouth area increased, and never a winter went by without the Sound being strewn with ships' timbers and rigging. At the height of a heavy easterly gale on 5 December 1838, the Boston schooner *Commerce* left the Hamoaze for the Cattewater to take in ballast. When off the Hoe, the wind veered and she was forced to anchor, but later dragged and went ashore under the Citadel. No sooner had she been refloated at high water than the gale swung southerly and she went ashore for a second time, eventually going to pieces. That same afternoon the French brig *Colosie* entered the Sound, anchoring between St Nicholas Isle and the shore, but parted her cables and was wrecked in Sandy Bay. Her mate gallantly attempted to swim a rope ashore but was drowned in the attempt, the remaining crew eventually being rescued by the revenue cutter *Harly*.

It is interesting to note at this stage that although the number of merchant vessels lost was on the increase, incidents involving naval ships had taken a sharp, inexplicable decline. Only three warships were lost during a ten-year period, and two of these, the 74 gun, 3rd rate *Talavera*, and the 26 gun *Imogene*, were the result of a severe dockyard fire. In September 1840 a blaze, thought to have started in one of the saw pits, spread to the old Adelaide gallery and in addition to causing the loss of two warships was a national calamity, since it destroyed some of the most historic and valuable relics of the Royal Navy. In the Adelaide gallery were stored the mementoes of many a hard-won battle and famous men; in addition to literally scores of figureheads, there was the flag under which Nelson had fought and died at Trafalgar, the banner carried by the *Queen Charlotte* at the bombardment of Algiers, and other irreplaceable items. The flames which devastated almost half the dockyard soon set fire to the heavy coating of tar on the *Talavera*, *Imogene* and *Minden*, only the last being saved by the efforts of twelve fire engines.

At the south-east corner of Plymouth Sound, where the high cliffs of Wembury sweep towards the Yealm estuary, lies the Great Mewstone, a tall rocky island, some half a mile offshore. Already mentioned in connection with previous wrecks, the island has been the scene of several others. The Jersey-owned smack *Industry* was lost here on 16 January 1851, and on 26 December 1852, a 206 ton brig from London with a general cargo, the *Ocean Queen*, went down on the Little Mewstone with the loss of 14 of her 15 crew. It was here, too, that the first steamer wreck in the vicinity of Plymouth occurred, on 13 October 1854, despite a calm sea and perfect visibility. The London-registered *Ajax*, with a general cargo and almost 300 passengers, hit the rock in broad daylight and became a total loss. In the report rendered by the local coastguards, the duty officer wrote: 'it was either done purposely, or else from sheer culpable negligence.' Perhaps he was influenced by the knowledge that the same captain had lost another steamer, the *Minerva*, in August. Twelve years later the fishing vessel *Matilda* was passing the Mewstone on 1 March 1866 when she struck the engines of the *Ajax* which still lay just awash, and sank. From the crew of three, only a boy, William Bunce, survived.

Evidence of an early wreck on the Mewstone comes from a number of iron cannon on the seabed and currently an underwater archaeological survey is being carried out to determine its identity, a task made difficult by the presence of pieces of the *Ajax* in the area, plus the remains of another steamer, the *Rothesay*, which sank on 15 October 1877. This 332 ton coasting vessel, built in Hull in 1874, became a total wreck while on passage from Caen to Cardiff in ballast. She called at Dartmouth for bunkers and, rather foolishly, her captain took her to sea in the teeth of a gale. Unable to weather the force eleven wind, she was blown inshore, struck a rock and sank. At low water, a dozen or more holes were to be seen in her hull; in addition, both stem and stern posts had been broken off and the propeller shaft snapped.

It hardly seems credible today that anyone could make a home on the Mewstone, but it is a fact that, in 1774, a local man guilty of some petty misdemeanour was sentenced by a magistrate to be 'transported' to the island for seven years. He remained there quietly with his family for the entire period without once setting foot on the mainland. His daughter, known as 'Black Bess', elected to remain behind when the time came for the family to leave. She eventually married and had three children on the Mewstone before her husband was drowned after falling off a rock.

Located eight miles offshore, the Eddystone reef needs no introduction since its infamous reputation is well known. It was Walter Whitfeld who first proposed a lighthouse here in 1691. It was to be built at his own expense provided certain patent rights were granted in return, but the government declined his offer. Already the scene of numerous wrecks, in 1696 the *Snowdrop* hit the rocks and disappeared with her crew of 60, followed by the brig *Constant* on Christmas Eve of the same year. The latter had belonged to a London mercer named Henry Winstanley, who was merrymaking at his home with fellow aldermen when two survivors from the wreck arrived and demanded admittance, having walked from Plymouth. This was the second vessel Winstanley had lost to the Eddystone and he vowed 'that no vessel of mine will cross the Channel whilst this menace to life and property remains without a beacon'. Patents were sought, building began in 1696, and for four years the tarred timber and stone construction rose above the surface, the first light being displayed on 14 November 1698. During a routine visit, Winstanley was marooned in the lighthouse by bad weather and forced to stay the night. During the hours of darkness of 27 November 1703, huge seas toppled the entire iron structure into the boiling cauldron around the reef, taking its keepers and builder to their death.

That the Eddystone light was missed is in no doubt, for only days after its destruction a richly laden Virginian, the *Winchelsea* was wrecked with few survivors. For three years the Eddystone remained unmarked, then, in 1706, the Trinity Brethren obtained permission from Parliament to build, or grant a lease to have built, a second beacon, the latter option being taken up by Capt Lovet for a period of 99 years. Just why Lovet chose John Rudyerd, the proprietor of a silk shop on Ludgate Hill, to design his lighthouse is uncertain. Nevertheless, this son of a Cornish labourer produced a design, the beacon was built, lit in July 1706, completed in 1709, and lasted for 46 years.

During the early hours of 2 December 1755 the tower was found to be on fire, and one can well imagine the awful predicament in which the keepers found themselves as they retreated from the flames. Red-hot sections of iron, blazing timbers and molten lead poured down on them, and one keeper died after ingesting the liquid metal, a 7oz piece of lead being found in his stomach, which is preserved in the Royal College of Surgeons, Edinburgh. The lighthouse was again completely destroyed and, Capt Lovet having since died, his interest was acquired by Robert Weston who obtained the services of John Smeaton for the next attempt to tame the rock.

Smeaton's tower was the only one to withstand gale after gale without damage, and it continued to do so for the best part of 125 years, when it was replaced by the existing building. The old lighthouse was dismantled and re-erected on the Hoe, where it still stands.

If the record of vessels actually lost on the reef itself is sparse, it is well compensated for by the dozens that have been lost in the vicinity, vessels such as the *Mary Laing*, carrying coal from Newcastle to Quebec. She sprang a leak on 30 April 1851 and attempted to reach the lighthouse, but when within a few miles, her pumps choked and she sank. Similarly, the Brixham schooner *Faith*, also coal-laden, sank close at hand on 6 September that same year after collision with the Plymouth-owned sloop *Fear Not*. In 1853, on 21 February, the emigrant ship *Bolton*, Capt Darby, on passage from Plymouth to Sydney, ran down and sank the pollacca *Thomas and Nancy* within sight of the reef, whilst the brig *Aire*, of Goole, foundered when overwhelmed by a gale on New Year's Day 1861.

Risk of collision, even today, is an occupational hazard for fishing vessels which choose to work the grounds south of the Eddystone, and a great many local boats have been lost with all hands. The *Little Florie*, a London brigantine built at Littlehampton in 1862, was on passage from her home port of Nassau on 26 January 1864 when she struck and sank an unlit trawler three miles off the lighthouse, and to this day the vessel remains unidentified. Similarly, the Glasgow-registered *Haiti* and Plymouth trawler *Gazelle* collided on 3 March 1864, and the Norwegian *Ceres* was run down and sunk by a ship that failed to stop on 18 August 1864. Two years later, the locally owned sloop *Constantine*, having picked up a cargo of pigs at Treginier was south-southwest of the Eddystone when the smack *Spring*, of Faversham, ran into her. The larger vessel's bowsprit, main boom and several sails were carried away, in addition to starting a serious leak. With distress signals flying, the *Constantine* limped into Plymouth, settling lower by the minute, until off Drake's Island she filled and sank on 3 March.

Only one steamer has been lost on the Eddystone reef itself, this being the 501 ton *Hiogo* of Sunderland. She left London for Japan on 28 September 1867 and all went well until off Start Point. It was during the second mate's watch that the Eddystone light was sighted, but when informed, in accordance with his orders, Capt Bainton refused to go on deck or to allow any alteration of course. Incredible though it may sound, the second mate continued to plead for instructions for a further hour and, even when the steamer was within yards of the reef, would not order a change of course himself, with the result that the *Hiogo* struck on the north side and became a total loss. At the subsequent Board of Trade enquiry the certificates of both master and second mate Johnson were suspended for twelve months, for having by joint default contributed to the loss of their ship.

An unidentified shipwreck, possibly an old naval vessel converted into a prison hulk, c1850, but more likely to be an old merchant vessel since the gunports appear painted only.

Meanwhile the Sound continued to claim vessel after vessel, despite the completion of the breakwater. The 80 ton sloop *Ocean*, of Boston, hit the structure on 2 February 1853 and literally fell apart, fortunately without loss of life, while the British ironclad HMS *Cossack*, had a narrow escape in October 1854 when she went ashore at Penlee Point. Under orders for Sheerness for repairs before joining the North American station, she hit the Draystone when leaving the Sound, stove in her forward bilges, broke off her forefoot and false keel, and badly damaged her engine. Admiralty tugs pulled her off the same day, returning her to Devonport for expensive repairs. Only a short distance away the *Mary Ann*, of Looe, was in collision with the steamer *Nile* on 24 November 1854, the former sinking with the loss of one life. Ironically, the *Nile* was herself lost on the Stones reef, near Hayle, Cornwall, only a week later.

A most unusual wreck at Plymouth was that of the 906 ton ship *Havering*, of London, lost as a direct result of mutiny. Built on the Tyne in 1849 the *Havering*, Capt Rickaby, left London on 8 March 1860 for Hong Kong with Government stores. By 30 March she was well out into the Atlantic but leaking badly, having encountered repeated gales. Her crew then refused to obey any orders which would take the vessel further from home, demanding that they turn back to have the leaks repaired and their quarters and bedding dried out. Capt Rickaby attempted to compromise, offering to get the carpenter to do his utmost, but the crew still refused to work. A pilot was taken on board from a passing cutter to act as an independent witness, while the ship's Articles were read, part of which referred to the punishment for mutiny. This had no effect on the crew, and the *Havering* turned back for Plymouth.

On arrival in the Sound, she was inspected by the company surveyor, who found nothing wrong with the ship, but still the refractory crew refused to sail. The captain then went ashore to seek legal aid, but whilst in Devonport obtaining a warrant for the crews' arrest, was advised that his ship was ashore on Batten reef. Returning on board by means of a pilot boat, Capt Rickaby learnt that his crew had stood around and done nothing as the ship dragged her anchors and went up on the rocks. Some of the men were persuaded to man the bilge pump, but gave up after half an hour, went below with the remainder to collect their belongings and walked off, leaving their ship to become a total wreck.

The majority of steamship wrecks in the Plymouth Sound area have occurred in the vicinity of Shag rock or the Mewstone. The *Ajax* and *Rothesay* have already received mention, but only a short distance from their remains are those of the Bristol Steam Navigation Co's *Constance*, lost on 21 January 1888, and the *Nepaul*, wrecked on 10 December 1890. Registered at Bristol, the 563 ton *Constance* went ashore in calm conditions, but even so three of her crew died, unlike the more fortunate individuals aboard the P & O liner *Nepaul*, all 147 of whom were saved. She was by far the largest steamship to be lost near Plymouth, being 3,550 tons gross, carrying passengers and a general cargo from Calcutta and Marseilles. Shortly after the *Nepaul* struck, the trawler *Baroda*, which had been following in her wake, also grounded on the Shagstone, less than 90 metres clear of the wrecked steamship, and became a total loss.

Only the *Queen Victoria*, of Newcastle, can claim to have been wrecked right inside Plymouth Sound. Owned by Palmer Brothers, this 1,434 ton steamship was carrying a cargo of telegraph cable, shipped by Glass Elliott of Greenwich for the post office authority at Rangoon. The *Queen Victoria* put into Plymouth in early December 1860 for orders, and in accordance with her instructions proceeded on 2 January 1861 to Keyham dockyard to coal ship. Robert Williams, a dockyard pilot was taken aboard for the short journey to Devonport, and all went well until she reached the Vanguard buoy. Here she refused to answer her helm and went aground on Wilderness Point, in Barn Pool. Hawsers were secured to mooring buoys and tugs passed ropes, but despite every assistance she refused to move. The Master Attendant of the Dockyard was put in charge of salvage and for several days lighters, gangs of riggers, and sailors from HMS *Impregnable* were employed in pumping out fresh water and landing her cargo, but still she refused to be refloated. Even with huge cables beneath her hull and secured to lifting lighters to achieve tidal lift, she remained fast. Divers then reported that her hull had cracked in several places, all her stores and cargo were removed and she was broken up where she lay.

The south-westerly gale of 20 February 1861 deserves special mention. The first victim of the elements was the 270 ton French brig *Augustine*, which entered the Sound carrying wheat that afternoon and anchored. At 10.45 pm, at the height of the gale, her cables parted and she drifted towards Mount Batten reef. Just before she struck her crew lowered a boat, into which her master and five men clambered, but barely had time to get the oars out before the ship's mainmast fell on top of them, smashing the boat to pieces. But for the timely intervention of a Brixham fishing sloop which saved Capt Gautier and two men, all its occupants would have drowned. By 3 pm the following day, the wind having roared in from seaward for over 24 hours, the Sound was described as 'a fearful spectacle'. The entire breakwater was often buried beneath huge waves, whilst over 40 merchant and government vessels at anchor heaved and snatched at their cables. On shore, the locals gathered on the Hoe in their thousands, never having previously witnessed such a storm. The next ship lost was the American barque *Hiawatha*, Capt Hall, from New Orleans in ballast. Dragging her anchors, she collided with the *Joseph* and a French barque before bringing up on the west end of the breakwater.

The latter years of the 19th century were eventful as regards shipwrecks generally, for an ever increasing number of vessels were using the English Channel, the peak years for shipwrecks on the coast of the United Kingdom being 1864 for sailing vessels, when 1,741 were lost, and 1880 for

Following a severe gale on 22 November 1865, the Penzance schooner Mischief, *centre vessel of three in this photograph, with the Belgian brig* Espoir, *right, and the Prussian* Commerzieweathin Haupt, *left, drove ashore on Mount Batten and were wrecked.*

steamships. The *Speedy*, a 66 ton schooner of Waterford, carrying coal from Port Talbot, was off Plymouth making between six and seven centimetres of water an hour when her foretopmast collapsed, leaving her so disabled she collided with another vessel. HMS *Geyser* saved the three man crew then took the *Speedy* in tow, but she sank close to the breakwater light. Storm damage brought in the Swedish brig *Johann II* which lay quietly at anchor whilst essential repairs were carried out until, on 22 November 1865 a gale from the south-west caused her to part her cables and she drove ashore. In the same gale, the Penzance schooner *Mischief*, the Belgian brig *Espoir* and the *Commerzieweathin Haupt*, a Mecklenburg brig, were all wrecked on Mount Batten. November 1868 saw the Brixham sloop *Uncle Jack* lost on Drake's Island with all five crew, and a month later the *Cabot* dragged her cables until she fouled the Bideford brig *Flying Cloud*, causing both ships to strand on Batten reef.

During the construction of the breakwater, whilst a refuge for shipwrecked mariners was built on the eastern end, it was not envisaged that the crane erected close at hand would be an alternative means of saving three lives. Caught in the open sea on 26 January 1884 in what was said to be the most violent gale for ten years, the French lugger *Bon Pasteur*, of Noirmutier, carrying phosphate from Le Havre to Bristol, literally rolled her mainmast overboard near the Eddystone. She ran for Plymouth Sound but drove onto the breakwater 100 metres from the lighthouse. A huge sea then picked up the wreck bodily and washed her over the breakwater, but she became caught in the derrick structure. Her crew, by now already in the sea, managed to scramble onto the breakwater, where they climbed up the derrick, remaining there for four and a half hours. They later reached the safety of the lighthouse, the keepers hoisting a flag signal next day indicating 'assistance is required' which brought out the tug *Perseverence*.

Although gales continued to sweep the Sound, inflicting yet more damage and suffering, it was Batten reef that was the cause of the majority of wrecks and which, as a consequence, acquired a somewhat infamous reputation. In one 24 hour period over 8/9 December 1872, the *Eliza*, *Richelieu*, *Fearful*, *Curaccao Packet*, *Lorenz*, *Ornen & Fratelli* and the *Burghino*, all finished up stranded on the reef. Another notorious gale, which began on 14 October 1877 and lasted two whole days, not only put four vessels ashore in Deadman's Bay but also sank two others near the Hoe and wrecked the steamer *Rothersay* close to the Mewstone. This was the last occasion on which a vessel was washed clean over the top of the breakwater, the victim being the Newport barque *R.H. Jones*, of 726 tons, on passage from Bremerhaven to Newport in ballast. Seventeen of the 18 crew aboard lost their lives, in addition to Capt Roberts, his wife and young son. The sole survivor was a German seaman, Alfred Blom, who would certainly have lost his life as well but for the prompt and unselfish action of a naval petty officer named Barnes who, on hearing cries for help while on the upper deck of HMS *Turquoise*, leapt overboard in pitch darkness, and swam to the man's assistance.

Less than a month after the 1872 storm, more evidence of wreck was floating around the entrance to Plymouth and the Wembury coastline. This time it was currants, the cargo of the unfortunate *Western Star*, wrecked near the Yealm estuary on New Year's Day 1873. She was a

During the wreck of an unidentified barque at Balitham, near Plymouth, in November 1880 two crew members lost their lives, one of whom fell from the breeches buoy before reaching the cliff top, as shown in this early illustration.

Bideford schooner of 74 tons, built at Appledore in 1869, on passage from Zante to Plymouth. When close to the Eddystone and enshrouded in thick fog, her master, Silvanus Williams, spoke to the skipper of a sailing trawler who assured him that Plymouth lay to the north-east. When land was eventually sighted, Williams incorrectly identified it as Rame Head, altered course accordingly, and drove ashore.

Exactly how many steamers have gone down within a 15 mile radius of the Eddystone may never be known for certain, but the number is considerable. Thick fog on 4 April 1876 saw the 633 tons gross Cardiff steamship *John Boyle* creeping down Channel, her steam siren mournfully warning of her presence. From out of the murk another steamer loomed up, the *Emma Lawson* of Whitby, carrying cotton seed from Alexandria to Hull. She struck the *John Boyle* a terrific blow, cutting a six foot wide gash in her side forward of the poop. Capt Lewis of the *Emma Lawson* had the presence of mind to keep his engines at full-ahead, which effectively sealed off the hole and gave the 20 man crew of the sinking vessel time to clamber aboard his ship. As he backed away, so the *John Boyle* commenced to settle and 20 minutes later she sank like a stone. In this instance no lives were lost but on 16 October 1882 a more serious collision between the steamers *City of Antwerp* and *Constantia* caused the loss of both ships, with only the captain and three survivors from the former and none from the *Constantia*.

As the 19th century drew to a close, vessels continued to be stranded or wrecked at Plymouth with alarming regularity. An inshore collision close to Penlee Point on 29 November 1882 ended the career of the 307 ton barque *Ellen Rickmers*, one of the famous Bremerhaven fleet of Rickmer ships. The 15 year old wooden vessel, Capt Seghorn, carrying coconuts and ivory, ten crew and one passenger, took a pilot aboard and was about to enter the Sound when she struck the Weymouth brigantine *Guide* and sank in the fairway. One month later the fishing lugger *J.S.T.* of Looe sank in similar circumstances in the eastern entrance, after colliding with the *Agenoria* on 22 December. Batten breakwater, which served to protect the entrance to the Cattewater, claimed the 123 ton German brigantine *Valentin*, after anchoring close at hand on 12 February 1883, only to drag her anchor until she went ashore and broke up, while Rame Head caused the demise of the schooner *Nora Rosa* on 10 May that same year.

Not many vessels have been so fortunate as to have struck the Shagstone and got clear, but such was the luck of the Brixham ketch *Florence May* on New Year's Day 1886. Her crew abandoned ship thinking she would sink

The British s.s. Ariel, *stranded on the rocks in front of the 'Lion's Den', under Plymouth Hoe, 8 December 1896. She remained there for two weeks until refloated and saved, but was later torpedoed and lost off the Bishop Rock.*

any minute, but noticing she remained afloat they reboarded her and sailed into Sutton harbour, where she sank beneath their feet. Later, she was refloated and returned to service, unlike the French *Marie Blanche* which foundered in 15 metres between the breakwater and Picklecombe Fort on 16 September 1886. Her wreck constituted such a hazard to navigation that Capt Sutton, the Queen's Harbourmaster, ordered her destruction by explosives, her cargo of flints not being considered worth salvaging. On 8 October, after naval divers from the torpedo school had packed several hundred pounds of explosive inside the hull, she was blown to pieces.

The last gale of that century proved to be the worst for over 100 years. It reached its height within 24 hours, by which time the wind, accompanied by blinding snow, had reached hurricane force. This was the holocaust of early March 1891 now known as the 'Great Blizzard', which raged from the 9th of the month until the 13th and cut off the West Country completely regarding road and rail transport. Ships of all sizes were lost along the length of the south coast, but remarkably few in the Sound. The Admiralty sailing cutter *Julia* broke from her moorings, foundering near Stonehouse; the *Jane*, a ten year old fishing dandy, and the pilot cutter *Mystery*, were both sunk, whilst the Falmouth ketch *Katie* was blown from Batten quay across to Drake's Island and then ashore at Mount Edgcumbe.

All the royal dockyards have at some time or another experienced a submarine disaster, the first at Plymouth being the *A-8*. In company with torpedo boat *No 80* and submarine *A-7*, she left the depot ship HMS *Forth* at 8 am on 8 June 1905 and proceeded towards the mouth of the Sound for exercises. In near perfect sea conditions, both submarines passed through the western entrance, and commenced manoeuvres and diving drills in the vicinity of their escort. At about 10 am *A-8* went missing and, simultaneously, signals were received from the breakwater lighthouse and Fort Picklecombe to the effect that a submarine had been seen to sink in distress.

Fortunately, a local fishing boat in the vicinity lowered a boat and rescued Lieut Algernon Candy RN, her commanding officer, Petty Officer Waller, and Leading Stoker Watt. The officer had in fact saved Waller's life when he became exhausted treading water in leather seaboots. The only information the survivors could offer was that *A-8* was on the surface, 'running light' as it was called, when an explosion occurred inside the hull. She began to sink rapidly, after which a second explosion hurled all three men off her deck and into the sea.

Vice-Admiral Henderson, dockyard superintendent, assumed command of rescue operations and ordered out the tugs *Assurance* and *Perseverence* to the scene, accompanied by divers from HMS *Defiance*. The survivors confirmed that *A-8* had sunk with her main hatch open, but it was hoped that some of the crew might still be alive behind a watertight door, either in the bow or engine-room compartments. Sweep wires passed over the hull caught on the special lifting hooks fitted to all A-class boats since 1904 and by 1 pm the submarine was ready to be lifted. As the winches on the tugs commenced to lift the wreck a violent explosion came from the seabed and the sea around the salvage fleet boiled, after which loose gear and two wooden gratings floated up. In view of the risk, all

After unloading a cargo of Welsh coal at Plymouth, the Sunderland registered s.s. Vectis suffered a breakdown of her steering gear whilst leaving the Sound and was wrecked on the Rennies on 5 February 1912.

diving was suspended, and apart from a guard boat, the fleet returned to the dockyard.

Salvage work resumed at dawn on the 9th, when two mooring lighters, divers and riggers were put to work, the location of the wreck being midway between the breakwater light and Penlee Point, near Knap buoy, in 18 metres of water. By 5 pm on the 10th, the *A-8* was clear of the seabed and about to be towed away when a strongback snapped and she plunged back to the bottom, breaking every one of the lifting wires. Having slung and lifted the *A-8* in a remarkably short time, one wonders why the Navy then employed Capt Anderson, of the Western Marine Salvage Co, Penzance, to continue the work. Using the Company's salvage vessel *Lady of the Isles*, the *A-8* was brought to the surface on 12 June, moored in a

The Amazon river steamer Goyaz of Para, *was blown ashore in the infamous 'Christmas Hurricane' of 1912 under Jennycliff, Plymouth Sound, but was refloated and saved.*

sheltered part of the Sound, then moved into No 2 Dock. Capt Lees of HMS *Forth*, wearing a 'standard' diving suit and helmet, but without weights, entered the submarine through the forward hatch, and commenced the unpleasant task of searching the interior. After recording the position of every control and examining the damage caused by three explosions, he brought out 14 corpses.

A loose rivet found in the forepart of the submarine under examination in simulated pressure conditions, let in one ton of water in ten minutes and was probably the cause of this tragic accident. Following refit and overhaul, the *A-8* returned to service and survived the First World War, being eventually sold to Phillips of Dartmouth for scrap in 1920.

It was 1912 before another steamer was lost in the Plymouth area. This was the 907 tons gross, two-masted *Vectis*, owned by John Hill of Sunderland, which went on the Rennies on 5 February and became a total wreck. Later the same year, during the notorious 'Christmas hurricane', the schooners *Ottawa* and *Guild Mayor*, the Amazon river steamer

The self-propelled hopper barge No 42 which went ashore on Plymouth breakwater 13 September 1913. Refloated the following day, she sank off the breakwater lighthouse.

Goyaz, ketch *Johnny Toole*, and the Plymouth lifeboat itself, all went ashore, but none was lost. The 62 tons net *Johnny Toole* of Newport, built at Bideford in 1886, survived until 29 April 1918, when a German submarine sank her off Carnsore Point.

Another wreck attributed to the breakwater was the self-propelled hopper barge *No 42*, which sank twice on 13 September 1913. This 150 ton vessel, on passage from Cadiz to Southampton having recently completed a dredging contract in Spain, arrived off Plymouth in the dark. Flares were burnt for a pilot, but when these brought no response her master attempted to enter the Sound without assistance. From his position aft, Capt Bun saw a dark shape loom up ahead and called to the lookout, 'What is that black ahead?' The lookout had no sooner turned to ask, 'What black?', than the barge hit the breakwater, filled and sank. Next day, with her engine room and accommodation flooded, she was pumped out and refloated, then taken in tow by the tugs *Stag*, *Boarhound* and *Deerhound*, but quickly became low in the water and finally sank for the second and last time.

After a spate of submarine disasters between 1903 and 1912, the nation was shocked to hear of yet another on 16 January 1914, off Plymouth. This latest disaster concerned the *A-7*, lost whilst carrying out dummy torpedo runs against HMS *Pigmy*, a 100 ton fleet tender. For five long days the navy swept the area for the missing craft, finally locating her on 21 January in 42 metres depth four miles west-northwest of Rame Head or, more exactly, two miles offshore from Fort Tregantle. Divers reported that her stern was already embedded at least seven metres into thick mud and that no response had been made to signals tapped on her pressure hull. Wires were swept under the hull by the tugs *Alliance* and *Firm*, then passed to the Sheerness salvage lighter *YC94*, but the submarine refused to move. Bad weather prevented any further work on the wreck and by the 28th of the month the Navy was smarting from newspaper taunts.

The 14,000 ton battleship HMS *Exmouth* was then taken to the scene and her powerful capstans took the strain on the lifting wires, keeping them as taut as bowstrings for over half an hour in the hope of breaking the suction, but succeeded only in tearing away much of the *A-7*'s outer casing. For the last time the salvage crews went through the routine of passing wires under the hull, a task made more difficult by the submarine now having sunk into the seabed to conning tower level. Once again the *Exmouth* took the strain, lifting first on one wire, then another, attempting to ease the *A-7* from her grave. Suddenly the wires went slack and hopes ran high for success until divers reported that her hull had been torn wide open. Reluctantly, the submarine and its occupants were abandoned. The *Western Morning News* opened a fund for the dependents of the drowned crew, and by the time it closed the citizens of Plymouth were proud to announce they had collected the sum of £1,024 12s 6d.

Only one wreck of any consequence occurred at Plymouth before the outbreak of the First World War, this being the 91 ton schooner *Erna* of Bremen. It had been Capt Kuhlke's intention to enter the port of Charlestown, in Cornwall, to load china clay, but a severe south-easterly gale forced him back to Plymouth where she anchored in Jennycliff Bay. Next day, 21 February 1914, the *Erna* commenced to drag, eventually striking the south-western edge of Drake's Island. Huge breakers and near gale force winds prevented the Plymouth lifeboat from getting alongside, but when its coxswain realised the *Erna* was sinking, he anchored and then dropped back as close to the wreck as he dared. By this means all six crew were saved, leaving the schooner, valued at £1,750, to go to pieces where she lay.

Naturally, the outbreak of hostilities during 1914 saw a tremendous increase in shipping activity around Plymouth, but there were remarkably few wreck incidents and the only inshore loss was that of the requisitioned trawler HMS *Abelard*, lost when she struck a mine near the breakwater on Christmas Eve 1916. A number of ships were lost by enemy action offshore, near the Eddystone, and there were also several collisions, in one of which, on 30 November 1916, the Teignmouth steamer *Dartmeet* was lost after having been struck by the steamer *Swazi*.

Within twelve months of the armistice, the steamship *Spyros* was wrecked when she foundered off the Eddystone, and there were two wrecks on the breakwater, the first being the Grimsby schooner *Fair City*, carrying 50 tons of cut stone and clay ballast from Fowey. The *Fair City* was a relatively small vessel of only 72 tons gross, but the next sailing ship lost on the breakwater was a large four-masted barquentine of over 1,000 tons. This was the French-owned *Yvonne*, built at Fairhaven, in California, in 1900 and carrying 419 tons of selected logwood from Savannah le Mer to Havre. On 3 October 1920 she was caught by a severe gale close to the Eddystone and but for the prompt action of her deck watch in reducing canvas down to two small topsails and jib, she would almost certainly have been wrecked on the reef. As it was, she missed the rocks by less than a ship's length, drove straight for the Sound, and headlong into the breakwater. The sea pounded her unmercifully as she

The French registered barquentine Yvonne *which drove ashore on the southern face of Plymouth breakwater, close to the Shipwrecked Mariners Refuge on 3 October 1920, to become a total wreck.*

lay on her side. Fortunately, she carried radio equipment and her distress signals were soon answered by the arrival of the Plymouth lifeboat and several tugs, but none of them was able to get close to the wreck. The 19 crew aboard the *Yvonne* were instructed to put on lifejackets and jump into the sea, 17 of them being picked up by the lifeboat, one by the tug *Rover*, and one drowned.

In 1926 there was yet another submarine accident, this time in Devonport dockyard. The submarine was the *H-29*, which sank in less than one minute, drowning seven men. She was alongside a jetty taking in water ballast on 9 August when, due to negligence in overfilling, she sank so low that the sea entered an open deck hatch and she went down in twelve metres of water.

From then until the outbreak of the Second World War the majority of

The remains of a steel lifting barge, still unidentified, which was sunk on the 'Bridge' during the Second World War to effectively block the shallow channel leading inside Drake's Island and on to Devonport dockyard.

incidents were confined to strandings, such as that of the steamer *Kentish Coast* in Jennycliff Bay on 16 November 1928. She was refloated and towed away, but was found to be so badly damaged that she had to be scrapped. The *Umberleigh*, another steamer, went ashore in Bovisand Bay in 1930 but got off, and it was not until a German U-boat campaign was mounted for a second time that the wreck incidents again increased. An Admiralty motor fishing vessel, the *Encourage*, was sunk by mine on 5 October 1940, close to the breakwater, followed by the requisitioned trawler *Lord Inchcape* only 20 days later. The *Kingstone Alalite* was lost in the same manner, but these were small losses compared to ships like the steamer *Medoc*, torpedoed near the Eddystone on 26 November 1940 with the loss of 39 of her crew.

Seldom is a ship sunk deliberately, since they are normally lost by accident, but in the case of the *Glen Strathallan*, she carried no crew, no

The Norwegian cruise liner Venus, *of Bergen, on the rocks at Dead Man's Bay in Plymouth Sound on 22 March 1955. After disembarking 250 passengers she anchored inside the breakwater, but dragged and went ashore. She was towed off four days later and repaired at Devonport dockyard.*

cargo or stores, and represented no financial loss, being sunk with the owner's consent. Built as a steam trawler of 690 tons in 1928 at Selby, when her fishing owner went bankrupt, the millionaire Colby Cubbin bought her and she was converted into a pleasure yacht at a cost of £30,000. At the outbreak of the Second World War she was loaned to the Royal Navy as an escort vessel, then returned to her owner who used her for cruising around the Isle of Man and Scotland. Following Cubbin's death, she became a training vessel for Merchant Navy cadets as instructed in his will, which further decreed that when of no further service, she was to be scuttled in the Hurd Deep, north of the Channel Islands. Plymouth Ocean Projects, Fort Bovisand, at the time a recently established Underwater

Built as a steam fishing trawler, the Glen Strathallan *became a millonaire's yacht, served in the Second World War with the Admiralty, and on her owner's death was converted into a training ship, his will decreeing that when no longer of use, she should be scuttled. This picture shows her being sunk off Bovisand, Plymouth Sound, 27 April 1970.*

Centre, requested of the trustees that she be sunk near the entrance to Plymouth Sound for the benefit of trainee divers. This scheme agreed, the Science Museum was allowed to remove her engine complete for exhibition purposes, and on 27 April 1970 Captain Clucus of the Plymouth School of Navigation opened her seacocks and she sank 250 metres from the Shagstone. To the embarrassment of her new owners, she was then declared a navigational hazard to the many fishing vessels using the eastern entrance to Plymouth Sound, and Trinity House marked the site with a wreck buoy. The cost of maintaining this light-buoy then fell on the owners, who were also ordered to render the wreck safe. Fortunately, the first heavy seas of that winter completely demolished her.

Subsequent wrecks in Plymouth Sound have been generally small, and include the motor launch *Maejub*, wrecked under Fort Picklecombe on 6 December 1970; the ketch *Falcon*, lost with two children in Cawsand Bay

Carrying a cargo of granite chippings for road construction, the Hull *registered m.v.* Fylrix *took a heavy list in a gale, and reached Plymouth, only to sink in Jennycliff Bay, 22 November 1984.*

on 1 February 1971, and the 637 tons gross motor vessel *Fylrix* in Jennycliff Bay on 22 November 1984, which sank very close to where the freeze trawler *Nordzee* had gone down previously on 15 January 1979. The latter lay on the seabed for over a year before she was refloated, much to the disappointment of Fort Bovisand and local divers. The Hull registered *Fylrix*, carrying granite chippings from the Dean Quarry, Porthoustock, Cornwall, to London, developed a severe list in a gale ten miles south-west of the Eddystone, and was escorted into Plymouth by a Royal Navy frigate. After anchoring near Jennycliff, her list became worse in heavy seas, and early that morning she was abandoned as she started to capsize only 100 yards offshore, going down on her starboard side with her stern towards the shore. Declared a total loss, no immediate attempt was made to salvage her, and since she lay well clear of shipping, the

The Arctic Explorer, *an elderly trawler which was moored in Turnchaple Bay, in the Cattewater in February 1979, and sank at her moorings. Attempts to raise her in 1980 failed, but a second attempt was successful and she was broken up at Laira Bridge.*

harbour authorities allowed her to remain where she lay for the benefit of divers, the wreck partly uncovering at low water.

Two further losses, both in the vicinity of the Eddystone took place in the early 1970s, the fishing vessel *Robin John* foundering with the loss of all three crew after collision on 6 June 1972, and the Danish coaster *Merc Enterprise*, carrying a cargo of barley from Treport to Cork, abandoned in wind conditions force ten, subsequently sinking 17 miles south of the Eddystone light. Built as the *Vestlollik* in 1968 at Bremen, seven of her 18 man crew went down with the vessel in deep water.

2

Stoke to Prawle Point

The western extremity of Bigbury Bay is Stoke Point, situated four miles from the Great Mewstone at Plymouth, whilst its eastern end is marked by Bolt Tail. It is a bay which bears a striking but unfortunate resemblance from seaward to Whitesands Bay, to the west of Plymouth. Unfortunate, since over the years, countless numbers of masters and captains have mistaken one for the other and sailed towards what they fondly imagined was Rame Head, at the entrance to Plymouth Sound, only to find themselves embayed. Once confronted by the sheer cliffs of Bolt Tail, and with an onshore wind, there was little chance of escape.

The most interesting of the early wrecks in the area was the *San Pedro Mayor*, or *St Peter the Great*, a 29 gun vessel of the Spanish Armada of 1588. After successfully evading the English in the Channel, she was navigated round Scotland and down the west coast of Ireland, only to be blown east again into the English Channel to go ashore near Hope cove on 28 October. She has been described variously as a 'hulk', a 'hospital ship' and a 'galleon' – even a 'treasure ship'; but it would appear from evidence in the State Papers of both England and Spain that she was a 'hospital hulk', one of a small fleet of armed merchant vessels, led by Juan Gomez de Medina on board the *Gran Griffon*, which lost their leader when that vessel was wrecked on Fair Isle, north of Scotland. As a result, the officers on the remaining hulks found themselves both lost and confused.

This was not the only Spanish vessel of the period to be lost in Bigbury Bay. According to John Leyland: 'two of Philip, King of Castelle's shippes felle to wrack in this haven, when he was driven into England by tempeste.' The haven in question was either Ayrmer cove or the mouth of the river Erme, neither of which was exactly suitable as an anchorage for a ship of any size.

Until 1991, no physical remains of any historic wreck at the mouth of the river Erme had been found, but that year Stephen George, of Totnes, located an iron cannon 400 metres to the north of Mary reef whilst snorkelling. This gun, possibly French c1450-1500, was plugged with a

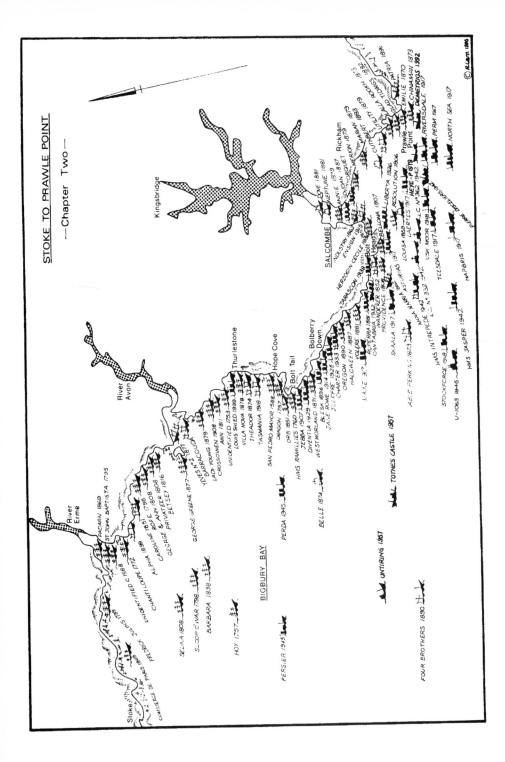

STOKE TO PRAWLE POINT

— Chapter Two —

© R. Larn. 1986

tompion and loaded with flint shot. This site, following a diving survey by members of the newly formed Bigbury Bay Investigation Team (BBIT), became designated under the Protection of Wrecks Act following the discovery of two more iron guns, shot and general 16-17th century artefact material, including coins and a lead pan weight bearing an English proof mark, found by Richard Larn, which suggest two wrecks, dated c1450-1500 and c1680-1715. No evidence has as yet emerged to link this site with the Spanish wrecks mentioned by Leyland, but interestingly, led directly to the discovery of what may be the oldest wreck site in Devon.

An extended survey of the East and West Mary reef took the divers some distance away, where they stumbled accidentally on a collection of possibly prehistoric tin ingots whilst using underwater metal detectors. A total of some 40 ingots of all sizes were found, which suggest they were lost in some long forgotten shipwreck, possibly as early as 2000 BC, although the British Museum have yet to confirm this date. Also designated as an historic wreck site, work has continued in both areas over the past three years, making exciting discoveries, which resulted in the divers concerned, led by Jim Tyson and Neville Oldham, receiving the Duke of Edinburgh's Award.

Other wrecks offered rich pickings, particularly a Dutch galliot of 100 tons, lost on Thurlestone Sands in January 1750. Laden with wine, brandy, coffee and indigo, from Zante to Hamburg, this vessel went ashore late one evening: 'it was with difficulty that the country people were kept from plundering it. On the Saturday evening, as many as 10,000 people congregated around this wreck, coming from all parts of the county for the sole purpose of stealing what they could of the remainder of the cargo, and were only kept at bay by the arrival of soldiers from Plymouth. The ring leader of the mob got killed, being drunk and falling on a soldier's bayonet, and got fixed to it.'

Prior to this, the *Dagger*, another valuable wreck, went ashore in 1736 in the mouth of the river Avon. At a manor court held at Hope during April 1737, the steward recorded in the court roll: 'George Hamblin of Orford Jefford, took up a graper, about 50 weight, at the place the *Dagger* was cast away; also, one John Piles, another small gun.' This court, composed of 13 respectable men, had the task of settling all disputes regarding salvage or property, unless claimed by an owner. Throughout the land, the right of wreck, originally vested in the Crown, was sometimes made over by special grant to the lords of local manors. The Courtenay family's claim existed from 1416 and their right of wreck was confirmed by Edward VI and Elizabeth I, later to be re-established by Lord Devon after a bitter dispute shortly before the first Merchant Shipping Act was passed in 1854. The rights of this family extended from Dartmouth Castle to the eastern shore of the Avon, below Aveton Gifford, and 'as far out to sea as a man on horseback could see an umber barrel'.

Whilst seldom exercised today, following the discovery of the two historic wrecks in the Erme estuary in the early 1990s, Mr A.J.B. Mildmay-White elected to exert his authority as Lord of the Manor of the Hundred of Ermington, challenging HM Customs and Excise in the High Court regarding ownership of artefacts recovered. Possibly for the first time in 50 years the rights of a lord of the manor regarding wreck were exercised, and upheld, Customs and Excise acquiescing to his claim.

On 8 October 1757, a valuable hoy was driven ashore in Bigbury Bay and lost with all hands. Her cargo of 6,000 gallons of brandy in barrels was saved, unlike the rich cargo of the *Chantiloupe*, which was stolen when she went ashore in 1772. Homeward bound from the West Indies, the only survivors were a seaman and a wealthy female passenger named Burke, said to be related to the famous Edmund Burke. Wearing a great deal of valuable jewellery she attracted the attention of the wreckers: ' . . . the savage people from the adjacent villages, who were anxiously waiting for the wreck, seized and stript her of her clothes, even cutting off some of her fingers, and mangling her ears in their impatience to secure the jewels, and left her miserably to perish.' Buried in the foreshore, her body was later uncovered by a dog and exhumed, when it was proven the unfortunate woman had been alive when cast ashore and deliberately murdered.

A macabre reminder of the loss of the *Chantiloupe* came to light in 1900, when children digging in the sand uncovered a skull and several bones from a shallow grave. They were pronounced the remains of a black man, almost certainly one of the crew of this tragic wreck.

Reminiscent of the *Marlborough* incident on the Manacles reef, also in the early 1800s, was the stranding of the *George & Ann* of Exeter, near Ayrmer cove, on 23 October 1808. Chased inshore by a French privateer which had been lurking around the Plymouth area for weeks, the British vessel stood in for the mouth of the Avon and reduced sail. As the enemy vessel drew closer, the helm of the *George & Ann* was put hard over, giving the crew the satisfaction of seeing the privateer strike a shallow rock and founder, until they, in turn, found themselves stranded close at hand. Less than one month later the military transport vessel *Selina* foundered in deep water on 21 November, to be followed by the *Ann*, a West Indiaman, bound for London from St Kitts, lost on 30 April 1811, and the *Betsey* on 11 January 1816. The last of these was carrying 65 French prisoners of war, 23 of whom drowned. Information concerning yet another early wreck of September 1812 has come down to us via Charlotte Bronte. Her mother, Maria Branwell of Penzance prior to her marriage, put all her possessions aboard a small sailing ship which was lost in Bigbury. In a letter dated 18 November 1812, she wrote, 'my box was dashed to pieces by the sea, and all my property except a few articles were swallowed up'.

During the next 50 years, Bigbury was the setting for a great many shipwrecks. In 1838 the brig *Barbara* was lost; *John*, a Bideford-registered snow, stranded on the Blackstone rock in November 1824; the Exeter-owned *Caroline* was wrecked near Challaborough on 20 December 1851, and on 11 December 1869 the French brig *Commerce de Paris*, Charles Chilbourg master, drove ashore midway between the Erme and the Yealm. Homeward bound from Rio de Janeiro with coffee, cotton, tapioca and dye wood, the 618 ton vessel anchored in Bigbury Bay during a gale, which was followed by thick fog. During the early hours of the morning she began to drag, and at high water went beam-on to the beach and bilged. Several bales of cotton and a large number of hides were salvaged, and the threat of plunder by the Devon wreckers was sufficiently strong to justify the eight policemen brought in by the French consul, all of whom were armed with pistols.

With the law guarding the only worthwhile wreck, the locals were obliged to look elsewhere for their 'Godsends', and were soon attracted east to Blackpool Sands, in Start Bay, where newspapers were excitedly reporting the finding of valuable gold coins of Edward III, Henry IV, and Charles and Louis of France; specie from some long-forgotten wreck of the 1400s. Over the winter of 1995-6, when the depth of Slapton Sands was much reduced by north-east gales, a large number of gold and silver coins of Charles II and James II (1649-88) were uncovered on the beach.

A January gale in 1877 saw the loss of the *George Green* at Challaborough, and on 14 October that same year the Santander schooner *Yves No 2* was smashed to pieces in the breakers of Ayrmer cove. When still a mile from shore, a huge wave swept Capt Pedro Albano to his death, and before mate Resende could take charge of the situation the schooner struck the shore. The breakers made short work of the wreck and the beach was strewn with timbers and ruined casks of flour, but not before the local rocket brigade had saved the remaining six crew.

The wooden barque Lady Young, *of Liverpool, was driven ashore in a gale at West Down Point, near Bantham, Bigbury Bay, on 26 October 1879. Her crew were saved by breeches buoy, the vessel going to pieces a few days later. Burgh Island in the background, is today dominated by a large hotel.*

The next wreck was considerably bigger, being the Liverpool barque *Lady Young* of 598 tons. She had left Cardiff for Hamburg on 20 October 1879 but, six days later, lost her foretopmast and a great deal of canvas when off Devon. Realising that his ship had been blown into Bigbury and embayed, Capt Watkins ordered distress rockets to be fired. These were sighted and answered by the Hope Cove coastguards, who hurried with their apparatus to West Down Point, near Bantham, where the entire crew were taken off by breeches buoy, but lost all their belongings. Next day, John Nabsly, the ship's steward, volunteered to return aboard to gather up anything of value. He regained the vessel via breeches buoy but, on return, fell out of the chair and met his death on the rocks below.

Few wrecks have no survivors at all, and the fact that there were none in the case of the brigantine *Crossowen*, led to much speculation. Registered in Glasgow but owned in St Austell, the *Crossowen* was found abandoned on the beach on 7 May 1908 with her sails set but less than a metre of water in the hold, having embarked a cargo of china clay at Par only the previous day. It was assumed that shortly after sailing she encountered dense fog which blanketed the south-west and lost her way. None of her seven crew were seen alive again, drowned corpses being found later close to the mouth of the Avon. A possible explanation is that she struck Burgh Island, whereupon her crew, thinking that she was sinking, abandoned her, only to be overwhelmed in the breakers on Bantham bar. Six bodies were buried together in Thurlestone churchyard, together with that of a boy who, although not part of the official crew, was presumed to have been aboard.

It is a strange fact that the largest of the wrecks in Bigbury Bay remained unidentified until 1969, 24 years after it had foundered. This was the steamer *Persier*, built in Newcastle in 1918 by the Northumberland Ship Building Co as the *War Buffalo*, a First World War 'Standard (B class) ship' of 5,030 tons gross. As far as the official records of the Second World War are concerned, the *Persier* ended her days near the Eddystone, after being torpedoed on 11 February 1945, but in fact she sank close inshore, bringing to a close a chequered career that was dramatic to the end.

On 8 February 1945 the *Persier* left Cardiff, loaded with foodstuffs for Belgium, on what was to be her last voyage. Designated convoy BTC 65, the ships were forced by rough weather to shelter first at Lundy, then Clovelly, and it was 11 February before they reached the Eddystone.

An alert lookout spotted *UB-1017*'s periscope, but the torpedo the German submarine had fired was already on its way towards them. An immense column of water several hundred yards away indicated a premature explosion, and a second torpedo went astern of the *Persier*, but at 5.25 pm a third struck No 2 hold, exploded, and the vessel began to list heavily. With his ship's engine now stopped, Capt Mathieu ordered the boats lowered during which time he inspected the damage, only to find the forward holds completely flooded and 1,500 tons of soap mixed up with tinned meat and dried egg powder.

The evacuation of the *Persier* can only be described as disastrous, since by now her engine had started itself due to a defective valve, and could not be stopped. Both Capt Mathieu and Commodore Wood boarded No 1 lifeboat which, in lowering, became unhooked from its falls at one end and hung vertically, throwing its occupants into the sea. A liferaft was released

Torpedoed off the Eddystone on 11 February 1945, the s.s. Persier (ex-War Buffalo) was abandoned, but with her propeller still turning steamed herself into Bigbury Bay at night where she foundered.

but became entangled with some obstruction and was dragged along, half in and half out of the sea. Lifeboat No 3 got away full of men, but drifted into the still turning propeller and was smashed. Number 4 boat, with no plug fitted and filling rapidly, was lifted clear of its hooks by a wave, leaving two men clinging to the fall blocks, and also drifted into the turning propeller.

The one boat that did get away intact went to the rescue of the men swinging on the empty falls, and both were rescued, but a stoker sliding down from the boat deck caught his foot, fell head downward and drowned. In going to his assistance, the same boat drifted astern, was cut in two by the propeller and its occupants thrown into the sea. Only one lifeboat now remained afloat and of the many rafts and Carley floats released, every one either drifted off empty, or else sank. The defective engine control valve which had caused so much loss of life then functioned correctly for a while and the engines were stopped, but not for long. HMS *Cornelian*, an anti-submarine trawler, then commenced to depth charge a sonar contact close at hand and the resultant explosions started the steamer's engine off again. Several escort vessels, seeing the *Persier's* predicament, closed in, taking off the remaining crew and leaving her to sink.

During the hours of darkness, the *Persier* must have continued to steam towards the shore, sinking slowly as she went, until she foundered in Bigbury Bay. She could well have waited a further quarter century before discovery had not fishermen located her on their echo-sounding equipment and passed the information to a local diver. In May 1970 her bell confirmed identification, the diver reporting that she lay on her side, a four-inch stern gun still mounted, with two machine-guns on the bridge.

At the extreme eastern end of Bigbury Bay, where the cliffs climb towards Bolt Tail, lie Thurlestone sands and Hope cove, both of which have a long association with wreck. The German brigantine *Theador*, carrying timber and cotton from the West Indies, was wrecked at Thurlestone on 14 February 1874, simply because a depleted crew were unable to manage the ship. She had encountered severe weather for three days prior to entering Bigbury Bay, during which her deckhouse galley had been washed overboard, along with her master and mate, leaving insufficient crew to handle the sails.

Similarities between Bigbury and Whitesands Bay have already been mentioned, but to mistake Bolt Tail for Land's End is not so excusable, as was the case with the *Villa Nova* in 1879. Capt Little was in command of this Ardrossan brigantine, in ballast from St Malo to Cardiff, when a choked pump forced her to seek shelter and whilst attempting to round what was thought to be Land's End, she went ashore and broke in two.

The largest wreck to take place in Bigbury Bay was the Belgian steamship *Louis Sheid* (ex-*Kendal Castle*, ex-*Ultor*), lost in Beacon cove. Built in 1920 for the Rickmers Line, this 6,057 tons gross vessel was close at hand when the Dutch motor vessel *Tajandoen* was torpedoed in the Channel on 7 December 1939, rescuing 62 crew and passengers from a sea of blazing oil in which six died. The *Louis Sheid* was on passage for Antwerp with grain when she went ashore in Bigbury Bay the same day. Refloated and beached at Thurlestone she broke in two, but was later heavily salvaged so that only her double bottom remains in the shallows.

The coastline then gives way to stark, rugged cliffs and the ancient

The Antwerp registered s.s. Louis Sheid *which drove ashore near Thurlestone, Bigbury Bay 7 November 1939, whilst carrying a general and grain cargo, and 62 survivors from a torpedoed liner in the same convoy.*

fishing village of Hope which nestles in the lee of Bolt Tail. Hope cove is aptly named, for hope is what it offered the generations of seamen shipwrecked around this notorious promontory. It has been said of the area: 'there is scarce a cove but holding stout timbers, legends of silver ingots, pieces of eight, moidores, doubloons and dollars.' Whilst the occupants of the cove have witnessed many tragedies over the centuries, none compare with the loss of the *Ramillies* in 1760, a 1st rate king's ship of 90 guns and a crew of 720.

In January 1760 she was ordered to join Boscawen on Channel blockade duty, and in company with the flagship *Royal William*, *St George*, *Sandwich*, *Princess Amelia*, *Venus* and the cutter *Hawke*, *Ramillies* left Plymouth on 6 February. On the 11th, the fleet was caught on the open sea in a fearful south-westerly gale, so severe that the admiral recorded in his log, 'we could seldom carry even a topsail'. Not surprisingly, on the 14th the seven vessels were scattered far and wide, each having received its share of storm damage. It was 16 February before it was known that the *Hawke* had foundered in mid-Channel with all hands, and the *Ramillies* had gone to pieces near Bolt Tail with less than 24 survivors.

The latter had been forced to heave-to on the 14th due to severe leaks, and had lumbered away to the east before the wind until her master estimated they were off Plymouth, when the ship stood in towards land which lay somewhere ahead over an indistinct, heaving horizon. When land appeared, it was mistakenly identified as Looe Island and the warship steered further east, seemingly towards Rame Head and safety. Only then was it realised that the island was Burgh, in Bigbury Bay. Now embayed, her captain and officers expressed their fears at even attempting to weather Bolt Tail, but the sailing master insisted all was well and ordered all canvas set in an attempt to stay ship. Under tremendous strain, the mainsail split from top to bottom; the main sheets had no sooner been let go than the whole mainmast came crashing down, followed shortly after by the mizzen. Orders were then given to anchor and for all sail to be taken down, followed shortly by instructions to cut down both foremast and bowsprit.

Devoid of all top hamper, the *Ramillies* rode easily at two anchors, half a cable's length from shore, remaining in this position until 6 pm when both cables parted and she drove towards the shore. A hastily dropped sheet anchor briefly checked her progress, but this soon parted and she drove ashore. Mountainous seas broke clean over her, sweeping all before them, throwing men into the sea or else to their death amongst the rocks. Survivors described the scenes on deck as pitiful. The captain of Royal Marines went off his head, marching up and down the poop deck, singing and exclaiming, while the ship's boatswain, who had taken his small son to sea with him, attempted to save his life by throwing him towards the shore, only to see his brains dashed out on the rocks. The only commissioned officer to survive the wreck was Midshipman Harrold; he escaped over her stern, taking with him a party of eight seamen. The last man to reach safety was a William Wise, who literally threw himself off the deck as the ship went to pieces under him.

Over 700 men and women died in the wreck, and next day Bigbury Bay was a mass of floating wreck and bodies. The stern of the *Ramillies* was jammed into an inlet near Bolt Tail on the seaward side, a cove which today bears the name of the ship. Initially several of her guns were

Fog caused the loss of the steam collier Jane Rowe, *of Gelfe, Sweden, when she went ashore near Lantern rock, under Bolberry golf course on 28 February 1914, where she went to pieces.*

recovered, after which the wreck remained untouched until May 1906, when Stephen Chapman, a diver resident at Hope cove, agreed to visit the site. It was again visited in the 1970s, when Peter McBride, his two sons and Jill and Bob Michaels, all sport divers, commenced excavating the wreck, making spectacular recoveries of gold and silver coins, shoe buckles, personal items and ship fittings, now on display in the Charlestown Shipwreck and Heritage Centre, Cornwall.

In later years other wrecks occurred in almost the same cove, but these were steamers of a more modern age. In the meantime, the small sailing vessel *Orb*, Davey master, with granite from Falmouth for Hull, filled and sank two miles west of Bolt Tail on 26 September 1851. Another total wreck was the London barque *Westmoreland*, on 14 July 1871, which went ashore in dense fog one and a half miles east of the Tail. This 456 ton vessel, built at Sunderland in 1858, was carrying a valuable cargo of sugar, rum, coconuts, fustic and logwood worth £12,000, most of which was lost.

The first of a long succession of steamships to go ashore on this part of the Devon coast was the Russian oil tanker *Blesk*, carrying petroleum from Odessa to Hamburg. On 1 December 1896 she hit the Graystone rock in fog and settled down until the sea lapped her upper deck, spreading oil over the immediate coastline and well up into the Kingsbridge estuary. Fog also caused the loss of the steam collier *Jane Rowe* of Gelfe, in Sweden. Built by Palmers of Newcastle in 1889 and launched as the *Mary Thomas*, she was renamed *Barto* when first she changed hands, and later, when sold yet again, was renamed *Jane Rowe*. As such she went ashore three-quarters of a mile west of the Lantern rock, under Bolberry golf links, at 5.45 am on 28 February 1914.

Carrying 3,000 tons of burnt ore, loaded at Oran for Rotterdam, the wreck was first sighted by the *Kingsbridge Packet* which plied between Plymouth and Salcombe. A hawser was passed between the two vessels but all efforts to pull the *Jane Rowe* clear failed. Meanwhile, news of the wreck had been passed to both the Hope cove coastguard and lifeboat by rabbit trappers on the clifftop, but despite a speedy launch the lifeboat could be of no assistance. The steamer had gone ashore on the only stretch of sandy beach hereabouts and hopes ran high that she would be saved, but even the combined efforts of the tugs *Boarhound*, *Dencaba*, *Venture*, *Totnes* and *Dragon* proved futile. By evening, having been driven high up the beach and now on top of some rocks, the *Jane Rowe* was found to be leaking badly and it was obvious she was finished.

Next morning, the rocket brigade fired a line across the wreck – now only 135 metres offshore – which was secured high in the foremast and a breeches buoy rigged. The entire crew were then taken off, the first to come ashore being the ship's cabin boy, who brought with him a kitten; the second was a seaman carrying the ship's cat, and the third struggled across holding a large dog.

The wreck of the *Jane Rowe* was followed by an unprecedented shipping disaster in the early hours of 18 March 1907, when two large liners went ashore in the West Country, one in Devon, the other in Cornwall. Unprecedented, not only due to the extraordinary coincidence of time and location, but also because they carried between them 611 passengers and crew, yet not a single life was lost. The Cornish wreck was the *Suevic*, which stranded on the outer Cledges rocks, at the Lizard. In Devon, the Elder Dempster West African mail steamer *Jebba* overshot the

WRECKED S.S. JEBBA.

The Elder Dempster liner Jebba, *of London, lies stranded beam-on to the cliffs near Bolt Tail, 18 March 1907. All 155 passengers and crew were saved, but the ship went to pieces.*

Eddystone in fog and stranded near Bolt Tail, only yards from where the *Ramillies* and *Blesk* had been lost. Carrying specie, ivory, palm oil, fruit and mail to a total value of £200,000 and with 79 passengers from Nigeria and the Gold Coast, plus a crew of 76, mostly Droo boys, the *Jebba* ended up beam-on to the cliffs less than 30 metres offshore. On board the liner, the boiler fires had been drawn to prevent any explosions, since there were already several feet of water inside, and everyone went to their lifeboat stations. There was no panic or disorder among either passengers or crew, and all calmly awaited the captain's instructions. Although the Hope cove lifeboat had already been launched, two local fishermen, Isaac Jarvis and John Argeat, risked their lives by climbing down the 60 metre sheer cliff face in the dark to help rig two bosun's chairs. Many a ghost must have stirred that night, for the rescuers were great-grandsons of the men who had hauled survivors from the *Ramillies* up those self same cliffs some 147 years earlier.

Everyone from the wreck reached safety without serious injury, 38 by

The South Shields registered tug Joffre, *stranded in fog under West Cliff, south-east of Bolt Tail on 27 May 1925. She was refloated three months later and worked until 1966 when she was broken up for scrap.*

means of the rocket apparatus, and 117 by lines rigged by the two fishermen, both of whom later received the Albert Medal for bravery. There was much interest ashore in the pets landed by the crew. First came the ship's cat, then two chimpanzees and several parrots, while the last three coloured seamen each carried a monkey wrapped in a blanket. Although the Hope lifeboat stood by until the last person was safely ashore, its services were not required, neither was any use made of the ship's lifeboats.

When the two local heroes proudly stood before Edward VII to receive medals, it did not escape the king's notice that these were the second and third such awards made to Devon men, Samuel Popplestone, of Start farm, having received the very first Albert Medal from Queen Victoria in 1866, for gallantry at the wreck of the *Spirit of the Ocean*.

The loss of the *Jebba* was by no means the end of an era; the small steam tug *Joffre* stranded close to the remains of the steamer *Jane Rowe* on 27 May 1925, remaining ashore for three months before being refloated. Four years later, on 12 February 1929, the British steamer *Deventia*, carrying soda from Fleetwood to London, went ashore during an east-south-easterly gale, was refloated, but was later scrapped.

Between Bolt Tail and Bolt Head lie five miles of the most stark, beautiful and inaccessible cliffs on the south coast of Devon. A particularly tragic five miles, since they have brought a premature end to at least three dozen recorded wrecks, and probably many others. A memorial in the churchyard at Malborough is a reminder of one such wreck, the homeward-bound British West Indiaman *Dragon*, Capt Gleast, from Jamaica to London, lost at Cathole on 22 August 1757. Three boys and a girl, all from the same family, in addition to four of the crew, were drowned. The *Lintor Ken* is reputed to be the rather unusual name of another early loss, but no details survive, not even the year. She is said to have carried a cargo of walnut wood and marble statues which provided many a local manor with decorative materials, and for years fishermen maintained that, in favourable conditions, marble blocks could be seen on the seabed.

Another London-owned West Indiaman, the *Bellona*, from Surinam with a valuable cargo, was lost on Bolt Head during September 1807, and on 19 November 1808 the transport *Providence*, homeward-bound from Corunna with troops and stores. Others during the following years include the *Nelly* on 27 July 1852; the *Wanderer*, a 91 ton schooner; the *Anna Maria*, offshore from Bolt Head on 23 July 1862, and an unidentified French brig in 1869. A fearful south-westerly gale put the brig ashore and only the corpses of her crew, barrel staves, and a claret-stained area of sea marked her passing. So strong was the wind that night that spray went clean over Bolt Head and contaminated fresh water in a cart standing outside the coastguard station, half a mile inland.

One of the dozen or more steamers lost between Bolt Head and Bolt Tail was the *Ruperra*. Owned by John Cory and Sons of Cardiff, she was carrying 1,529 tons of cotton seed from Alexandria to Hull when she went ashore just east of the Hamstone at 5.15 am on 27 January 1881. Within minutes the level of water in her forward hold had reached one and a half metres and both ship's boats were lowered. One rowed round to Hope cove; the other, with the captain and first mate aboard, stood by the wreck for over an hour until it was obvious the ship could not be saved, her loss being attributed to a defective compass. Although the first of four lifeboats stationed at Hope, all of which were named *Alexandra*, was in service at the time, it played no part in any wreck incident from its installation on 28 February 1878 until the morning of 18 January 1887.

At 7.30 pm on 17 January, the full-rigged ship *Halloween* of London went ashore in Sewer Mill cove. She had left Foochow on 15 August with 1,600 tons of tea. Despite being one of the fastest sailing ships afloat, having reached Sydney in 69 days on her maiden voyage in 1870, bad weather slowed her down and 155 days at sea passed before the Eddystone was sighted on her starboard bow. A course of south-east was set to clear the Start by some eight miles, yet two hours later she struck inside of the Hamstone rock. Heavy seas broke over her, quickly gutting both cabin and forecastle and forcing her crew into the rigging. There they remained, in relative safety, but when a stay parted and the mizzen mast became unsafe the men returned to the deck. Flares were burnt, rockets and guns fired, even a bonfire lit on the poop deck, but still no one ashore was aware of the wreck until daylight.

John Ford, of Southdown farm, was the first to sight her, and it was his messenger who roused the Lloyd's agent at Salcombe and escorted him back along the cliffs overlooking the scene. Meanwhile, Second Officer McLean and able seamen Wigil and Gorse volunteered to swim ashore to get help, but the latter drowned in the attempt. It was 10 am before the Hope cove lifeboat arrived, when 19 numbed and exhausted men, more dead than alive, were taken off and landed safely. At high water, the deck of the *Halloween* was completely submerged, and three days later local newspapers reported that her back had broken, all three masts had gone overboard, and that her valuable cargo now lay on the beach as a massive barrier, some three and a half metres high in places. Although the underwriters compensated the owners for the loss of cargo, valued at £40,000, the ship itself was uninsured and represented a severe loss to Messrs John Willis & Co, of Leadenhall Street, London.

Mention has already been made of a wreck carrying walnut and marble, the *Lintor Ken*, lost hereabouts. There is no reason to doubt the authenticity of this information, but at the same time there is a remarkable similarity between the cargo mentioned and that of the Italian barque *Volere*, of 464 tons, blown ashore and wrecked by a south-westerly gale on 6 March 1881. The *Volere*, whose master, Gavagnin, was also part owner, carried marble and selected timbers from Genoa for London, and went ashore in Sewer Mill cove with the loss of five crew and one

Registered at Genoa, the Italian s.s. Liberta, *drove ashore on the Mewstone under Bolt Head during a gale and thick fog on 15 February 1926, her crew being saved by the rocket apparatus before the vessel broke in two.*

passenger. Her marble cargo was salvaged in July 1996.

The 844 ton French steamer *Soudan*, with 24 crew, eight passengers, and a cargo of pig nuts from Senegal, was only a few hours from her destination of Dunkirk when she struck the Hamstone rock in thick fog on 27 June 1887. Her remains lie close to the bar, at the entrance to Salcombe. Tugs attempted to get her into the harbour, but she foundered at the entrance. Two Belgian salvage steamers, the *Berger Wilheim* and *Newa*, were engaged to raise the vessel and for two whole months worked on the wreck, but every attempt to refloat her failed and she became a total loss.

Dense fog, which blanketed the south coast from Land's End to Portsmouth on 7 August 1888, saw the *City of Hamburg* go ashore half a mile to the west of Sewer Mill, beneath South Down cliffs. After establishing that his ship was well and truly stranded, Capt Lamont was firing a distress signal when the gun burst, inflicting fearful injuries which later necessitated amputation of his right arm. The first lifeboat lowered

The Spanish steamship Cantabria, *carrying iron ore from Bilbao, lies almost underwater in Steeple Cove, Bolt Head, 13 December 1932.*

from the *City of Hamburg* was swamped and lost; the second, with the injured captain and five others aboard, managed to reach Salcombe; the third boat landed at Mothecombe, a fourth being taken in tow by the Salcombe rowing lifeboat *Lesty*. At 4 pm the following day the steamer was successfully refloated by the tug *Power* and towed away to Plymouth.

Also refloated and saved was the 12,000 tons gross hospital ship *Asturias*, which had been deliberately run ashore on 20 March 1917 after being hit by a German torpedo, which killed 45 crew and nurses. Prior to the outbreak of war, the *Asturias* had been a Royal Mail liner and was one of the first merchant vessels to be requisitioned by the Admiralty. Fortunately, she had already disembarked a large number of wounded troops from Salonika at Avonmouth and was on passage up-Channel when attacked. Her identity could not have been in doubt, since every light on deck was burning and huge red cross emblems were painted on either side of her hull and floodlit.

Other losses or incidents included the 4,073 ton Barclay Curle-built

Another French trawler, the Tarascon, *went ashore in Steeple Cove on 22 March 1938 in fog, but was refloated when pulled off literally by hand, her crew using blocks and tackles.*

Liberta, ashore and wrecked on Bolt Head during fog on 15 February 1926; followed by the *Cantabria* of Spain, in Steeple cove on 13 December 1932, with a cargo of iron ore from Bilbao to Newcastle and only 25 days later, the steam drifter *Charter*, under Cathole cliff. The *Charter* went ashore between the remains of the *Jane Rowe* and the site of the *Joffre's* stranding, and at low water her boiler can still be seen.

Between Bolt Head and Prawle Point lies the entrance to Salcombe, a sheltered port and anchorage downstream from Kingsbridge. The port, besides its lawful and more general commercial activities, was at one time a centre for smuggling and saw a phenomenal traffic in contraband between France, the Channel Isles and Devon. In common with other ports, the coastguard and revenue system brought it under control, and the locals were forced to turn to the more lawful occupations of pilotage, fishing and shipbuilding, with the result that the district prospered.

On 13 December 1806, the American ship *Resolution*, London to St Lucion, was wrecked near Salcombe in an unspecified location, as was the Helford-built cutter *Louisa* in March 1859, while the *Industry* was lost on the sandbar there on 20 October 1862. The *Western Daily Mercury* of 16 October 1877 reported that on the previous day a vessel, believed to be French, had come ashore near the Rickham coastguard station, but that no bodies had been found, nor had the identity of the vessel been established. Later, she proved to be the *Pauline*, and local fishermen recovered a total of seven bodies out at sea.

Two years later, on 16 January, the 242 ton wooden barquentine *Annie* was stranded and lost on the bar; an unfortunate end to this Salcombe owned and crewed vessel, en route from Bahia with 390 tons of sugar in bags. She attempted to enter port in a deplorable, storm-damaged condition, having lost her bulwarks, longboat, figurehead, cutwater and foretopmast. After striking the bar she anchored, but had insufficient water under her keel and went to pieces as she pounded on the bottom. The Salcombe lifeboat rescued the master, Edward Patey, and his mate, the remaining six crew being taken off by a local boat.

A fouled anchor chain and a strong southerly wind combined to drive the 23 ton sloop *Brothers* ashore at Cove Point on 29 March 1881. She soon filled and sank along with her cargo of limestone, and similar circumstances caused the loss of the two year old cutter *Dove* which was last seen at anchor on 16 May 1881, then disappeared and presumably sank. Two years later, at the end of January, the Blackstone rock almost claimed the Liverpool barquentine *Chittagong* which put into Salcombe after losing her deckhouse and two hands in an Atlantic gale. She struck the bar and leaked so badly that it became necessary to run her ashore. Similarly, the *Amy*, a Dartmouth schooner carrying devi-devi from Riohacha, also went ashore on the eastern side of the harbour entrance on 8 November 1883. Following the *Amy*, the Plymouth schooner *Ensign* became one of the few total wrecks after striking the Blackstone on 30 January 1915.

In 1916, the worst lifeboat disaster Devon has experienced came when the Salcombe boat overturned on the bar, drowning 13 of her 15 crew. Launched on her sixth and last service on 27 October 1916, the *William and Emma*, which had been on station since 1904, was called out by the Prawle coastguards to attend the wreck of the Plymouth schooner *Western Lass*, ashore in Lannacombe Bay, near Start Point. Sea conditions were bad when the lifeboat left and no doubt Coxswain Distin had some anxious moments before they reached deep water. The lifeboat was still within sight of Salcombe estuary when a message arrived to say that the Prawle rocket brigade had already saved the schooner's crew, but with no means of communicating with the lifeboat it continued all the way to the scene of the wreck on a wasted journey. It seems strange that it could pass close to both the Prawle coastguard lookout and the signal station without some attempt being made to turn the crew back, but such was the case.

By the time the *William and Emma* arrived back at the entrance to Salcombe her crew were wet through and exhausted, and their condition probably influenced the coxswain to attempt the bar when, in different circumstances, he might well have waited another hour. As the lifeboat approached the line of breakers, a huge wave overtook it, lifting the stern high in the air, and lookouts on the cliffs saw the boat slew sideways down the slope, fall beam-on to the sea and capsize. Unfortunately the tide was on the ebb and the overturned boat and its crew were swept seawards. Edward Distin, brother of the coxswain and one of the only two survivors, regained the boat by hauling himself along the sea anchor rope, followed by William Johnson. Eventually they managed to reach an offshore rock, to which they clung until a weighted cane, attached to a line, was thrown to them from the shore. They were by then so weak that brandy had to be lowered to them before they could summon up strength enough to pull down a heavier rope, by which means they were dragged ashore and saved, but spent many weeks in hospital recovering from the ordeal. It was a major disaster for the town to lose 13 of its men in this tragic manner, yet within two months a new volunteer lifeboat crew had

The last of many 'tall-ships' wrecked in the West Country, the Finnish four masted barque Herzogin Cecilie *struck the Hamstone on 25 April 1936, but sank in Starehole Bay, near Salcombe.*

been found, and by April 1917 a new boat, the *Sarah Ann Holden*, was on station.

One of several ships sunk by enemy action off Salcombe in the First World War was the West Hartlepool steamer *Teesdale*, of 2,470 tons gross, torpedoed when three miles south of Salcombe on 15 June 1917. Bound for Gibraltar with Tyneside coal aboard, she was beached and refloated after repairs, but eventually foundered three miles north of Saltburn, Yorkshire, while on passage to the Tees for permanent repairs.

Another First World War victim, which has since received a great deal of publicity, was the Atlantic Transport Co's steamer *Maine*, torpedoed and sunk off Salcombe on 23 March 1917. Built in 1904 by Hendersons as the *Sierra Blanca*, the war risk insurance fund paid out £19,429 on her loss, a sharp contrast to the £38,000 purchase money paid to the Sierra Shipping

Co in 1913, and the £100 which the Torbay branch of the British Sub-Aqua Club paid for ownership of the wreck in 1961. The prize these amateur divers sought was not her cargo of chalk, cow and horsehair, goatskins or seeds, but her 6.5 ton bronze propeller, which was eventually brought to the surface by the naval boom defence vessel *Barbastel* in April 1963. During 1969, several champagne bottles, still tightly corked and full, were salvaged by divers, their contents still drinkable despite 52 years under water.

Although the famous *Herzogin Cecilie* was not the last of the old 'tall-ships', she was certainly amongst the last half-dozen and the last big sailing ship wrecked in the south-west, apart from the *Maria Assumpta* near Padstow in 1995.

Her last passage was the unofficial grain race from Australia in 1936, when she reached Falmouth in 86 days, seven whole days ahead of her nearest rival, the *Pommern*. Two days after she had reached Cornwall the grand old 'Duchess', as she was affectionately known – her figurehead being that of the Duchess Cecilie, daughter of the Duke of Oldenbourg – struck the Hamstone rock, eventually to became a total wreck. How she came to be there will never be known. In his deposition to the Receiver of Wreck, Eriksson wrote: '. . . loss due to fog and possible magnetic attraction, plus the presence of sufficient tidal impulse to set the vessel right off course.' There was a great deal of newspaper talk and correspondence suggesting that the cliffs had a high iron content which had caused this and many other wrecks in the area, but the same has been said of every cliff from North Foreland to Land's End at some time or another.

As soon as she struck, her anchors were let go but failed to hold, and the 3,111 ton ship swung round, her stern crashing against other rocks, close to the spot where the tea clipper *Halloween* had ended her days. Capt Eriksson fired off distress rockets which were sighted by the local coastguard, who in turn alerted the Salcombe lifeboat, but the first person to see the wreck from ashore was Jack Jarvis, a resident of Hope cove, who spotted her outline through the now thinning fog. He hailed the vessel, but the crew only shouted back, 'Get some tugs!' Dawn on the 25th brought out everyone who could find an excuse to attend the wreck, most of them sightseers.

A breeches buoy was rigged from the clifftop and used to land personal belongings and baggage, which were promptly rifled by members of the public and everything of value stolen. Twenty-two members of the crew were then taken off by the Salcombe lifeboat, leaving only the captain, his wife, both mates, and four seamen aboard. The Customs officers, on learning that these eight intended to stand by the wreck, impounded every drop of spirits and every cigarette, and in a bout of zealous officialdom even slaughtered the pet piglet whose corpse was flung overboard and floated around the vessel for days. They then boxed up and took away the ship's cats, but lost some of their enthusiasm when faced by the captain's Alsatian dog, Paik, who took an instant and obvious dislike to the intruders.

For seven long weeks the *Herzogin Cecilie* lay on the rocks while from the clifftops tens of thousands of spectators stared down at her, the last sailing-ship wreck most of them would ever see. Local farmers made a good thing out of the incident by charging people to cross their land, and the coastline between Bolt Head and Tail was visited by more people than at any previous time in its history. Salvage was technically possible, even after seven weeks, and various authorities were approached for funds and assistance. Finally, it was agreed that the cost of salvage would be offset if the owner, Gustaf Eriksson, would give British deck-officer cadets and apprentices the opportunity to serve aboard, and a general appeal was launched, headed by a donation of £500 from Canada.

A great deal of the grain cargo had been discharged from the wreck in good condition, but more than half still lay rotting and fermenting in the hold, its stench quite appalling. Capt Eriksson naturally wanted to get his ship into Salcombe harbour, where she would have complete shelter while temporary repairs were carried out, but fearing wholesale pollution of local beaches with the holiday season on hand, the local council insisted that she be beached in Starehole Bay at the mouth of the estuary.

On 19 June she was successfully refloated amidst great cheering from the watching crowds, taken to the supposedly sandy cove, and run ashore. University students on vacation volunteered to assist in clearing the rotting grain, and by 27 June had reduced the original 4,242 tons to less than 1,500. It was a close-run thing, and had the ship not worked herself into the sand and settled down on a hidden reef, she might well have survived the south-easterly gale of 18 July which caused her to break her back. Similarly, had the Salcombe authorities allowed her inside the harbour a month previously, she would have discharged her cargo in half the time, completed repairs and sailed.

Assisted by work gangs from ashore, the remaining crew helped strip the wreck of all her fittings. Her figurehead and saloon, complete with

Ashore on the eastern side of Soar Mill Cove, near Salcombe, on 20 July 1972, the Dutch motor coaster Lenie *ran ashore in fog whilst carrying china clay from Par to Rotterdam. She was refloated the same day with the assistance of the Salcombe lifeboat.*

upholstery, curtains, lamps, clock and barometer, were donated to the Maritime Museum at Alands, Finland, and on 24 September the wreck was sold to Messrs Noyce, a Kingsbridge scrap metal dealer for £225. By January 1939, the *Torquay Times* reported that all four masts had gone overboard and that the wreck had broken into four separate pieces.

East of Salcombe, on Rickham sands, is where the Liverpool full-rigged ship *Meirion* went ashore in thick weather during the early hours of 7 September 1879. An iron ship built at Sunderland only the previous year, she had left Rangoon for London, commanded by Capt William Williams, on 13 March. With her holds full of rice and cutch, she was flying round the Cape of Good Hope in the teeth of a gale when she was flung on to her beam ends and suffered considerable damage. Her cabin was completely flooded and just about all the furniture and provisions aboard were destroyed, while able seaman Taylor was washed from off the upper deck and lost overboard. As she passed the Eddystone on her way up Channel, the wind swung from the south-west to south-east, forcing her inshore, and she was unable to weather the Prawle. The local rocket apparatus was used to save her entire crew, and the tug *Heron* made two attempts to pull her off, but failed.

From this point the cliffs run out towards Prawle Point, the southernmost extremity of Devon and the eastern boundary of this chapter. A German barque, the *Emilie*, went on the rocks here in dense fog at 8 pm on 29 May 1870 and eventually went to pieces. Bound from Iquique to Falmouth for orders, the 290 ton vessel, carrying saltpetre and a crew of 13, refused to go about after she had been sailed too close to the

The Dutch s.s. Betsy Anna *which went ashore in fog on 17 August 1926 on Prawle Point. She was refloated 47 days later and taken in tow for Cowes, but foundered in heavy weather off Portland Bill.*

Stranded in fog on Gara Rock, between Salcombe and Prawle Point on 11 April 1934, the French trawler Touquet *was refloated and saved three days later.*

shore in making a landfall. An anchor with 15 fathoms of chain was dropped, but the cable parted and the barque went ashore. The following day the crew returned to the scene intending to reboard her at low water and collect their belongings, but it was a wasted trip; the *Emilie* had already broken up and little remained above water.

Close at hand, on Gammon Head, are the remains of another victim of fog and the second tea clipper lost in the vicinity of Salcombe. This was the famous *Lalla Rookh*, lost on 3 March 1873. She was on passage from Shanghai to London with the first of a new season's leaf tea, 1,200 tons in all, plus a further twelve tons of tobacco, one passenger, a crew of 20 and a stowaway. They had left China on 22 October and made good time to the mouth of the English Channel, but were then slowed down by fog so dense that the helmsman could not even see the forecastle. They ploughed on past Cornwall and the Eddystone, completely blind to anything ahead, and her lookouts neither saw nor heard anything until Prawle Point loomed up only yards ahead. The *Lalla Rookh* struck just once, then

The Belgian fishing trawler Amelie-Suzanne, *which drove ashore on rocks in fog near Bolt Head, Salcombe, 1 April 1972 and went to pieces.*

drifted into a small cove where the mizzenmast fell clean through her bottom plates and she filled. Thomas Groves, the mate, lost his life when the first of the ship's boats launched was swamped; the only other victim was a stowaway, who was thought to have died from dysentery in his bunk before the ship went ashore. Prawle Point coastguards rescued 15 of the crew by breeches buoy, the remainder saving themselves by jumping onto the rocks and scaling the cliffs.

Other losses around Prawle Point include the 1,292 ton ship *Glad Tidings*, and the barque *Patria*. Registered at St Johns, New Brunswick, the *Glad Tidings* had some 1,900 tons of raw linseed on board from Calcutta. Charles McMillan, her master, calling at Falmouth for orders, was redirected to Amsterdam and was passing Salcombe when he mistook a light there for the Start. Thinking he was at least five miles offshore, he altered course to the north and soon after, the ship crashed on to the rocks a quarter of a mile west of Prawle. Some sparks from a distress flare fell into the lazarette and fire quickly spread throughout the ship. Nineteen of the crew were saved, but two drowned when they attempted to swim ashore. Nine years later, on 22 March 1888, the Porsgrunn barque *Patria* also went aground here to become a total loss, the victim of incorrect information given by a pilot vessel.

During the First World War there were several losses. Among them, the galliot *Kilkelina* drifted onto the rocks at Galmpton in January 1915 and broke up, and the schooner *St Clair*, two miles west of Mothecombe in Bigbury Bay, was lost with a cargo of coal in February 1915. The fishing ketch *Pursue* was sunk by a German submarine using 'bombs' in April 1917; the Norwegian steamship *Havbris* was torpedoed by *UB-32* in July 1917; and the steamships *Laertes*, of 4,451 tons gross, and *Newlyn* were both sunk by *UB-31* south of Prawle Point that August. In the last year of the war, the Brixham trawlers *Irex*, *Leonora* and *Rosebud*, were all sunk by German submarine, as was the steamship *Uskmoor* in March 1918, followed by the *Stockforce*, *Bretagne* and *Lord Stewart*.

The Second World War claimed the steamship *Talvaldis* on 9 July 1940; the fishing drifters *Intrepede* and *Pierre Descelliers*, both on 13 August 1942; the landing craft *LC(BB)-332* and *LC(BB)-362*, both on 19 September 1942; and the steam tug *Empire Harry*, along with the two barges she was towing, in June 1945.

In recent years, the old Dartmouth paddle steamer *Totnes Castle*, one of a quartet of such vessels laid up during the Second World War, which ferried passengers up and down the river Dart from 1948 to 1962, herself became a wreck. After a short period as accommodation ship for a sailing school which failed, she was bought for scrap by a Plymouth company, but sank off Bigbury Bay whilst under tow on 9 November 1967. The latest loss in this area was the Belgian fishing trawler *Amelie-Suzanne*, stranded and lost off Bolt Head in fog on 1 April 1972.

3

Prawle Point to Scabbacombe Head

Prawle Point occupies the same position in Devon as does the Lizard in Cornwall, both marking the southernmost extremity of their respective counties and both renowned for their one time Lloyd's signal station. Ships passing up or down Channel reported their progress to first one and then the other of these squat, white-painted buildings, whose telegraph link with Lloyd's of Leadenhall Street in London, played such an important part in seaborne trade.

As with the Lizard station, which has a phenomenal number of wrecks in its immediate vicinity, so Prawle Point has seen a quite remarkable number of incidents, both to the west and on the formidable stretch of coast reaching east to Start Point. Fittingly, one of the most famous shipwreck rescues in the whole of Devon took place here, a quarter of a mile west of the Start, on 23 March 1866, which led to the introduction by Queen Victoria of the Albert Medal for gallantry.

The London barque, *Spirit of the Ocean*, 578 tons, built by Jones & Co, was running down Channel in bad weather, bound for Halifax, Nova Scotia, when an attempt was made to reach the shelter of Dartmouth harbour. An offshore wind from the north-east caused the barque to fall off and she drifted away across Start Bay in great danger of becoming embayed should the wind change. She did just manage to scrape past Start Point itself, but then a submerged rock brought her to a shuddering halt and, shortly afterwards, the *Spirit of the Ocean* broke in two. On board were 24 passengers, 18 crew, and a valuable general cargo, including a large quantity of tea. The wreck occurred in such an inaccessible location that it is doubtful if anyone on board would have survived had not Samuel Popplestone, a Start Point farmer, actually seen her go ashore. He was instrumental in not only informing the Hallsands coastguard of the wreck, but risked his own life by climbing down the sheer face of the cliffs to save two men. It has often been stated that these were the only survivors, but in point of fact four men escaped alive, the mate, the bo'sun, and two seamen. A memorial to the 38 dead was erected in the form of a stained glass window in the south transept of the church at Stokenham.

Two and a half years later, on 10 December 1868, another disastrous shipwreck involving a sailing vessel took place, midway between the remains of the *Spirit of the Ocean* and Prawle Point, with a heavy loss of life. This was the 735 ton Liverpool-registered *Gossamer*, a full-rigged ship built by Alexander Stephen & Sons at Glasgow in 1864, and a vessel of considerable fame. She also had taken part in the annual tea races from Shanghai to London, and only two months before her loss had been the second vessel home from China. Now outward bound for Australia, the *Gossamer* left London for Adelaide with a general cargo, 24 crew, five passengers, and the master's wife aboard. Her passage west from the Downs was very stormy and Capt Thompson was obliged to remain on deck for one day and two whole nights without sleep. Whether or not this was over-zealous devotion to duty or distrust of the Channel pilot's ability is uncertain. Pilot Grant had joined the vessel at Gravesend and was to remain on board until the ship reached Plymouth, where additional passengers would be embarked.

In great need of rest, the captain finally went below to his cabin when the *Gossamer* was off Dartmouth, but had his sleep disturbed twice within the hour by the chief mate, who informed him that the pilot refused to set topsails. Much later, at the Board of Trade inquiry held at the Seven Stars inn at Chivelstone, a village about eight miles from Prawle, there was indisputable evidence that the pilot was not only under the influence of drink, but also negligent in refusing to set more canvas.

Meanwhile, on board, the sound of chain running out through both her hawsepipes was the first knowledge Capt Thompson had of the danger facing his command. For a full 20 minutes the *Gossamer* held to her anchors, then simultaneously, both cables parted and she went ashore. Unfortunately, she missed a shingle beach by less than 135 metres, hit some rocks and went to pieces, drowning 13 persons. In a desperate attempt to save his bride of only two weeks, the captain lashed his wife to a spar and was seen by watchers on the clifftop to be supporting her in the water. Neither survived, and it was assumed that they had been struck by falling wreckage and killed.

By Sunday 13 December, eight bodies, including those of the captain and his wife had been recovered and laid out in the belfry of Chivelstone church. Many relatives of those aboard visited the scene to recover

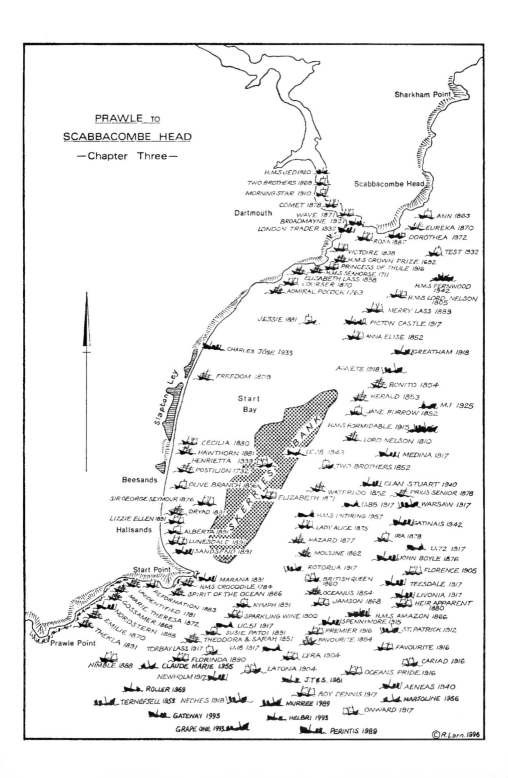

PRAWLE TO
SCABBACOMBE HEAD

—Chapter Three—

Sharkham Point

H.M.S JED 1920
TWO BROTHERS 1868
MORNING STAR 1910
COMET 1878
WAVE 1871
BROADMAYNE 1921
LONDON TRADER 1937

Scabbacombe Head

Dartmouth

ANN 1863
EUREKA 1870
DOROTHEA 1972
ROSA 1887
TEST 1932

VICTOIRE 1838
H.M.S CROWN PRIZE 1692
PRINCESS OF THULE
H.M.S SEAHORSE 1711
ELIZABETH LASS 1858
COURSER 1870
ADMIRAL POCOCK 1763

H.M.S FERNWOOD 1942
H.M.S LORD NELSON 1805
MERRY LASS 1889

JESSIE 1891

PICTON CASTLE 1917
ANNA ELISE 1852
GREATHAM 1918

CHARLES JOSE 1933

AGNETE 1918

FREEDOM 1809

Start Bay

BONITO 1854
HERALD 1853
M.1 1925
JANE BURROW 1852
H.M.S FORMIDABLE 1915
LORD NELSON 1810
MEDINA 1917

CECILIA 1880
HAWTHORN 1881
HENRIETTA 1939
POSTILION 17..

UC.18 1943

TWO BROTHERS 1852

Slapton Ley

S K E R R I E S   B A N K S

Beesands

OLIVE BRANCH 1856

CLAN STUART 1940
PRIUS SENIOR 1878
WARSAW 1917

SIR GEORGE SEYMOUR 1876

WATERLOO 1852
ELIZABETH 1871
U.85 1917

DRYAD 189.

LIZZIE ELLEN 1891

H.M.S UNTIRING 1957
LADY ALICE 1875
GATINAIS 1942
IRA 1878

Hallsands

ALBERTA 1891
LUNESDALE 1891
SANDSEND 1891

HAZARD 1877
MOLLINE 1862

U.72 1917
JOHN BOYLE 1876

Start Point

ROTORUA 1891

FLORENCE 1905

MARANA 1891
H.M.S CROCODILE 1784
REFORMATION 1883
SPIRIT OF THE OCEAN 1866

BRITISH QUEEN 1860
OCEANUS 1854
JAMSON 1868

TEESDALE 1917
LIVONIA 1917
HEIR APPARENT 1880

UNIDENTIFIED 1781
MARIE THERESA 1872
GOSSAMER 1868
NORDSTERN 1888
EMILIE 1870
THEKLA 1891

NYMPH 1891
SPARKLING WINE 1900
UC.51 1917
SUSIE PATO 1891
THEODORA & SARAH 1851

H.M.S AMAZON 1866
SPENNYMORE 1915
PREMIER 1916
FAVOURITE 1854

ST. PATRICK 1912
FAVOURITE 1916

Prawle Point

TORBAY LASS 1917
FLORINDA 1890
NIMBLE 1888   CLAUDE MARIE 1955
NEWHOLM 1917

U.18 1917
LATONA 1904

LYRA 1904
J.T.&S. 1961

CARIAD 1916
OCEANS PRIDE 1916
AENEAS 1940

ROLLER 1969
TERNEFJELL 1953   NECHES 1918
GATEWAY 1993
GRAPE ONE 1993

MURREE 1989
HELBRI 1993
PERINTIS 1989

BOY DENNIS 1917

MARJOLINE 1956
ONWARD 1917

© R. Larn. 1996

property or identify the dead, but literally thousands of pounds worth of goods found their way into the hands of the wreckers. A detachment of police and troops had to be sent for and, under the leadership of Superintendent Vaughan and Captain Mauthom of the coastguard service, attempted to save as much cargo as possible and prevent further looting. But it was already scattered far and wide, giving spectators ample opportunity to help themselves.

Pilot Grant, who caused the wreck in the first place, was found guilty of manslaughter at the local sessions, remanded on bail of £350, and sent for trial at the Exeter assize the following March. Whilst much of her cargo was salvaged at the time, that remaining was investigated by sport divers until the 1980s when Stephen George, the same diver who located the Erme estuary historic wreck sites, found many interesting relics in the remains of her iron hull. Joined by members of the Northampton BS-AC who made up the Bigbury Bay Investigation Team, they uncovered a wealth of interesting artefacts, at the same time stumbling across a much earlier, forgotten wreck nearby which held hundreds of items of mostly silver and pewter jewellery. The identity of this early wreck, possibly c1780, remains unknown.

If the *Gossamer* provided the locals with clothing, then the next wreck, that of an Italian brig, gave them fuel at a time of year when it was most appreciated. The *Marie Theresa* of Genoa, Nicola Bozza master, left Newcastle for her home port with 850 tons of coal in late November 1872. On 4 December, when 15 miles west of the Start, a green light appeared on her starboard bow. This vessel then altered course directly towards the Italian until both sidelights were clearly visible. Shortly afterwards, she struck the *Marie Theresa* a terrific blow on her port side, cutting her planking down to the waterline, then backed off and sailed away. In imminent danger of foundering, the brig was headed inshore and beached one mile east of the signal station, where she broke up very quickly. Fortunately, no lives were lost amongst the crew of twelve, all of whom landed at Lannacombe Bay in their own boat.

Seemingly, that was the end of the incident, but what was to follow must surely be unique in wreck history. The Italian crew of the brig were quartered overnight at an East Prawle inn and gave no trouble until next morning, when, for reasons unknown, they began to quarrel amongst themselves. One of the seamen then went berserk and stabbed three of his shipmates with a knife. With no policeman in the village, the only authority to whom the landlord could look was the coastguard. When

Carrying a cargo of china clay from Par to Velsen, the m.v. Heye-P *stranded on Prawle Point during a gale on 17 December 1979, and subsequently broke up in heavy seas.*

eventually one of them appeared in uniform, the half-crazed seaman mistook him for the law and fled towards the coastguard station and houses. The duty officer at the station opened the door in answer to his knock, only to be violently assaulted and stabbed five times in the chest. His wife, attracted by her husband's shouts, was also stabbed three times, and another officer and his wife 14 times between them. As the assailant left the building, he was confronted by the chief boatman and another officer, both of them armed with cutlasses. They, too, were attacked, whereupon the senior of them drew his cutlass and, choosing his moment, felled the Italian with a single blow from which he later died.

Such incidents were, of course, exceptional and the majority of wrecks received little or no publicity in 19th century newspapers, especially if their cargo was as singularly unattractive as the 70 tons of boulders on

The Panamanian m.v. Demetrios, *broken in two on the rocks on Prawle Point, 18 December 1992 after breaking away from a tug in a gale, whilst under tow for breaking in the Mediterranean.*

board the Fleetwood schooner *Utility*, which went ashore near Prawle during a south-easterly gale on 3 January 1879. Capt Sumner and his crew of five managed to get away in the ship's boat when the 20 year old vessel broke up. In the same area, the Swedish barque *Thekla*, 378 tons gross, was wrecked on 8 May 1891, and might well have been joined by the steamer *Pinedene* on 17 January 1901 which had lost her propeller in a collision, but for strenuous efforts made by local tugs.

The names of 23 known ships lost on Prawle Point include the Amsterdam owned Dutch East Indiaman *Boot*, wrecked 8 November 1738. Homeward bound with a cargo valued at 33,853 guilders for Hoorn and 33,638 guilders for Enkhuizen, of her 80 crew only two were lost. Two hundred and forty one years later, on 17 December 1979, the Ramsey registered coaster *Heye-P*, went ashore during a gale almost on top of the remains of the *Boot*, directly underneath the coastguard station.

The largest wreck on Prawle Point was the Panamanian motor vessel

Demetrios (ex-*Long Lin*), which broke from the tug *Nastorozhenny* on 18 December 1992 at the height of a gale, and drifted four miles before going ashore on the rocks 95 metres west of Prawle Point where she broke her back. On passage for breaking in the Mediterranean, she had only just left a Dunkirk ship repair yard where leaks had been repaired. As if to prove that the Devon instinct for wrecking was not dead, people in their hundreds descended on the broken ship, and the local police confiscated many items looted from her bridge as they were brought ashore.

Start Point, which lies three and a quarter miles east-north-east of Prawle, is easily identified from seaward by the five hillocks, each about 60 metres high, that give it a rugged cockscomb appearance. Since it represents a turning point in coastal navigation, it is not surprising that a great many vessels have come to grief there, either on the rocks or in the immediate vicinity. In 1781, on 26 January, the same day that the brandy-laden *Wierkelyk* was lost at Plymouth, an unidentified ship was wrecked on the Start and all hands lost. Three years later the *Crocodile*, a 6th rate, 24 gun man o'war, was also wrecked here, with 200 dead, whilst returning from the West Indies.

Even more lives were lost in the disastrous collision between the emigrant ship *Favourite* and the *Hesper* on 29 April 1854. The former was carrying emigrants from Bremen to Baltimore when, in heavy rain and rough seas, she was struck by the American vessel on her starboard side. Capt Hoegman of the *Favourite* was asleep in his bunk at the time and reached the upper deck, still in his night clothes, just as the *Hesper* was beginning to pull clear. To abandon his passengers and command at such a critical moment was unforgivable, yet without a moment's hesitation he leapt for the receding bows of the *Hesper*, gained a handhold, and scrambled to safety, his example prompting the first officer and four seamen to follow suit.

As the gap between the two ships widened, so the sea poured into the hold of the *Favourite* and the 191 despairing emigrants and the ten remaining members of her crew were left to their fate. A combination of extreme darkness and rough seas prevented the *Hesper* from effecting any sort of rescue. She remained in the vicinity all night, but at daybreak not a trace of the sinking vessel was to be found. The six men who had so cowardly abandoned their ship were the only survivors from the original complement of 207.

Collision at sea was, of course, common in those days, and another occurred that same year, on 17 September, involving the Norwegian barque *Oceanus*, commanded by Capt Norbeck, and an unidentified American schooner. Carrying 500 tons of rice from Akyab, the *Oceanus* of Kristiansund was run down and cut clean to the waterline off Start Point. The colliding vessel, after backing off, refused to render any assistance and stood away down Channel. Fortunately, the Brixham lugger *Hero* was on hand and took off the *Oceanus*'s master and some seamen, the remainder landing from their own boat at Gun cliff, in Lyme Bay. The only casualty was a seaman who was killed outright when the foremast collapsed and struck him on the head. Another incident involving collision off the Start took place on 7 August 1862 when 16 men drowned; this was when the *Moulin* and *Daphne* ran into one another. But when, a year later on 25 May 1863, the *Lovely Lady*, an Aberystwyth schooner, was struck a fatal blow by the barque *Korswein*, the sea claimed only her cargo, 128 tons of salt.

As the volume of sea traffic along the coast increased during the second half of the 19th century, so did the number of shipping incidents. Ironically, not a single steamship was involved until 1866 when, by sheer coincidence, steamship struck steamship, these being the collier *Osprey* and the sloop HMS *Amazon*. The 1,081 ton warship, built at Pembroke Dock only 14 months previously and armed with two 64 pounder cannons, had the worst of the collision and foundered, but without loss of life. On 28 February 1868 the Truro schooner *Samson*, with 50 tons of lime on board for Hull, was run down and sunk during a rain-storm by the brigantine *Mercury* of Llanelly; the *Lady Alice*, a Salcombe schooner carrying coal, was sent to the bottom by the German steamer *Nuonburg* on 10 October 1875, and the second steamship to founder from the same cause was the 633 ton *John Boyle* of Cardiff, on 4 April the following year, after striking the Whitby steamship *Emma Lawson*.

Inshore incidents must not be forgotten, since in 1881 the 295 tons gross wooden barque *Hawthorn*, of Arbroath, was wrecked on Start Point during a west-southwesterly gale, the only vessel over 200 tons to be stranded until 1888. This was the German steamer *Nordstern* of Bremen, loaded with wine from Malaga, ashore on 13 January. Her crew took to their own boats and were partway to Salcombe when met by the lifeboat *Lesty*, out on her first service. The German seamen refused to board the lifeboat and continued rowing towards the harbour entrance, but were taken aback by the huge breakers over the bar. Eventually, a member of the lifeboat's crew was put into each of the two boats to act as a pilot, and the procession gained the inner harbour without incident.

Of the many disastrous storms that have swept over the West Country, few, if any, could have equalled the violence of the 'Great Blizzard' that lasted from 9 to 13 March 1891. Not even the hurricane of 1866, which caused so much damage in the Torbay area, or some of the earlier gales that lashed Plymouth Sound, could match this holocaust. Of the many vessels lost in Devon, four were wrecked in the Start Point area. Of these, the worst in terms of lives lost was the steamer *Marana* of Liverpool, a 2,177 tons gross, iron-hulled ship built by Aitkens of Glasgow in 1880. Her last voyage began on 1 March when she left the Victoria docks, London, with railway sleepers for Colombo, under orders to coal ship at Swansea en route. She reached the western end of Lyme Bay during the afternoon of 9 March and shortly afterwards was overtaken by the easterly hurricane which came roaring up astern.

Despite near blizzard conditions, which completely blinded both lookouts and helmsman, the *Marana*'s captain kept her at full speed, with the result she plunged onto the Blackstone rock, tearing off both rudder and propeller. Realising that she must break up, her crew took to two boats; the captain, chief engineer, steward and three mates in the smallest, the remaining 22 men in the larger, port side lifeboat. In rowing west towards Prawle, they became separated, the smaller boat frequently disappearing from view in the troughs of huge waves. Nothing of this boat nor its occupants was ever seen again. The larger boat reached Horseley cove, a mile north-east of the coastguard station, but no sooner had the craft turned bows-on to the sea than it capsized. Some of the occupants managed to grasp the lifelines and hang on until she righted herself, but were thrown off when the sea capsized the boat for a second time. Only four stokers survived the ordeal, all of whom gained the shore by scrambling over Mal rock. One of the men, in an advanced state of exhaustion and unable to walk the short distance to Prawle village, was left in the care of two companions, the fourth member going for help.

He reached Prawle at 10.30 pm, a half frozen bewildered figure, unable to make himself understood amongst the several households roused from their beds. Fortunately, the significance of a soaking wet stranger knocking on doors at night was not lost on them, and a search party was immediately despatched. Despite scouring the beaches and cliff tops, it was the best part of three hours before the three Swedes were discovered behind a stone wall. Next day, Prawle coastguards struggled out to Start Point, no mean achievement with deep snow obscuring the path and filling deep crevices. Here they found the broken steamship and five corpses floating in the sea, in addition to hundreds of wooden railway sleepers, which were later salvaged and sold. One of the four survivors died from exposure, and nine days later, after the snow had melted, the frozen body of a fifth crewman was found close to the main cliff path.

At the height of the storm, a Hallsands lookout saw a hooker or mackerel boat in the breakers, and the keel of such a craft came ashore to support this story, followed by five bodies, one of which had an artificial foot. This last feature identified the wreck as the smack *Alberta* of Padstow, which had left Par for Gloucester with china clay. How she came to be so far east of her course will never be known.

The same evening that the *Marana* was lost the three-masted schooner *Lunesdale* went ashore at Hallsands. Bound for Lancashire with whiting, the 141 tons gross schooner was flung beam-on to the sea and bilged. Her four man crew were already in the rigging, but by the time the local fishermen and coastguards had linked arms in a human chain and reached the wreck, only the master remained alive. Drenched and cold from their immersion, the fishermen had hardly reached their homes before another wreck was reported. This was the *Lizzie Ellen*, a Chester schooner carrying china clay from Charlestown to London. Driven before the gale, she was wrecked at the foot of a cliff north of Hallsands, her mate and two seamen being the sole survivors. Her terrified, screaming cabin boy, who refused to leave the rigging and jump into the sea to be rescued, cost her master his life, since he remained behind persuading the lad to leave, and they drowned together when the wreck went to pieces.

But worse was to come. Another sailing ship was lost during the early hours of 10 March, with no survivors, and by the time the coastguards reached the beach it was all over and the vessel smashed to pieces. Lettering on her forecastle showed the victim to have been the 1,035 ton, iron full-rigged ship *Dryad*, which had left Shields for Valparaiso on 3 March. Built on the Mersey by Roydons in 1874, the *Dryad* normally carried a crew of 22, but her owners confirmed one man had been left behind. It is possible that another wreck occurred at Hallsands in the gale, as lights were seen offshore at the height of the storm. Next day a piece of broken timber bearing the words, '*Nynph* of T-' was found, but could have come from anywhere.

Less than a month later, the 642 ton steam collier *Sandsend* was lost on the Start in dense fog, bringing the total number of wrecks at Start within 30 days to six, probably seven. Since then the sea has almost completely demolished the village of South Hallsands, which was abandoned after a

86

The 15,000 ton battleship Formidable, *a Majestic class warship, which was torpedoed and sunk with a heavy loss of life off Start Point on New Year's Day 1915.*

particularly bad storm and tide during the First World War. It is quite remarkable that it was ever possible to work fishing boats from off this rugged beach, even in good weather, yet in the old days, the village had a thriving fishing community and kept a number of Newfoundland dogs, magnificent creatures which had been trained to swim out beyond the breakers and bring the end of a rope ashore in their teeth.

Of the many warships lost around the Devon coast, by far the largest was the 15,000 ton battleship *Formidable*, which was torpedoed and sunk with a very heavy loss of life on New Year's Day 1915. Launched at Portsmouth on 17 November 1898, the *Formidable* was built as a Majestic class warship, which embodied many of the improved Canopus class features, making her one of the most powerful ships of her day. Part of the Channel Fleet, the *Formidable*, in company with other capital ships, was steaming in line ahead towards the west in the face of a gale. At 3 am, when off Start Point and last in the line, *Formidable* was hit on the port side by one, possibly two torpedoes, fired by the German submarine *U-24*; she settled down with a list to starboard and sank within 45 minutes.

Sea conditions were so bad that only four of her boats could be launched. Of these, one capsized, throwing its occupants into the sea. A second got clear with 70 men aboard who were picked up by a light cruiser, whilst the third, a pinnace with 60 survivors, made for Lyme Regis. Before this boat reached the shore, nine men had died from exposure and wounds, all of whom were buried in Lyme cemetery. One young seaman, presumed dead, was covered by sacking, which attracted a dog to sleep on top of the 'corpse', the animal's warmth revived him and it is understood that he was still alive in 1975 and visiting the area every year.

The last of the four boats to leave the *Formidable* was a launch carrying 69 seamen and one officer, Torpedo Gunner Hurrigan. They drifted out to sea and the boat might well have foundered, since it had a hole in one side stopped only by a pair of underpants. Fortunately it was seen by the Brixham trawler *Provident*, skipper William Pillar, who carried out a daring rescue in very difficult conditions. He took his boat alongside the big navy launch four times in all, saving everyone aboard, and landed them safely at Brixham. A tablet commemorating the rescue of 18 officers and 183 men from the *Formidable* was placed on the obelisk on Brixham quay, where it served also as a memorial to her captain and at least 648 dead. The tablet has since been removed and is believed now to be inside the Town Hall.

Other war losses in the vicinity of Start Point included over 30 steamships, the trawling ketch *Favourite* (BM240), sunk by submarine gunfire in September 1916, and many fishing boats of the Brixham fleet.

A distinguished war loss was the *Medina* of 12,350 tons gross, which once had the distinction of serving as a royal yacht. During the evening of 28 April 1917, having left Plymouth for London early that same day on the last leg of a passage home from India via the Suez Canal, for part of which she had carried Lord and Lady Carmichael, the retiring Governor of India, she was torpedoed in her engine room and sank within 45 minutes. Six of her 'black gang' lost their lives in the explosion, being the fourth engineer and five native firemen. She sank in over 60 metres of water, taking to the bottom a general cargo which included tin, and all Lord Carmichael's possessions. Her tin was salvaged in 1932, and in 1986 Consortium Recovery Ltd using the salvage vessel *Holgerdane* retrieved large quantities of personal effects, including letters, masonic jewels, clothing and Oriental objets d'art, which were sold by Sotheby's at an auction held at Billingshurst on 26 May 1988.

The war was not completely one-sided in this area, however, since a number of German submarines were also destroyed hereabouts. The *UC-51* was submerged off the Start, waiting for targets, when on 17 November 1917 some sort of accident caused her cargo of mines to explode. The Admiralty-requisitioned trawler *Lois* was on patrol in the area at the time and her crew were startled to hear a massive underwater explosion, after which the submarine appeared on the surface close at hand, then rolled over and sank. A number of intact horned contact mines floated to the surface, accompanied by a great deal of oil, rubbish and human entrails; positive identification came from a German seaboot marked with the name 'Edward Metzger'. It was a British minefield in much the same area off Start that brought about the end of the *U-18* the same day as the *UC-51* was lost, and previously the *U-85* on 12 March, and the *U-72* on 12 May.

Apart from a few fishing boats sent to the bottom by scuttling charges, the Norwegian steamer *Livonia*, torpedoed on 3 December 1917 with the loss of 23 crew, and the *Agnete* on 29 April 1918, were the last of the war losses.

It was mid-November 1925 when the nation learned of another accident involving a British submarine, the fourth since the war had ended. It was the massive *M-1* that had gone missing, feared lost, somewhere off Start Point, and half the Royal Navy was out searching for her.

The *M-1* and eight other conventional boats were placed in reserve as part of the fifth submarine flotilla attached to HMS *Dolphin*. On 12 November 1925, having been brought up to operational standard, the *M-1* put to sea accompanied by the *H-22*, *H-29*, *H-30*, *H-34*, the parent vessel *Maidstone*, and the tender *Alecto*. At some time during the exercise the *M-1* failed to surface and a full-scale search was initiated. A German salvage company offered the use of their deep-diving armoured dress, and went down to 76 metres on many occasions, even to 70 metres at night when tidal conditions were favourable, but found nothing.

The first clue as to the fate of the *M-1* came from the merchant ship *Vidar*, of 2,159 tons gross, after she had docked at Stockholm. Her master, Capt Anell, reported that at approximately 7.45 pm on 12 November, when in position 49.59° N, 03.55° W, his ship had struck a submerged, or partially submerged object. Examination of the *Vidar* in dry dock showed

The Belgian collier Charles Jose, *of Antwerp which stranded on Slapton Sands, 17 December 1933. After her cargo of coal was discharged onto the beach, she was refloated and saved.*

her stem to be badly bent over to port, with several rivets gone and plating damaged. There were also traces of grey paint with no possible connection with the steamer's own colour scheme. A large Japanese steamer, the *Aden Maru*, passed close to the *Vidar* and on the same track at the instant of the supposed collision, and may have been involved, but she neither stopped nor reported any unusual occurrence.

After three weeks of fruitless searching the hunt was officially abandoned on 2 December, but the wreck has since been relocated in deep water by the authors, using magnetometer and side-scan equipment, which clearly shows the submarine sitting upright, its huge twelve inch gun still in its turret forward of the conning tower.

During the Second World War the twin-screw steamer *Aeneas* sank offshore from the Start after having been bombed on 2 July 1940. Built during 1910 at the Belfast yard of Workham Clark, the *Aeneas* had already survived the previous war as a troopship, as well as a stranding on Rathlin island. The *Clan Stuart* also went to the bottom, not as a result of enemy action but through collision with the *Orlock Head* on 11 March, which also went down. Since then the only incident of particular interest was the scuttling of HM submarine *Untiring* on 25 July 1957. During 1945 she was loaned to the Greek Navy and renamed *Zifias*, but on return was considered obsolete and selected for sinking as an asdic training target in deep water.

During research into wrecks in this area, a great many names and dates were uncovered but seldom was a location given other than 'lost in Start Bay', or 'near Dartmouth'. The stretch of coast between the Start and Dartmouth measures about ten miles, and along with the great Skerries bank lying offshore must have been the scene of many a shipwreck. Known incidents range from the *Postilion* at Beesands in 1732, to the salvage craft *LC(S)-18*, which broke from her tow and went ashore on the Skerries on 4 December 1943.

At the end of the 12th century a considerable business grew at Dartmouth out of shipbuilding and repairs. The first street in Dartmouth was the 'street of the smiths', which still survives, but in its original form ran parallel to Millpool, then a creek or inlet, said to have been a quarter of a mile long, separating Hardness and Clifton. Ships once tied up alongside the wall of St Saviour's church, but this was at a time when Dartmouth was a centre for privateering, and when every shipload of cloth sent down from Totnes outward bound was matched by two shiploads of fish from Newfoundland and another three full of European wines coming in.

Which particular wreck brought the renowned diver Jacob Johnson to the area in 1629 is not known, but it appears that he was 'forbidden to use his endeavour at Dartmouth by the Mayor and Town Clerk'. In August of the same year, Johnson petitioned the Lords of the Admiralty and obtained a warrant to employ his art and industry by diving in the harbours and creeks of the Isle of Wight, the Lizard in Cornwall, Ireland, and elsewhere, for the recovery of bullion, cannon, anchors and cables. By September he was back in Dartmouth and raised five pieces of ordnance, but was not allowed to proceed 'unless he would compound with the town'. This is the first reference to diving in the area, but it was not long before local men became interested in its possibilities. During the summer of 1716, a Nathaniel Symens of Totnes was able 'to remain submerged in the river Dart before 100 persons for three-quarters of an hour, but

In ballast from London to Newport News, the Swansea registered tanker Broadmayne *stranded in thick fog on the Kingswear side of Dartmouth harbour 1 January 1921, where she broke in two, only her bow section being refloated.*

complained that though a great number of gentlemen were present, he received but one crown from them all'.

Twenty lives were lost on 9 February 1692 when the 26 gun, 6th rate man o'war *Crown Prize* was lost outside the harbour entrance, and another Queen's ship, the 14 gun, 6th rate *Seahorse*, on 26 December 1711 'near Dartmouth'. Wrecks during the following century were mostly small and of less than 500 tons, such as the 31 year old schooner *Courser*, Fecamp to Torbay in ballast, stranded one mile west of the Dart estuary in Redlap cove on 13 February 1870 with the loss of five of her six-man crew.

Two rusting boilers and plating in the vicinity of Newfoundland cove are all that remain of what was the largest of the local wrecks at the time. The oil-tanker *Broadmayne* of London, outward bound for Newport

News, stranded in thick fog on New Year's Day 1921, close to the seamark on the Kingswear side. Weather conditions were so appalling, with a full gale blowing from the south-west accompanied by heavy rain, that the launching of the Brixham lifeboat *Betsey Newbon* had to be delayed until 2 am next day, by which time conditions had improved. Coxswain Sanders and Signalman Noraway went on foot to Brounston farm, from where they set out to search the cliffs and eventually located the wreck. They then climbed down the cliff face in darkness to a point from where they could communicate with the crew, but despite advice to remain on board until the lifeboat could reach them, 16 of the crew left the ship and clambered to safety. The fog continued so thick that even when the *Betsey Newbon* arrived off Dartmouth, her crew failed to see the wreck even after searching the rocks for six hours. Finally, at 5.30 am, a rocket fired from the deck of the *Broadmayne* attracted their attention and the lifeboat moved in to rescue 28 men still aboard.

The Brixham section of the rocket brigade made a gallant effort to assist, dragging their cumbersome wagon to John Brocks Mews, where three horses were requisitioned. The team then began the long haul up and over Hill Head road and were close to exhaustion when they finally reached the scene of the wreck, only to discover their rope ladders were too short to reach the rocks below. The wreck eventually broke in two, the forepart being refloated and towed into Mill cove where it was broken up, the stern section being abandoned.

Whereas the *Broadmayne* was broken in two by the forces of nature, the next steamship to be stranded at Dartmouth, the *English Trader*, was deliberately cut in order to save the greater part of the vessel. The lessons of ship surgery had already been learnt in the West Country when two other steamers, the *Highland Fling* and the *Suevic*, had been saved by this technique, and the removal of the *English Trader*'s bow section was relatively easy. Built by the Furness Shipbuilding Co in 1934 as the *Arctees*, she was one of the first three 'Arcform' vessels to be built to the order of Sir Joseph Islewood. It was while entering Dartmouth harbour on 23 January 1937 that she stranded close to the castle, and refused to move despite every effort by HM destroyer *Witch* and four tugs.

By 3 February rocks had pierced her forward tanks and it was decided to cut her in two, the operation taking just 19 days and the undamaged after section being towed into Dartmouth stern-first. She was then towed to Southampton, where tenders were invited for a complete repair, which entailed a complete rebuild from the boiler room forward. The Middle

The English Trader, *of London, wrecked on Checkstone ledge, under Dartmouth castle, after suffering a steering gear failure when entering the port on 23 January 1937. The lifeboat saved all 52 crew and she was refloated a month later, but only after her bow section had been cut away and left on the rocks.*

Docks & Engineering Co of South Shields secured the contract, and exactly 100 days later the *English Trader* was finished and ready for sea, a remarkable achievement considering that over 6,000 tons of cement in the bilges of No 2 hold had to be patiently chipped out before work could start. The abandoned bow section was later cut up and towed ashore for scrapping.

Wrecks to the east of Dartmouth, between the harbour and Scabbacombe Point, include the wooden brig *Eureka*, the auxiliary cutter *Test* and, more recently, several small fishing vessels. Carrying coal from Newcastle to Devonport, the *Eureka*, of 241 tons, was less than a year old when she struck the cliffs near Pudcombe cove on 6 February 1870, drowning three of her nine-man crew. The *Test* (BM93), was a local three ton vessel built at Exmouth in 1928, the foundering following collision with the excursion steamer *Duke of Devonshire* on 15 August 1932. Since then, a number of small, mostly local, fishing boats have been lost, including the crabber *Dorothea*, which went ashore in Newfoundland cove on 17 February 1972 with the loss of all three of her crew, and the 25 ton Brixham trawler *Catherine Allen*, two miles offshore on 28 October 1973.

The *Catherine Allen* capsized when a heavy trawl was being swung across her deck, and she foundered in 37 metres of water with a 13 year old schoolboy, Kevin Crocker, asleep in the stern cabin. Despite rescue attempts by the Fishery Protection Vessel *Kedleston*, divers from RNAS Culdrose, the motor cruiser *John Teast* and the navy salvage vessel *Pintail*, the boy unfortunately drowned.

4
Torbay and Brixham

The 25 miles of coastline between Scabbacombe and Hopes Nose, the geographical limits of this chapter, are taken up almost entirely by the wide sweep of Torbay. It was Lord Howe who exclaimed in 1795 that 'Torbay will be the grave of the Navy', having witnessed from the quarterdeck of HM man o'war *Queen Charlotte* no less than 27 warships in his fleet lose their anchors and cables in a gale, but fortunately his prophecy was incorrect. In fact, less than ten warships have been wrecked in this area, and not all these belonged to the Royal Navy.

Since Torbay is completely sheltered from westerly winds, it has been a popular anchorage and haven since earliest times. The Domestic State Papers contain many early references to Devon wrecks, but the earliest with a positive location relates to 30 November 1657, when a vessel was reported as being stranded in Torbay and 'Captain Pley and constables were recruited to prevent the country people making havoc with her'.

During the early part of 1745, Devon and Cornwall were asked to provide recruits for the West Indies expedition, and the transport *Tiger* left Plymouth with hundreds of raw troops aboard on 27 February. No sooner had the *Tiger* reached the open sea than she was overtaken by a hurricane, blown up Channel and wrecked under Berry Head. Troops and crew alike leapt overboard in an attempt to get ashore, but the majority drowned like rats and by morning 170 bodies lay strewn along the beach. Those who escaped attempted to reach Plymouth, where posters were already offering the public a reward of one pound for every soldier caught. At the same time Admiral Medlen's fleet, consisting of a large convoy and escort vessels, lying at anchor in Torbay, were driven to sea before the wind, every single vessel having had to cut its cable. The East Indiaman *Royal George* ran foul of the *Cape Coast*, which foundered but without loss of life. Another transport, the *Expeditious*, also went ashore under Berry Head and there was much confusion as to whether survivors were from her or the *Tiger*.

Of the warships mentioned earlier as having fallen foul of the Torbay

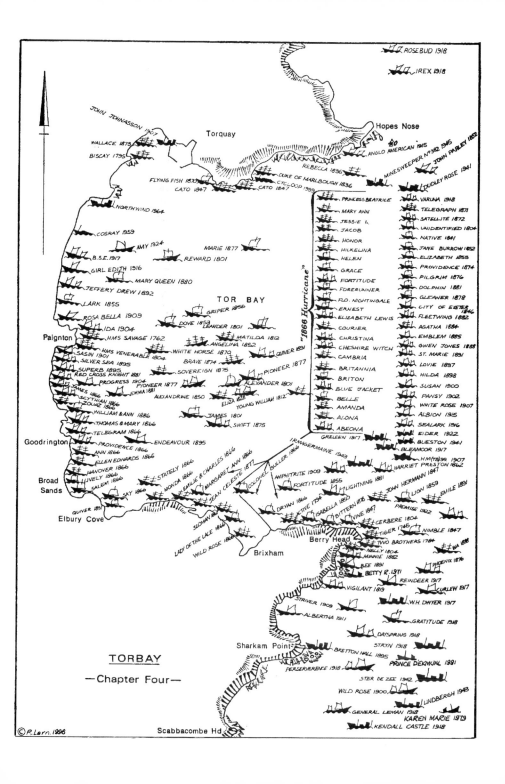

ROSEBUD 1918
IREX 1918

JOHN JOHNASSON 1907

Torquay

Hopes Nose

WALLACE 1873
BISCAY 1795

ANGLO AMERICAN 1915
REBECCA 1836
DUKE OF MARLBOUGH 1836
CYCLOOP 1959

MINESWEEPER N°382 1945
JOHN PARLEY 1852
DUDLEY ROSE 1941

FLYING FISH 1870
CATO 1847
CATO 1847

NORTHWIND 1964

PRINCESS BEATRICE
MARY ANN
JESSIE I.
JACOB
HONOR
HILKELINA
HELEN
GRACE
FORTITUDE
FORERUNNER
FLO. NIGHTINGALE
ERNEST
ELIZABETH LEWIS
COURIER
CHRISTINA
CHESHIRE WITCH
CAMBRIA
BRITANNIA
BRITON
BLUE JACKET
BELLE
AMANDA
ALONA
ABEONA
GRELEEN 1917

VARUNA 1918
TELEGRAPH 1871
SATELLITE 1872
UNIDENTIFIED 1804
NATIVE 1841
JANE BURROW 1852
ELIZABETH 1855
PROVIDENCE 1874
PILGRIM 1876
DOLPHIN 1881
GLEANER 1878
CITY OF EXETER 1846
FLEETWING 1882
AGATHA 1884
EMBLEM 1885
GWEN JONES 1888
ST. MARIE 1891
LOVIE 1897
HILDA 1898
SUSAN 1900
PANSY 1902
WHITE ROSE 1907
ALBION 1915
SEALARK 1916
EIDER 1922
BLUESTON 1941
BLEAMOOR 1917

COSRAY 1959

AMY 1924
MARIE 1877

B.S.E. 1917
REWARD 1801

GIRL EDITH 1916

MARY QUEEN 1880

JEFFERY DREW 1892

LARK 1855

TOR BAY

"1868 Hurricane"

ROSA BELLA 1909
GRIPER 1856

LIDA 1904
DOVE 1853
LEANDER 1801

Paignton
HMS SAVAGE 1762
MATILDA 1812

HMS VENERABLE 1804
WHITE HORSE 1870
ANGELINA 1852

SASIN 1901
BRAVE 1874
QUIVER 1891

SILVER SEA 1895
SOVEREIGN 1875
PIONEER 1877

SUPERB 1895
RED CROSS KNIGHT 1881
PIONEER 1877

PROGRESS 1904
ALEXANDER 1801

JAMES 1866
EMMA 1881
ELIZA 1828

SCYTHIAN 1866
ALEXANDRINE 1850
YOUNG WILLIAM 1812

ZOUAVE 1866
WILLIAM & ANN 1886
JAMES 1801

THOMAS & MARY 1866
SWIFT 1875

TELEGRAM 1866

Goodrington
PROVIDENCE 1866
ENDEAVOUR 1895

ANN 1866

ELLEN EDWARDS 1866

HANOVER 1866
STATELY 1866
RANGERMAINE 1943

Broad
Sands
LIVELY 1866
SALEM 1866
MONDA 1866
EMILIE & CHARLES 1866
AMPHITRITE 1909
COLONEL BULLER

LIGHTNING 1881

MARGARET ANN 1866
FORTITUDE 1855

LION 1859

HARRIET 1847
HM(T)399 1907
PRESTON 1862

JOHN HERMANN 1899
EMILE 1891

SKY 1866
JEAN CELESTE 1877
DRYAN 1866
ISABELLA 1806
PROMISE 1922

QUIVER 1891
KIVIE 1794
BITTERN 1870
VINE 1847

Elbury Cove
SLOMAN 1866
CERBERE 1804

LADY OF THE LAKE 1846
TIGER 1745
NIMBLE 1847

WILD ROSE 1868
Brixham
Berry Head
TWO BROTHERS 1784
BIA 1688

NELLY 1804
MINNIE 1882
PHOENIX 1876

BEE 1891

BETTY R. 1971

REINDEER 1917

VIGILANT 1819
CURLEW 1917

STRIVER 1909
W.H. DWYER 1917

ALBERTHA 1911
GRATITUDE 1918

DAYSPRING 1918

Sharkam Point
STRYN 1918

BRETTON HALL 1895
PRINCE DEKMUHL 1931

PERSEVERENCE 1918
STER DE ZEE 1942

WILD ROSE 1900
LINDBERGH 1943

GENERAL LEMAN 1918
KAREN MARIE 1979

KENDALL CASTLE 1918

TORBAY

—Chapter Four—

Scabbacombe Hd

© P. Larn. 1996

area, the first was the eight-gun sloop o'war *Savage* of 144 tons, ashore in February 1762, near Roundham Head. The small inlet in which the wreck took place is known to this day as Savage cove, but anything of the vessel that may remain will be well buried beneath the sand. The second warship to be lost was the *Cerbere*, a French gun brig armed with ten 18 pounder cannon. She had been captured by HMS *Viper* when off Mauritius on 29 July 1800. Under the command of Lt Patey, the *Cerbere* left Plymouth on 19 February 1804, but in working up Channel towards Dover she missed stays near Berry Head and went ashore during a northerly gale. Having no protruding keel and drawing less than 1.8 metres of water, the wreck lay very shallow, and all her guns and stores were readily accessible for salvage. Later that year, on 30 November, the brig *Nelly* of Teignmouth, carrying clay from Poole to Liverpool, also struck on Berry Head, bilged and became a total loss.

In the meantime, several wrecks had taken place within Torbay itself and the inhabitants of 'Torkay' as a 1771 edition of the *Exeter Flying Post* shows, were not slow to appreciate the value of a perishable cargo:

'The brig *St Peter*, William Causey, from London, laden with groceries from this (Exeter) city, having overshot her port and got opposite Torkay on Friday night last, 1 September, in a heavy gale to the eastward, drove ashore about a mile to the westward of Tor Abbey, and was dashed to pieces. The cargo was supposed to be worth £4,000, the greater part of which was lost, the crew being happily saved. Immediately on going to pieces, the country people came down in great numbers to plunder the wreck, and even robbed the captain of his watch; on which George Cary Esq of Tor Abbey, accompanied by his brother and several armed men, seized the ringleaders, of whom they immediately sent on board a man o'war, and by their endeavours saved all they could of the cargo, and secured it in their cellars.'

Whether or not the owners ever saw this cargo once locked away in Cary's cellar, is left to the imagination!

The last days of December 1778 saw many inhabitants of Brixham and Torquay on the cliff top at Berry Head, watching a fleet of 300 merchantmen sailing down Channel escorted by warships. Amongst these was the East Indiaman *London*, built by Perry at Blackwall in 1771. On passage to Bencoolen and China on her third voyage under Capt Webb, she carried 99 crew and 26 guns. On 28 December 1778 she collided with HMS *Russell*, of 74 guns, some two miles offshore and foundered within an hour, taking to the bottom a general cargo which included a large consignment of muskets for the Indian army.

The year 1748 brought a letter to the *Gentleman's Magazine* from a correspondent of Torbay giving news of another wreck, saying: 'This morning, 12 January, in thick snow and a hard gale of wind at south-east, the sloop *Two Brothers*, Capt West, from Plymouth to Portsmouth with eleven passengers, ran ashore about a mile to the westward of Berry Head and instantly went to pieces, only the captain being saved.' The next incident was on 12 November 1787, when a large Guernsey smuggling lugger was lost in Torbay and her crew of five drowned; the sloop *Active* was stranded and wrecked on 20 December 1794 near Brixham, and on 22 December 1795 George Cary performed yet another public service in connection with shipwreck. This was when the brig *Biscay* parted her cables and drove on to Tor Abbey sands, where she went to pieces. Her cargo, a valuable quantity of groceries, was, needless to say, lost almost entirely to the local wreckers. The ship's mate, four seamen and a boy, the only survivors, were taken in by Cary and given food and clothes, then sent out to help scour the coastline for the body of Capt Burgess, who was reported to be wearing a money belt, containing a large sum in gold. The corpse was found, but there was no sign of the belt.

A particularly severe gale on 12 April 1801 started another century of shipwreck incidents by adding four names to the list, the *James*, *Reward*, *Leander* and the West Indiaman *Alexander*; but these were minor losses compared to that of the *Venerable* in 1804, the third warship to be lost in the area. Considering the weather conditions and circumstances, it is remarkable that only three men lost their lives out of a crew of 555. It is also believed to be the only occasion on which a warship was lost because a seaman fell overboard. It was on 23 November 1804 that the fleet blockading Brest, under the command of Cornwallis, returned to Torbay, awaiting favourable winds. On the 24th, the flagship signalled an immediate departure just before dark, a decision which could not have been made at a more inopportune moment. None of the warships had received any warning of departure, no time was allowed them to shorten their anchor cables, most of the crews were at supper, and movements by large ships in the confines of Torbay at night was inviting disaster. On board the *Venerable*, a 3rd rate, 74 gun ship renowned throughout the navy as having remained loyal during the Nore mutiny, the call for 'all hands' brought them grumbling and unwilling to the upper deck, and within less than half an hour the ship was in trouble.

During the process of 'fishing' the anchor, a seaman slipped from the cathead and fell into the sea. As a boat was being lowered to rescue him, one of the falls was released prematurely, the boat was swamped, and suddenly a dozen men were floundering in the water, a midshipman and two seamen being drowned. A second boat was swung out and managed to save the remainder of the men, including the seaman responsible for the entire misadventure, but by now the *Venerable* had lost her position. She fell away to leeward and in the dark drifted down on to Paignton ledges, at Roundham Head, and went ashore. Distress signals were fired, but apart from HMS *Impeteux* and *Goliath*, the fleet was out of earshot. Both ships lowered every boat they had, thinking that the *Venerable* could easily be towed clear, but already the wind had freshened, causing the wreck to be thrown heavily against the rocks. Her masts were cut down, and had they fallen towards the shore they would easily have bridged the gap between ship and shore but, as it was, they fell to seaward and by 9 pm, when it was obvious she was doomed, the order was given to abandon ship.

Most of the ship's company owed their lives to the cutter *Frisk*, Lt Nicholson, which anchored as close as possible to the wreck. By daybreak, only the officers and 17 seamen remained aboard the *Venerable*, all of whom declared they would rather die than abandon their captain and ship. Only when her forecastle went under water, would the captain consent to leave, saving not only his own life but those of his devoted crew. Junior officers leading, the men boarded the waiting boats in almost leisurely fashion and by 6 am the wreck was deserted. Within an hour, she broke in two. Some reports state that a drunken marine was left to his fate on board, having been caught plundering some of the officers' chests and drinking their port, but this is untrue. Admiralty records in the PRO show that this man, the only member of the entire crew to misbehave, was court martialled on board HMS *El Salvador del Mundo* in the Hamoaze, Plymouth and sentenced to receive 200 lashes around the fleet.

To the everlasting shame of the inhabitants of Torbay, not a single boat put out from Brixham or Paignton to assist in the rescue, the locals being far too busy appropriating what they could for themselves, for which they were roundly condemned.

There followed a number of smaller incidents, such as the loss of the sloop *Matilda* and the brig *Young William*, both wrecked 'near Torquay' on 5 December 1819, leaving 14 cannon on the seabed; the *Eliza*, stranded and lost under Waldon Hill during 1828; but only the *Duke of Marlborough* wreck in 1836 was of any consequence. Formerly a Post Office packet vessel stationed at Falmouth, the *Duke of Marlborough* had achieved a measure of notoriety when commanded by Capt John Bull, since she was the ship which fought out a long engagement against the *Primrose*, another British packet, each mistaking the other for an American privateer. Following her purchase out of government service by Messrs Newman and Hunt, she was fitted out for a trading expedition to West Africa but, only a few days after leaving the Downs, sailed into Torbay in September 1836 so that Capt Putt who had some minor illness, could be taken to hospital. On 11 October, during a severe storm, she parted her main cable; her mate, Gluvias, ordered the second bower anchor to be dropped, but within half an hour it too parted and the vessel went ashore beneath a sheer cliff. From there she swung round, drifted into an inlet, and came to rest surrounded by rocks almost the height of her masthead.

The port shrouds of the mainmast were cut, which allowed the mast to fall against the cliff, and the mate and one seaman began to climb. Just as they reached the topmast futtocks, the wreck gave a lurch which dislodged the mast, crushing the seaman to death and throwing the mate to the deck. For a second time the mate clambered aloft, finally reaching the topmast and then the clifftop, badly cut and bruised. Of the seven men remaining aboard, none would brave that climb and all drowned when the *Duke of Marlborough* finally sank. Next day, when the mate revisited the site, he at first refused to believe that he had been capable of such a feat and swore he could never repeat it.

In the November following the wreck, Charles Deane, the celebrated inventor of the standard diving helmet, was engaged to raise the vessel, but recovered only part of her rigging, six cannon, and some fittings. It is worth noting that, from there, Deane moved on to the wreck of the *Venerable* and worked her when weather permitted until November 1848, when he committed suicide by cutting his throat in London. Many other salvage attempts on the *Duke of Marlborough* are recorded, the most successful being a party of divers on board the smack *Mary Ann* who, in April 1851, recovered many relics and valuables.

Following the *Marlborough* there was a profusion of wreck incidents, commencing on 9 February 1846 with the *City of Exeter*, which took the ground whilst entering Brixham, filled and sank. This was followed on 18 March by the American barque *Nahant*, bound for Galveston with emigrants, which went ashore under Berry Head. Not a single life was lost in this incident, and while another vessel was being chartered her passengers and crew were housed in the old poor house at Baker Hill. The

Nahant, in fact, floated clear at high water and was later found half awash off Poole cove, but she was so badly damaged that she was towed into Torquay harbour and broken up in the shallows. On 3 January 1847 the *Cato*, Sprague master, attempted to enter Torquay harbour without a pilot, struck the bottom, and soon afterwards only her masts were showing above water. An Admiralty cutter, the *Nimble*, was another victim of Berry Head when she went ashore without loss of life on 20 February following, and the Brixham trawling sloop *Vine* foundered on 27 October after being run down by the full-rigger *Brunswick*, near the Shoalstone.

Before the year 1847 came to a close Berry Head claimed yet another victim, the *John Mermann*, Capt Leprenz, Hamburg to Sierra Leone, which missed stays on 19 December and went on to the rocks. Within 24 hours she had fallen on her beam ends and become a total loss. Her cargo consisted of coloured handkerchiefs, blue beads, and general barter goods for the natives of Africa, relics of which still survive in Brixham.

Elbury cove, now popular as a holiday beach, saw a sailing ship ashore with its stern section ablaze on 9 December 1861. Fire had been discovered on board the *Sloman* by the captain's daughter when they were some 25 miles west of the Start. Two Brixham smacks, the *Sophia* and the *Charles*, helped her into Torbay and managed to beach her in the shallows. As the fire continued to spread she was towed off at high water and taken into Brixham harbour, where holes were cut in her sides through which the local fire brigade pumped water. Much to the surprise of the harbour authorities, no assistance was forthcoming from the crew, seven out of eight of whom were drunk and more interested in fighting amongst themselves than the fire. Although the ship was not completely gutted, she was badly damaged, losing all her sails, mizzenmast, stores and spare gear, and was sold for breaking. Although the name *Sloman* appeared on her bows, lifebelts and boats, it transpired that she was in fact, the *Eliphat Greely* of Maine, her master having assumed a false identity to confuse American privateers.

Of all the gales that have swept through Torbay, none matched the fury of the great hurricane of 1866. On Wednesday, 10 January, a total of 74 vessels were at anchor within Torbay, the majority of which had already attempted to leave, only to be forced back by gales from the south and west, which lasted for a month. A great calm then fell over the western counties and most of the ships at anchor made preparations to sail, just as soon as there was sufficient wind. By afternoon, a full gale was blowing

The dramatic scene on the outside of Brixham Pier after the Great Hurricane of 10-11 January 1866, when more than 40 vessels were lost in Torbay. The vessel in the background is the barque Wild Rose of Whitby, *carrying a cargo of wheat.*

yet again, and within a period of three hours had swung, in turn, from south to south-west, then to south-east, finally settling in the north-east. It was the wind, which reached almost 100 mph accompanied by driving snow and hail, that caused most of the damage. In total darkness, the vessels at anchor heaved and pitched until their cables parted, after which they blundered into each other, were hurled against the breakwater at Brixham, or else drove ashore.

A number of captains attempted to reach the open sea where they stood an infinitely better chance of weathering the storm, but in so crowded a roadstead this was impossible. Those that made the harbour safely were the *Tangerine*, *Florence* and *Nightingale*, but at least seven others got no further than the breakwater. Two barques, the *Wild Rose* of Whitby, 208 tons, and the Antwerp-registered *Leone*, drove from their moorings and collided with several other vessels, causing them also to go adrift. No less than eight ships ground themselves to pieces against the outer wall of the breakwater, where they were later joined by the *Colonel Buller*.

At anchor a mile offshore was the *Cambria* of Exeter, 107 tons. She, too, parted her cables, and within ten minutes became a total wreck. In that short space of time she was involved in six collisions before striking the pier. Fortunately, her mast overhung the stonework and her crew were able to scramble to safety; seconds later, no recognisable part remained.

It was the same throughout the length of Torbay; beaches strewn with broken ships, corpses, and items of cargo everywhere. In Oxen cove, where four vessels lay stranded, the only thing of value remaining was the mast of the trawler *Salem*. Likewise, Churston cove and Elbury were a mass of tangled wood and scattered cargo, all that was left of two vessels sunk in deep water. At Broadsands, where six or seven ships were ashore, four were intact and later saved, but lay amongst the wreckage of those less fortunate.

Next day, the storm having abated somewhat, it was possible to take stock and to establish with some degree of accuracy how many vessels and lives had been lost. Of the original 74 ships at anchor, ten were still at their moorings, though much battered and leaking. A further ten were safe inside Brixham harbour, eight were ashore with every chance of being saved, 41 were total wrecks and five had simply disappeared. It was therefore assumed that 46 vessels were lost in the gale, with 73 lives. Many of the corpses washed ashore were fearfully mutilated, some beyond recognition, being found amongst the rocks without heads or limbs.

Many acts of bravery were performed that night, not least by the wives of Brixham fishermen, who carried bundles of wood, straw, and other combustible material, even their bedding, to the pier head. There they lit and maintained a beacon, guiding many to safety. Police constable Amstey waded out into the surf near Brixham and, with the aid of a line, saved the crew of the *Thomas and Mary*, while a fisherman named Mills rescued 14 people from wrecks near the breakwater. Another local named Matthews went over the edge of a steep cliff on the end of a rope at the height of the gale, literally plucking several men from a wreck, the same feat being repeated at Broadsands. For well over a week following that awful night, gangs of men were recovering items of cargo and corpses.

The next incident occurred on 23 March 1866 when, during a gale almost the equal of January's, the Welsh schooner *Mary Louisa* of Llanelly went ashore on the beach near Paignton pier. Her crew lowered their only boat but would never have made the shore without the assistance of Samuel Wills, a local seaman, who waded out into the surf and took their line. Driven higher and higher by successive waves, the wreck eventually finished up at the back of Torbay House, 180 metres from where she struck.

One of the most dramatic shipping incidents at Torquay concerned the *Wallace*, which caught fire and came so close inshore that she threatened the whole waterfront. The *Wallace* of Boston, after discharging petroleum at Antwerp, was on passage back to Key West when she was forced to seek shelter from the weather in Torbay, on 2 January 1873. Between 3 and 4 am on 6 January, fire was discovered in her forehold, which her crew tried to extinguish but without success. Signals for assistance went unanswered, so attempts were made to sail her to Paignton Sands where she could be scuttled. While standing across Torbay, the wind changed and she was blown north until she grounded 100 metres west of Sulyarde Terrace, settling across the town's main sewer outfall.

Until now the fire was confined to the forepart of the *Wallace*, but it quickly engulfed the entire vessel, putting the safety of the town itself at stake. Today the site of the blazing wreck is occupied by the Torbay Hotel, which at one time was on the waterfront but due to reclamation is now some distance from the sea. Every fire appliance in the area was summoned and soon the entire harbour was full of smoke and flying sparks. With the possibility that the *Wallace* might have to be scuttled, the Torquay Military Volunteers brought a carriage gun across from Corbyn Head and prepared to fire into her waterline. A fire engine was also put aboard the barge *Tavistock* and towed to windward of the burning hulk, so that water could be played on the fire from both sides, but it made little difference and the *Wallace* burned for two whole days and nights before becoming a total loss.

Since there was once a time when Brixham could boast of a fishing fleet in excess of 300 vessels, it is not surprising that a great many of these came to grief, usually being run down and sunk offshore. The 27 ton *Brave*, lost in Torbay on 14 June 1874 was a typical case; *Providence*, 34 tons, was run down off Berry Head on 29 July the same year; the Dartmouth sloop *Swift* foundered at her moorings in Brixham Roads on 28 March 1875. These were followed by the 56 year old sloop *Phoenix* on 21 April 1876; the *Pilgrim*, run down by an unidentified ship on 28 July 1876; and the *Dolphin* on 6 August 1881 following a collision with the barque *J.B. Sproutt*.

Although the *Shamrock* of 1851 was the first steamship to be involved in an incident in Torbay, the first steamship wreck was the *Bretton Hall*, which went ashore on Mudstone beach, near Sharkham Point, on 6 December 1885. Registered and owned in Liverpool, she was on passage to Newport from Antwerp, intending to take aboard 2,000 tons of coal. Steaming through dense fog at eleven knots, her captain had every confidence in his dead reckoning, which placed the ship well south of both Prawle and Start Points but was, in fact, 13 miles in error. After going ashore, her distress rockets were sighted by Harry Parker, a local miller, who after obtaining several lengths of rope managed to pass them across to the wreck from the clifftop, and by this means 36 Lascars and Portuguese seamen, out of a crew of 50, got ashore. Although the Brixham lifeboat was launched its services were not required, although it later assisted in the recovery of valuable cargo.

Following the abandonment of the *Bretton Hall*, a party of 50 local fishermen went on board, remaining there all night, probably in hope of some salvage award. After a night on the beach she began to take in water rapidly and was abandoned with her stern completely submerged. Her cargo included 450 tons of best Belgian malleable iron, used in sword making, which was of little interest to the waiting crowd. As she broke up 50 tons of general cargo was released into the surf and literally thousands of people scavenged along the beach, picking up packs of playing-cards and boxes of eau-de-cologne, much to the frustration of the Torbay Customs officers.

As the 19th century entered its last decade Torbay was faced with the full fury of the 1891 blizzard, which appears to have either been accurately

The Brixham fishing smack Vesper, *drove on the rocks north-west of Black Head, near Ansteys cove, Torquay, in dense fog on 12 December 1902. Her crew rowed ashore in their own boat, but the vessel became a total loss.*

forecast or anticipated, since only two vessels were reported as being in difficulties, namely the *Emilie* and *Quiver*. At 3 pm on 10 March the former, a 16 year old Cherbourg brig, drove ashore directly beneath Berry Head House, less than 100 metres from the coastguard lookout. Her crew of eleven were all taken off by breeches buoy, the last to leave being Capt Viget, who at the last minute insisted on going below to collect his umbrella! The *Quiver*, a Brixham cutter of 48 tons, was at her moorings and empty when the gale struck, parting her cables and she drifted ashore in Oxen cove.

No further incident of any note occurred until 1907 when, in June the naval torpedo-boat HM *TB-99* was lost on trials, some four and a half miles off Berry Head. Built by Thornycroft's in the late 1880s, this steel-hulled 15 ton warship was armed with two torpedo tubes and a machine-gun. At the time of her loss she was being used to evaluate a new design of propeller which, during a fast run, vibrated so violently that she sprang a leak and sunk.

Salvage operations were in progress by mid-July, with the gunboat *Spanker* and the tug *Etna* in attendance. Diver Trapnell, aged 48, went down in 'standard dress' to 45 metres and within minutes reported over his telephone that he had located the propeller and shaft, and that it had broken away from the main hull. He asked for a rope to be sent down, to which the item could be attached, when, without warning, his voice became weak and strangled and he advised his attendant that both his air line and breast rope were entangled in the wreck. A second diver went down who took two hours to free Trapnell, after which the second man returned to the surface bleeding from the nose and in a state of complete exhaustion. By now, Trapnell had spent almost three hours at 45 metres, which was outside any decompression tables at that time, so that bringing him to the surface slowly with periodic 'stops' in an attempt to avoid the 'bends' was a matter of guesswork, taking five hours in total. Once back on board and undressed, Trapnell was unable to stand up and was put to bed on the *Etna*. Next day he was transferred to Torquay general hospital, but became delirious and died from a combination of decompression sickness, shock, and physical exhaustion. Later that year both sections of the wreck were salvaged and taken to Devonport.

The war years saw considerable U-boat activity off Torbay and over 1917-18 at least five steamers were torpedoed and sunk in the area. The *W.H. Dwyer* of Sunderland, was sunk on 26 August 1917. One month later the *Greleen*, built by Harland & Wolff for the Haenton Shipping Co in 1894, was sent to the bottom with 19 lives lost on 22 September, to be followed by the *Bleamoor* on 27 November, the *Styrn* on 10 June 1918, and the *Kendall Castle* on 15 September 1918, all less than four miles from shore and in the same area.

Between the two world wars there were very few incidents. A pair of destroyers went ashore on Roundham Head and Preston beach respectively on 12/13 December 1920. The crew of the Torbay and Brixham lifeboat no doubt imagined themselves in for a busy night, until they learnt that the warships were the German *T189* and *S24*, carrying only six steaming crew between them. They were under tow by the London tug *Warrior*, from Cherbourg to Teignmouth for scrapping, when both parted their tow ropes and stranded in Torbay. The *T189* broke her back and had to be abandoned on the rocks, but her partner was patched

Stranded near Torquay on 22 December 1964, the Danish m.v. Northwind, *takes a severe battering from rough seas in the shallows, but was later refloated and saved.*

up and towed away, despite nine metres of her bow being badly buckled. Three steamers went ashore between 1922 and 1929, namely the *Eider*, beached near Berry Head after springing a leak on 2 March 1922; the *River Lagan* on 8 January 1924, on Goodrington beach; and the Spanish *Sebastian* on Broadsands, 6 December 1929, but all were refloated and saved.

In more recent years, the large Dutch steel barge *Cosray 10*, one of three under tow by the tug *Cycloop*, broke adrift and was wrecked beneath the cliffs at Daddyhole Plain on 5 December 1959. A Danish motor coaster, the *Northwind*, had a lucky escape on 22 December 1964, when a north-easterly gale forced her ashore on Hollacombe beach, between Paignton and Torquay. She lay beam-on to a 27 metre high cliff, from where a breeches buoy was rigged and Capt Kirkeby and his five crew speedily rescued. When the weather abated she was successfully refloated, having suffered virtually no damage, as was the *Trinity Navigator*, a tanker of 42,844 gross tons, which went ashore on the north side of Berry Head at 3.30 am on 2 March 1971, the last shipping incident near Torbay to date, apart from the motor-boat *Betty R* in May 1971 and a local pilot boat, the *Tanrogan* in January 1972.

5

Torquay to the Dorset border

It is not necessary to be a connoisseur of shipwreck to appreciate the marked change in wreck incidents from here on along the south Devon coast, as the coastline swings north-east towards Lyme Bay and the Dorset border. Although this chapter in fact embraces the longest single stretch of Devon's coast, the wreck incidents diminish not only in number but also in tonnage, the most obvious decline being in 'deep-water' sailing ships and steamers. Vessels passing up or down Channel normally set course between St Catherine's Point on the Isle of Wight, and Prawle Point, or the Start, which keeps them well clear of Lyme Bay. Only those unfortunate enough to become embayed before a south-easterly gale or, in more recent times, coasters entering or leaving Exmouth and Teignmouth, were in real danger. Consequently this area is far from notorious for its shipping losses.

The majority of incidents occurred around Teignmouth, which in bygone days enjoyed not only a brisk interchange of trade with Newton Abbot but also supported a large shipbuilding industry. It was even considered of sufficient importance for de Tourville's ships to select it as a secondary target for attack in 1690, after being thwarted by unfavourable winds from attacking Plymouth. The French swept in and sacked East Teignmouth, leaving it almost completely destroyed, but it was soon rebuilt.

A remarkable underwater find which may be related to the sacking of Teignmouth, or possibly as early as the Spanish Armada of 1588, was made in July 1975 by Simon Burton, a 13 year old schoolboy, whilst snorkelling off the seafront. Spear fishing at St Michael's, he discovered a 'long green sort of pipe thing' which proved on recovery to be a 3.35 metre long bronze saker cannon, weighing over a ton, one of two such guns found eventually. Loaded with stone shot and powder and sealed with a wooden tompion, it had been cast by Sigismondo Albeirghetti of Venice between

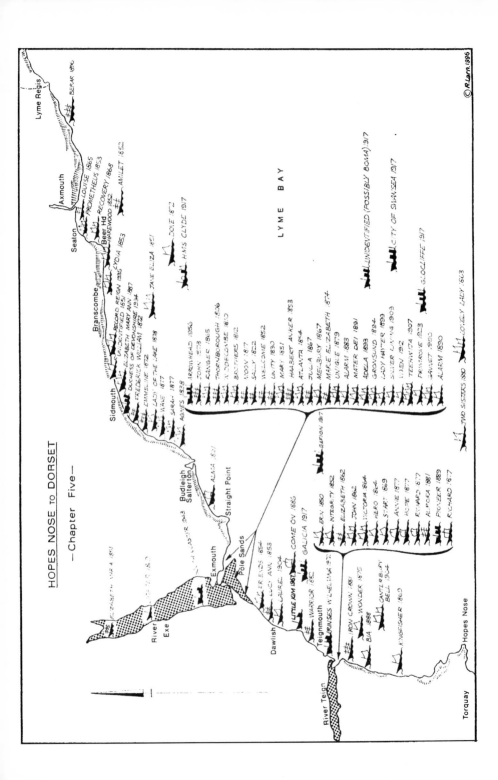

HOPES NOSE TO DORSET

— Chapter Five —

© R.Larn.1996

1580 and 1620. Other finds from this site, now designated a Protected Wreck, include additional guns, stone shot and personal items including a beautiful gold seal, but the identity of the wreck still remains a mystery.

The wreck of the *John*, of Lympstone, in 1573 appears to have been the subject of the earliest full wreck account recorded in any detail. There then follows a considerable gap in time, until the late 1700s, when we hear of a privateer named *Bellona*, belonging to an ironmonger named Leake, of Exeter, which foundered in sight of Teignmouth after leaving port on 5 September 1779. Sixty-one years later, in 1840, a Teignmouth trawler brought ashore a piece of the wreck in late September, having found the remains of the *Bellona* near Clerk rock. Another West Country privateer, the 16 gun *Thornborough*, Capt Crowte, fell victim 'to the high rocks off the land at Orcombe' on 2 November 1806. During a hard gale from the south-west, the schooner-rigged vessel was sighted off Exmouth bar in distress, having lost her foretopmast and jib boom. After striking the rocks, she bilged and sank, her first lieutenant, Mr Salter of Topsham, and two seamen getting ashore. At 9 pm the same day, the deck parted from the rest of the wreck and a further nine men were saved, but her captain and two men drowned.

On 16 November 1812 the Cardiff collier *Brothers* was wrecked on Orcombe Point, followed by the *Moon*, carrying pipeclay for Topsham, at the same spot, during February 1817. Both losses were directly attributable to bad weather, but the next wreck, if we are to be influenced by public criticism, was brought about by the reluctance of Exeter pilots to put to sea when it was too rough. The 73 ton Exeter schooner *Friends*, on passage from Hartlepool with £100 worth of coal aboard, anchored off Exmouth on 3 January 1854 while her master burnt flares for a pilot to come out, but received no response. A strong north-easterly wind was blowing at the time, which soon increased to force ten on the Beaufort scale. Unwilling to enter the Exe at night without assistance, the master attempted to reach the shelter of Torbay, but struck the ground and had to beach his ship between Dawlish and Langstone rock. The crew of five were saved, but the schooner, valued at £400, quickly went to pieces. In their defence, a spokesman for the local pilots stated to the Board of Trade, that 'they never went to sea at all on such occasions'.

Further south, in Babbacombe Bay, was where the American full-rigged ship *Caroline* of Charleston was stranded on 12 March 1860, the largest vessel to go ashore in the locality. Having discharged her cargo from America at Hamburg, she loaded railway iron and sailed for Cardiff.

In dense fog, Capt Haynes mistook Straight Point for Land's End and turned inshore. When close to the Gull rock, the *Caroline* was sighted by a local fisherman named Harris who put out in his own boat to warn them of the danger, but before a tug could be called the *Caroline* went ashore and was badly holed forward. Valued at £30,000, both wreck and cargo were sold to a syndicate of ten local men for the ridiculous sum of £250. To the original owners' intense chagrin, they landed and sold the entire cargo of iron at a handsome profit, then proceeded to refloat the ship, refitted her, and returned her to service!

Only five years later, on 29 April 1865, the remains of the *Friends* were joined by those of the Brixham fishing trawler *Ranger*, which leaked so badly that she had to be put ashore, where she went to pieces. During 1867 there was a particularly unfortunate incident on the Pole sand, at the entrance to the Exe. This concerned the Exmouth brigantine *Julia*, of 148 tons, owned by a Mr Norrer, which was carrying 240 tons of Newcastle coal consigned to P. Varwell at Exeter. She was driven on to the bar by a furious south-easterly gale on 5 January, striking at the back of the Pole, nearly opposite the lifeboat station.

There was considerable delay in launching the lifeboat and even then, because of the tremendous surf running, it was necessary to drag her seaward with ropes. The lifeboat *Victoria* was no sooner afloat than she drifted away upriver, and the exertions of her crew proved futile against the wind and tide. Within 15 minutes of going ashore nothing of the *Julia* or her seven-man crew was to be seen, and the hundreds of spectators ashore had only been able to watch in horror as she quickly disappeared. A small boat, belonging to the 'preventative officers', was launched and manned by Exmouth fishermen, who reached the brigantine where the lifeboat had failed. Only one man remained alive, Adam Stewart of Aberdeen, who had shipped aboard at Shields at the last minute to replace a seaman who had run away. Of the remainder, the body of Capt Canham was the only one recovered, being found by HM cutter *Nimble* between Exeter and Lympstone.

There followed a great many incidents on both the Pole sand and Teignmouth bar, during which the lifeboat saved a great many lives and vessels, the majority of them fishing boats or small coasting ketches. Typical was the 76 ton wooden smack *Melbury*, which became a total loss on Exmouth bar on 19 November 1867. An unnamed lighter sank in Exmouth Bight during the November of 1869, the French sloop *Marie Elizabeth* was yet another victim of the Pole sand on 25 February 1874, and on 14 October 1877 a southerly gale sank the luggers *Annie, Hope* and *Richard.* Another wreck of larger proportions was the London brigantine *Warrior,* carrying coal, which stranded on the beach on 7 January 1882. Built in America in 1853, the *Warrior* was one of a fleet of 28 ships owned by Hall Brothers of Newcastle.

Collisions at sea in other areas of Devon were frequent occurrences but rare off Teignmouth. One concerned the three-masted schooner *Scud* which was cut in two by the steamer *Blanchard* in 1885. A Guernsey-registered vessel, the *Scud* had been in the hands of a shipbuilder in order that she could be lengthened. On completion, she loaded china clay at Melbury docks and sailed for Leith. On 12 January the lights of another vessel were seen ahead. As the two vessels got abeam of each other the *Blanchard* inexplicably turned towards the *Scud* and ran her down. She sank in less than two minutes, fortunately without loss of life, the prompt action of her mate saving the captain, who was trapped with both legs broken under the fallen mainmast.

One stranding prior to the First World War, was the Russian schooner *Tehwija* of Riga on 10 October 1907. From Lappvik to Exmouth with a cargo of timber, she went ashore on the outer Pole sand. The Exmouth lifeboat made several attempts to reach the wreck but was beaten back by huge seas. An urgent call was sent to the Teignmouth lifeboat for assistance and after an exhausting row the *Alfred Staniforth* reached the schooner and saved her eight-man crew, the Russian vessel going to pieces shortly after.

Wartime incidents were confined mostly to 1917, in which year four large steamers were sent to the bottom by enemy action at the western end of Lyme Bay. The first and by far the largest was the Pacific Steam Navigation Co's liner *Galicia,* of Liverpool. This twin screw, 5,922 tons gross vessel, built by Swan Hunter of Newcastle in 1901, struck a mine and sank in 15.5 metres depth on 12 May. The Teignmouth lifeboat, assisted by a tug, brought ashore 50 passengers and crew, the remaining nine being taken off by a naval patrol boat. During mid-August the *Glocliffe,* of 3,281 tons gross, was torpedoed and sunk off Exmouth, and on 25 September the *City of Swansea* went down with her cargo of Newcastle coal. Exactly one month later the Norwegian *Gefion* met the same fate, sinking in 20 metres in a position given as 50.32.40° N, 03.21.42° W. Since then, the only incidents of note have been the wreck of the *South Coaster* and the stranding of the *Arrowhead.* The steamship *South Coaster,* of Cardiff, went ashore on the Pole sand on 13 December 1943.

The Cardiff steamship South Coaster, *went ashore on the Pole Sand on 13 December 1943, was refloated and beached in the shallows within the Exe estuary, close to the railway line that runs along the Warren, where a single mast and her bow section can still be seen.*

Refloated by Admiralty tugs and beached in the shallows close to the railway line that runs along the Warren, she was partially scrapped where she lay, but her mast and hull still show at low water.

An unusual 'wreck' incident – if that is the correct description – was reported in local newspapers during 1907. On 31 May the Brixham fishing ketch *Skylark* was some eight miles south-east of Exmouth when her crew spotted what they thought was a hayrick floating on the surface. Drawing closer, they found the object to be a derelict army observation balloon and four hours were spent in chasing the partially deflated balloon all over the sea before it was finally secured and the 'catch' examined. Attached to the balloon was a wicker basket, containing nothing but an officer's riding crop. Not appreciating the implications, the crew of the *Skylark* resumed their fishing and it was three days before they reported the incident on return to port. A massive search was immediately launched, the balloon being identified as having come from Aldershot, manned by two officers of the Royal Engineers, but no trace of them was ever found.

From Exmouth to where the border between Devon and Somerset meets the sea, a little to the west of Lyme Regis, lies a quiet and peaceful stretch of coast with an infamous reputation for smuggling but few wrecks. An expression once common in these parts stated that: 'Sidbury financed, Branscombe landed, Sidmouth found wages, and Salcombe carriers.'

It has been the practice of Sidmouth, Beer and Seaton, along with other small ports, to work small coastal craft directly off the beach, embarking or landing cargo over the side at low water using horse-drawn carts. Such operations always involved an element of risk, since a sudden change of wind direction or a ground swell could spell disaster. The loss of the *Samuel*, in August 1812, was typical. She had partially discharged her cargo of coal at Sidmouth when the wind swung onshore and though every effort was made to save her, she was wrecked on Otterton ledge, near Budleigh Salterton. The number of vessels lost in this manner are legion: a Guernsey-registered schooner, the *Agnes*, was wrecked on Sidmouth beach on 19 March 1838; the *Jane Eliza* of Caernarvon, carrying pipeclay, was lost on Chit rocks on 15 January 1851; the *Harewood* on Beer Head, 16 June 1852; the *Amulet* near Seaton, 28 October 1852; the *Lydia* at Seaton Sluice, 17 March 1853; *Prometheus*, another Seaton wreck, 29 November 1853; the Penzance brig *Louise*, also at Seaton on 8 February 1865, and many others.

The practice of landing passengers and cargo over the side brought about the total loss of a once well known excursion steamer, the *Duchess of Devonshire*, on 27 August 1934. After being laid up for some time when the Devon Dock, Pier & Steamship Co of Exeter found her no longer economic, she was bought by a local syndicate headed by a Capt Coleberd in 1933, and employed on excursion trips between Seaton and Torquay. She arrived at Sidmouth shortly after noon on 27 August with 40 passengers aboard, some of whom wished to disembark. This necessitated running her ashore and rigging a small gangplank, over the bow. A heavy sea lifted her stern and swung her beam-on to the beach, and she stranded on top of some concrete slabs. At low water the obstructions pierced her hull and she commenced to fill. Eventually the hole was plugged and her pumps started, but she refused to be refloated and had to be abandoned,

The broken bow section of the Italian barque Berar, *in Charton Bay, near Seaton, on 7 October 1896, the vessel having gone ashore whilst carrying a timber cargo, in fog and wind conditions force 9.*

eventually to be broken up for scrap. As late as 1950, some of her bottom plates were uncovered by the sea and later removed by the local council.

Since then, the motorised topsail ketch *Record Reign*, a famous 'Q' ship in the First World War, stranded on 8 February 1935, was the last vessel lost in similar circumstances. She got off course in fog and after striking an offshore rock was beached at Littleham Shute. Offshore, the deep water wrecks include the Admiralty requisitioned trawler, HMS *Clyde*, lost in collision off Sidmouth on 14 October 1917, and a still unidentified wreck eight and a half miles from Sidmouth church. The latter could well be the Liverpool steamer *Boma* of 2,694 tons register, thought to have been torpedoed in position 50.32.10° N, 03.14.12° W.

Only one further wreck remains to be mentioned on the few remaining miles of the south Devon coast, and this is the Italian barque *Berar* which went ashore in fog on 7 October 1896. She carried a massive quantity of sawn timber, en route from Baga to Swilley, and shortly after going ashore broke in two, allowing the cargo to float away to cover local beaches for miles. She struck a rock mid-way between Culverhole Point and the centre of Charton Bay, and it was here, during 1972, that her remains were relocated by John Moore, a diver employed by the Unit of Coastal Sedimentation, based at Taunton.

6

Hartland to Westward Ho!

Situated at the extreme north-west corner of the county, Hartland Point dominates the entire 60 or so miles of North Devon coastline facing the Bristol Channel, stretching from Marshland Mouth east to Glenthorne. Although a mere 106 metres in height, compared with the Great Hangman and Holdstone Barrows which are both in excess of 304 metres, the cliffs at Hartland offer some of the most impressive and spectacular coastal scenery in the whole of England and Wales. Rightly called 'the sailors' grave', it is an area notorious for shipwrecks and steeped in legend.

Despite documentary evidence of wreck here as early as 1321, when a sailing vessel was lost near Clovelly, with an unidentified vessel wrecked at Hartland Quay in 1641, the details are sketchy, as is to be expected, and it is not until the mid 1700s that specific details can be found. The first named wreck in the area appears to be the *Anne*, lost on Hartland Point in May 1753, whilst on passage from London to Bristol.

In 1821, a tremendous October gale put 40 fishing vessels ashore near Clovelly with the loss of 35 lives and an unspecified number of boats; again, in October 1838, a similar incident claimed a further 21 lives and 14 locally-owned fishing craft. These losses were followed by that of the *Auspicious* of Ilfracombe, Portreath to Neath, wrecked at Hartland on 21 October 1842, then the *Sir R.R. Vyyan* on 8 March 1845, but it was not until 1851 that a vessel of any size is recorded as lost.

This was the Finnish ship *Pollux*, of Bjorneborg, which left Dublin for Alexandria on 4 November in ballast. Shortly after her departure from Dublin she encountered a furious gale, her ballast shifted, and she went over on her beam ends. Righted after her crew cut away her main and mizzen masts, the vessel drifted helplessly into the Bristol Channel and it was 6 November before she was sighted by two pilot skiffs off Devon. The pilots went aboard to offer their assistance, but to their astonishment, instead of welcoming their help, the crew of the *Pollux* promptly abandoned ship, leaving the locals to get the vessel into Clovelly roads as best they could. Next day the crew of the *Pollux* returned aboard, with the

120

exception of Captain Lindstrom who claimed urgent business elsewhere. For reasons best known to themselves, the crew refused to render any assistance to the pilots and the Clovelly smacks which were still struggling to get the ship into Bideford. Twice en route she grounded but got off, and in desperation the Lloyd's agent requested the help of a steamship or tug. Less than half an hour after the *Pollux* had been taken in tow, a member of her crew deliberately cut the towing hawser, and she finished up on the beach at Clovelly close to the pier.

Repudiating her as a wreck, the local Receiver of Wreck insisted that everything possible should be done to save the vessel and her contents. He ordered her ballast to be discharged, all spirits and stores unloaded and placed under lock and key, and before nightfall she was once more afloat. She was then towed a short distance offshore, anchored and left empty for the night, but within hours a full north-easterly gale was blowing. She rode safely until 10 am next day, then both cables parted and within ten minutes she was ashore and going to pieces, her remains later auctioned off as firewood.

There was great concern when large pieces of wreckage, thought to be from a foreign vessel of some 150 tons, were found among the rocks at Hartland on 10 February 1852, but a search revealed nothing and the wreck was never identified. On 24 March 1857 the crew of the St Ives schooner *Sarah* managed to row themselves to Clovelly in their own boat, leaving their vessel to break up on the rocks, one of the few contemporary instances of the entire complement of a wrecked ship being saved. Another schooner, the Brixham owned and built *Fame*, of 85 tons, was wrecked at Hartland on 14 March 1866, and 17 days later the first steamship wreck in the area occurred. The wooden paddler *Queen* was well known locally, having been in the Hayle to Bristol packet service for 14 years.

The *Queen* left Bristol on 29 March with 116 crew, 37 passengers and 100 tons of general cargo on board, calling at Ilfracombe only. She sailed at 10.30 pm, and followed her normal westerly course for an hour and 50 minutes as usual, which took her five miles past Hartland, where the mate ordered a new course of south-west by west. Shortly afterwards, to his horror, steep cliffs loomed ahead and the vessel struck the Tinge rock a terrific blow. She backed off and headed for Ilfracombe, but when the ship's carpenter reported a metre of water in the hold, she was run ashore at Clovelly, a ship's length from the pier head. It was obvious that she was seriously damaged, and all on board were safely ferried ashore. Work

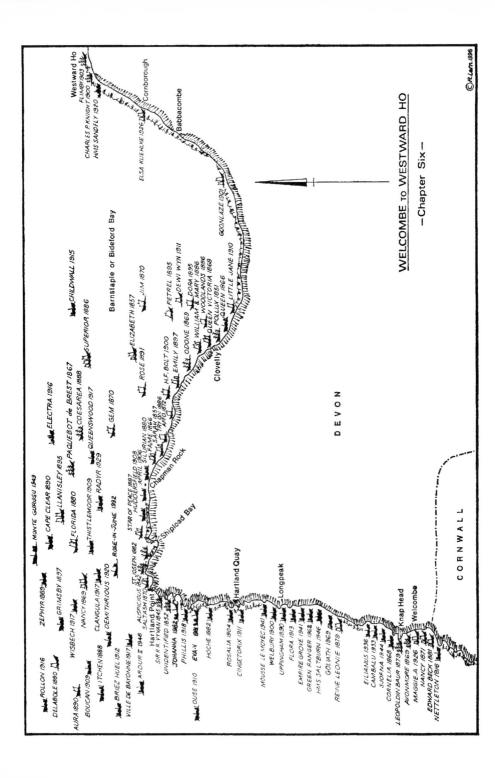

WELCOMBE TO WESTWARD HO

—Chapter Six—

©R.Larn.1996

began next morning on the removal of her cargo, continuing uninterrupted until the Wednesday, when she broke her back and went to pieces. The inevitable Board of Trade enquiry opened on 1 May in the Guildhall at Penzance, where Capt Spray, despite his excellent record, was found guilty of neglect for not using the lead and line, and of having failed to keep and maintain a ship's log since the day he had assumed command of the packet, and was reprimanded.

Although there had been lifeboats at Appledore since 1825, the Manby mortar life-saving apparatus at Clovelly was for many years considered sufficient to cover the entire Hartland area. Then, in the 1860s, there was such a succession of small wrecks that public attention was drawn to the need for an additional lifeboat at the western end of Barnstaple Bay and a local subscription fund was opened. On 22 August 1868 the polacca schooner *Queen Victoria* of Bideford was blown ashore at Clovelly and wrecked. Another schooner was to follow, the 91 ton *Nancy*, which foundered off Hartland on 18 March 1869 with the loss of all six crew, and on 12 September a Genoese barque named *Odone* was lost at Portledge. On this occasion it was the local coastguards who went to her rescue; they manned the station's galley and went out beyond the line of breakers from where they were able to guide the twelve Italian crew and one passenger to safety in their own boat.

The first Clovelly lifeboat, the *Alexander & Matilda Boetefeur*, arrived at her new station on 18 June 1870, the new station boathouse and lifeboat having been purchased through a legacy of £10,000 given as a direct result of the loss of the *Odone*, but, for reasons unknown, did not attend the wreck of the Plymouth schooner *Saltash* which stranded at Hartland on 28 August that year with the loss of all five crew. It was, in fact, October before the lifeboat was put to use, when it went out to rescue the crew of the herring boat *Gem* which had sunk in bad weather, and but for its intervention the crew of another fishing vessel, the *Sisters*, would also have been lost. During 1871, the Clovelly lifeboat herself had a lucky escape when she capsized in a gale during an exercise launch. Fortunately, all the crew wore regulation lifebelts, so that not one of them was lost.

Although the records of the Royal National Lifeboat Institution show that the Clovelly boat went out to a great many wrecks, for every occasion it was launched there were an equal, if not greater number, when it remained in its house unused. A typical instance concerned the steamer *Silurian*, of 1,252 tons gross, which struck Chapman rock, two and a half miles east of the point, on 2 September 1880. Built at Newcastle in 1876 and owned in Salonica, Greece, the *Silurian* was carrying patent fuel from Cardiff, which previously had been her port of registry. Some three months later, on 23 November, the 50 ton Jersey schooner *Florida* was run down offshore by the French steamer *Charles Godard* and sank, and on 1 July 1882 the *Hoche*, another French steamship, was wrecked two miles south-west of the headland, near Spekes Mill mouth. Two other vessels went ashore at Hartland that same year. The French-owned brig *St Joseph*, on passage from St Malo to Swansea in ballast, stranded on 10 September to become a total loss, but the fishing lugger *Start*, stranded on 7 December, was later refloated and saved.

There followed an almost frightening number of wreck incidents, starting with smacks and coasting ketches of less than five tons, followed by larger sailing ships, and finally a number of steamers. The Plymouth schooner *Star of Peace*, of 142 tons register, was rated locally as a 'proper wreck' when she struck the Hartland rocks on 18 February 1887, while carrying copper ore and zinc ash. Among the steamships were a number which went almost unnoticed locally, such as the *Itchen*, registered at Southampton, 193 tons gross, which foundered off Hartland on 28 August 1888, and the Waterford Steamship Co's *Zephyr*, which sank somewhere between Lundy and the mainland on 29 September 1889. She ran headlong into a severe gale off Lundy while carrying coal from Cardiff to Flushing. The sea tore away her engine-room skylight, flooded the tiny boiler room and extinguished the fires, so that her complement of 16 crew and one passenger were forced to abandon ship. They got away in one lifeboat and a small dinghy, both of which reached Ilfracombe. The following year the Newcastle-owned *Cape Clear*, outward bound from Liverpool to Rosario and St Vincent with a general cargo, also went down in the same area, between 20-23 January, but with a tragic loss of life.

Exactly mid-way between Hartland and the border with Cornwall stands a bleak and desolate point known as the Longpeak, which claimed the 1,431 ton steamer *Uppingham* of London on 23 December 1890. From Cardiff to Port Said with coal, she developed engine trouble when off Bude and, after setting auxiliary sail, put about for Lundy where Capt Lilley hoped to find shelter. Her engine then failed completely and she drifted helpless on to the rocks, with the loss of eight of her 28 crew. One of the survivors was second officer Teck who, by coincidence, was on board another steamship, the *Welbury*, of West Hartlepool, which was wrecked almost on top of the *Uppingham*'s rusting remains on 24 April 1900.

Although salvage tugs were available at both Lundy and Ilfracombe on 4 October 1895, there was no way in which they could be contacted from out at sea since these were the days before radio communication was available. The result was that the Norwegian brig *Haabet* had to be abandoned and allowed to drift ashore at Croyde, where she became a total loss. Her distress signals were sighted from the cliffs above Clovelly, and the lifeboat was quickly launched. The brig was found to be leaking badly, with most of her canvas blown away and not one boat left intact, so the lifeboat took off her crew of nine, together with the captain's young daughter. Another set of distress signals sighted by the Hartland lighthouse keepers on 13 August 1897 indicated that the Cardiff collier *Grimsby* was in trouble a short distance offshore. Again the crew of the Clovelly lifeboat found her full of water, and as she was in imminent danger of foundering, her four passengers and 13 crew were taken off.

The stretch of high cliffs between Clovelly and Westward Ho! is a particularly fearsome place on which to be wrecked. Even today, the cliffs are virtually uninhabited, and in 1901, when the *Goonlaze* was lost there with tragic result, the area must have been desolate indeed. It was the body of a seaman, found on 5 February in a field at Peppercombe, four miles east of Clovelly, that first indicated a vessel had gone ashore. A search of the coastline showed a mass of wreckage concentrated below Cockington Head, but no sign of survivors. So completely had the sea demolished the wreck that it was some time before it was identified as the Hayle schooner *Goonlaze*. In time, the corpses of all four of her crew were found, only one of whom had managed to scale the 90 metre high cliff before he, too, succumbed from exposure and injuries. It appears that the schooner came into Bideford Bay to shelter and was unable to get clear when the wind veered to the north-west. Possibly she parted her cables and stranded so close under the cliffs that her distress signals went unseen.

The year 1904 marked the beginning of a long series of steamship wrecks, almost as if Hartland was some monster with an insatiable appetite for ships and men. The first of these was the Italian-owned *Rosalia* which, on 27 May, crashed on to the rocks at Hartland Quay in dense fog, tearing such holes in her bottom there was no hope of salvage. Unlike the *Goonlaze* incident, her presence could neither be mistaken nor ignored since she stranded immediately in front of the naval-manned coastguard station. Had the *Rosalia* been driven a further 180 metres over the rocks, her bow would have destroyed the parapet surrounding the station and lookout post. It was fog that also brought about the end of the

The Italian Rosalia *lies a total wreck only yards from the old coastguard station at Hartland Quay, after stranding in fog on 27 May 1904.*

Abril on 16 February 1906. This Spanish steamer, loaded with 1,700 tons of coal from Cardiff, went ashore in the Beckland Bay area, close to Chapman rock. She filled so quickly that her crew of 20 promptly abandoned ship in two lifeboats, the larger of which, with 16 men aboard, reached Clovelly. The smaller boat, unable to make headway against the tide, went missing for a time, but was later found by a steam tug which had put out to assist the Clovelly lifeboat. Built at Campbeltown in 1897 by Cuncliffe & Dunlop as the *Ardgour*, the 1,334 gross tons *Abril* broke her back and became a total wreck.

This service by the lifeboat *Elinor Roget* was its last on this station, and by coincidence its replacement, the larger twelve-oared *Elinor Roget II*, which arrived in June 1907, performed its first useful function in almost identical circumstances. This was at the scene of the wreck of the 2,055 gross tons *Huddersfield*, of Cardiff, on 27 January 1908. Yet another

The Spanish steamship Abril, *ashore in Beckland Bay, close to Chapman rock, Clovelly, on 16 February 1906. She went ashore in fog whilst carrying coal from Cardiff.*

victim of fog, she stranded under Gawlish cliff, west of the *Abril*. As with so many previous incidents, the first anyone ashore knew of the wreck was the arrival at Clovelly of survivors, in their own boat. By the time the *Elinor Roget* had reached the scene, huge ground seas were sweeping the steamer from end to end. She was already breaking up, and with no boats remaining intact the twelve men still aboard would certainly have drowned but for their timely rescue.

It was 2 November 1909 before the next incident occurred, the victim being the *Boucan*, of 1,216 tons gross and owned by Cie de Navigation d'Orbigny, which sank following collision with the *Salgia*. The 4,008 tons gross *Thistlemoor* foundered off Hartland exactly one month later, after being struck by a succession of giant waves which tore off all her ventilators and flooded her forward hold to such an extent that her bows were forced down and her propeller made ineffectual. Despite every assistance from another steamer, the *Arndale*, and the Clovelly lifeboat, the *Thistlemoor*, coal laden from Cardiff to Cape Town, went down in deep water, taking with her 23 crew including Capt Yeo.

The Cardiff registered steamship Huddersfield, *under the cliffs one mile east of Hartland Point, after going ashore in fog on 27 January 1908, whilst bound for the river Plate. Nine of her crew rowed a boat to Clovelly to raise the alarm, the lifeboat saving the other twelve men.*

Fifteen months were to pass before Hartland again echoed to the crash of distress rockets. This was in March 1911, when two more steamships were lost within 24 hours. During the evening of 2 March, a Mr Oatway, proprietor of the Hartland Quay hotel and leader of the local LSA team, noticed thick fog sweeping in from seaward. As a precautionary measure, a Mr Slute was sent up to the cliff lookout post to keep watch and had hardly reached his station before the deep bellow of a ship's siren was heard close inshore, followed immediately by distress signals. Fog hampered rescue operations and it was some time before the ship was located, driven deep into the ridges of rock at St Catherine's Point, only half a mile south from the old quay.

The 1,375 tons gross *Cingetorix*, of Antwerp, having struck at low water, lay some 640 metres offshore and presented so difficult a target for the rocket apparatus that its crew were obliged to climb down the cliffs to the rocks below. Even then, four rockets failed to send a line across the

WRECK OF THE S.S CINGETORIX OFF HARTLAND QUAY

The Belgian steamer Cingetorix, *of Antwerp, which went ashore at low water off Hartland Quay on 2 March 1911. She was the first of two such wrecks in the area within 24 hours, the second being the Cardiff collier* Ouse.

Belgian steamer's deck, and eventually it was a line fired from the wreck itself that established contact and enabled all 19 crew to be saved. On this occasion the Clovelly lifeboat, unable to weather Hartland Point, had to put back, its services fortunately not required. The sea quickly pounded the *Cingetorix* until only her bridge showed above water, and despite salvage attempts by the now famous Western Marine Salvage Co of Penzance, she went to pieces, scattering her cargo of 2,100 tons of steel sheet and billets on the seabed.

The very next morning, the Cardiff collier *Ouse* sank off Hartland, after developing a serious leak. Capt Wicklin and his crew of 13 saved themselves, but none of them had sufficient time to collect any belongings.

Two more steamers were added to the tragic list before the outbreak of the First World War; the *Briel Huel* on 9 March 1912, and the *Katina* on 23 May. Of these, the former was by far the largest being of 3,074 tons

129

The Greek steamer Katina *went ashore in fog during the night of 23 May 1913, whilst bound for Barry docks in ballast. Her crew walked ashore and climbed the 400 foot high cliffs at Elmscott, south of Hartland Quay. She was towed off by the tug* Etna, *beached at Clovelly, and then towed to Cardiff for repairs.*

register. Carrying coal from Barry, destined for Algiers, and with 39 crew and two passengers aboard, she struck the steamer *Tempest*, foundering as a result. The *Flora*, an Amsterdam-registered vessel of 725 tons gross, went ashore at Longpeak on 4 April 1915 and was wrecked, whereas the Greek-owned *Katina*, although badly damaged in stranding close at hand, was eventually refloated and saved.

Following the declaration of war with Germany in 1914, there was a tremendous increase in the demand for Welsh coal and the number of steamers entering and leaving the Bristol Channel increased a hundredfold in as many weeks. The commanders of U-boats found easy targets amongst these slow, and as yet, unarmed and unescorted merchant ships. Between 1914 and 1918, 268 vessels were sunk by enemy action in the Bristol Channel, but many others were lost by collision or wreck. In the immediate vicinity of Hartland Point, 20 losses were recorded, 18 of

With her name and neutral port of Amsterdam painted in large letters on both sides, the Flora *went ashore in fog under the cliffs at Longpeak, two miles south of Hartland Point, on 4 April 1915, her crew of 19 waiting for low water when they were able to walk ashore safely.*

which were steamers, enemy action accounting for 13. The *Childwall* of Liverpool, 593 tons gross, was in collision with the *Trinculo* on 1 April 1915 and foundered; the 2,413 tons gross *Nettleton* of Hull, in ballast, was wrecked in fog on 11 February 1916, south of Knap Head, only half a mile inside the Devon border. Although the Bude LSA team was summoned and struggled along the clifftop with their apparatus, by the time they arrived the crew of the steamer, assisted by two local youths, had rigged an improvised breeches buoy and got ashore safely. The underwriters later sold the wreck to Thomas Wall & Co, who carried out extensive salvage. These wrecks were followed by that of the *Electra* of Liverpool, 495 tons gross, sunk following collision with the steamship *Margaret* on 4 October

1916, and the Norwegian *Rollon*, which foundered following a leak on 27 October in a position given as four miles north by west of Hartland Point.

Of the war losses connected with this part of the Devon coast, the first were the French-owned *Ville de Bayonne*, and the British *Queenswood*, both torpedoed by *UC-65* on 16 February 1917. From that date onwards, hardly a month went by without some unfortunate crew having to row themselves ashore, more often than not reaching Clovelly harbour. A Newcastle steamer, the *Wisbech*, was sent to the bottom west of Hartland on 14 August, to be followed by the Cork Steamship Co's *Clangula* on 19 November. She sank in 24 metres, taking with her a general cargo, her master, and 14 crew, four miles south-west of the point. By far the largest vessel sunk was the 7,388 tons gross hospital ship *Rewa*, owned by the British India Steamship Co and on passage from Madras to Avonmouth with 287 crew and 279 patients aboard, only four Lascar firemen being killed when she was torpedoed on 4 January 1918 by *U-55*.

In the decade following the war there were less than a dozen occasions on which the services of the Clovelly lifeboat were required. One of these was to save the crew of the 140 ton Greek steamer *Dimitrios* (ex-*Ben Ledi*), which was on passage from Fowey to Liverpool with china clay. She sprang a serious leak when five miles east-northeast of Hartland on 4 September 1920 and foundered after her crew were taken off. The *Radyr* (ex-*War Tabard*) (ex-*Jura*) which went down with the tragic loss of all 21 crew on 7 December 1929, was a loss which remained in the memories of local lifeboatmen for years. An SOS radio signal from this 3,000 tons gross Cardiff collier was relayed to both the Clovelly and Appledore lifeboats, but seas were so huge that neither boat could reach her in time.

Mystery wrecks are not common, and for that reason an incident at Hartland on 4 January 1921 is worth special mention. A Mr Goaman, looking down at the beach from the overhanging cliffs at Elmscott, noticed a great deal of wreckage, and shortly after part of a large vessel, 37 metres long and with a twelve metre beam, was discovered on the pebbles. The timber and paintwork were fresh and carried neither marine growth nor barnacles, her galvanised ironwork shone as new, and the tar in her seams smelt strongly. With the wreckage upside down, a huge iron propeller could be seen on the end of a shaft and was thought by locals to be much larger than that of some of the steamers wrecked nearby. Yet there was no sign of an engine, only masses of electrical cable hanging down and she remains unidentified.

It was Knap Head, already well littered with wreckage, that claimed the

The Liverpool registered Eilianus *under the cliffs at Welcombe mouth, a little north of the Cornwall/Devon border. Carrying 800 tons of scrap metal she went ashore in fog on 16 June 1936 and became a total wreck.*

next casualty, the Liverpool coaster *Cambalu*, of 496 tons gross, which went ashore to become a total loss on 30 January 1933. Her bow section was still intact and showing at low water when she was joined by the 333 ton *Eilianus* (ex-*Wyke Regis*), in fog, on 16 June 1936. She had previously discharged her cargo at Dunkirk, then proceeded to Le Havre to take on board 800 tons of scrap steel, destined for Britton Ferry. Her crew drifted about in the fog all night, before coming ashore at Marshland mouth and scrambling up the cliffs.

War losses during the Second World War were small compared to those of 1914-18 and began on 30 September 1940 with HM tug *Comet*. A French collier, the *Mousse le Moyec*, was wrecked at St Catherine's Tor on 6 December, victim of a north-westerly gale which unfortunately coincided with a breakdown of her engine. Another victim of the elements

133

The armed Norwegian steamship Sjofna, *ashore near Hartland with a cargo of china clay in bags, on 23 November 1944. Seven men were saved by lifeboat, the remaining ten by breeches buoy from the cliff top.*

was the 320 ton Liverpool motor vessel *Empire Grove*, lost on the return leg of her maiden voyage on 18 October 1941. By late 1944, the bow section of the *Cambalu*, still intact, had remarkably been thrown against that of the *Eilianus*, so that they propped each other up. Incredibly, a third bow section appeared on site when the Norwegian steamer *Sjofna* stranded almost alongside on 23 November. She was carrying 500 tons of china clay in bags from Fowey to Larne, and both the Padstow and Clovelly lifeboats went to her aid, saving seven lives before the rocket line parted and heavy seas forced the boats to seek shelter. The Hartland LSA crew then took over the rescue and saved two more men, but the rope of the breeches buoy had to be cut to save the second man from drowning when it became entangled. Another line was fired but fell short, a second going straight into the wheelhouse where it broke the captain's right leg and set fire to the ship's cat! Eventually the injured captain, nine remaining crew and three animals, including one very singed cat, were landed safely, the *Sjofna* going to pieces shortly after.

After the war, on 10 August 1946, a small steam tug, the *Ardur II*, foundered off Hartland following a series of events so bizarre that one can hardly believe their authenticity. The flush-decked steam tug *Ardur II* was launched in 1912 by Heffled & Co of South Shields. Her subsequent career was uneventful, at least until 6 May 1946 when she was sold by Cowington & Sons Ltd of Chelsea to the Standard Lighterage Co of Liverpool, their intention being to use her on the river Mersey. Her new owners contracted with Tonmouth Lister & Co of South Shields to deliver the vessel. She was insured for £2,000 after inspection on 17 May but a number of serious defects were somehow overlooked. Her steam windlass was inoperative, her pumps defective, there were faults and blockages in her bilge lines and she carried no lifeboat, nor did she have Ministry of Transport permission to sail without one. In addition, her only liferaft was inadequate and there was not a single flare or distress signal on board.

Nevertheless, a certificate of seaworthiness was eventually issued and she sailed with a recently demobbed, temporary lieutenant (RNR) as master, plus a crew of four. What followed was a chapter of disasters that surely has no equal. She finally reached Newhaven at 8pm on 14 June with her engine making fearful knocking noises and on the instructions of the harbour master she was moored to a buoy. Her exhausted crew turned in but were rudely awakened next morning with the news they were sinking. Fortunately, they all got off just before she heeled over and went down.

By 28 June she was afloat again and had been repaired, cleaned out, painted, and leaks made good – or so it was thought. The *Ardur* left Newhaven on 28 July, but within five hours was again leaking so badly that she had to put into Yarmouth, on the Isle of Wight. So the journey continued. The final act came on 10 August, when she leaked so badly that her fires were extinguished, her pumps choked, and she sank one mile north of Hartland Point. With no flares or radio, the crew's only means of attracting attention was the steam whistle, and the captain continued to send S-O-S in morse code until the pressure failed. Although the tug was too far from shore for her whistle to be heard, an alert Hartland coastguard recognised the puffs of steam for what they were and called out the Clovelly and Appledore lifeboats, plus the Hartland LSA crew. Two of the tug's crew were rescued from the liferaft, the remainder from the sea, but despite prolonged artificial respiration the engineer died. A Ministry

The Admiralty Fleet Auxiliary tanker Green Ranger, *broke from the tug* Caswell *on 17 November 1962 in a force 10 northeast gale whilst on her way to a shipyard at Cardiff for a refit, and drove ashore at Longpeak, between Bude and Hartland, to become a total loss.*

of Transport enquiry was opened at the Temperance Institution Hall, Southampton, on 15 September 1947 and resulted in the new owners being fined £400 for negligence.

Four months after the *Ardur II* incident, an obsolete warship, the 710 ton minesweeper HMS *Saltburn* fell victim to the Longpeak on 7 December after breaking tow on her way to a scrapyard. Built in 1918 by Murdoch & Murray, the *Saltburn* was bought by a Mr Gifford of Bude, who broke her up where she lay, salvage being complete by 1948.

The *Green Ranger*, a Fleet Auxiliary tanker, was in tow of the tug *Caswell*, from Devonport to Cardiff for refit when, during the afternoon of 17 November 1962, in a force ten gale from the north-east, she broke adrift and went on the rocks half a mile south of Longpeak. Distress

The L'Orient registered trawler Goliath, *on the rocks only a short distance from the cliffs at Sandor, near Hartland, on 16 March 1969, the vessel going to pieces.*

signals from the tug were relayed to the secretaries of both the Appledore and Clovelly lifeboats and both launched, but only the more powerful Appledore could weather the point, where she began a search for the wreck close inshore. Sleet and driving rain reduced visibility to a few metres, so that the lifeboat crew went past the wreck without sighting it and continued to search right down to Knap Head. Here they met up with the destroyer HMS *Agincourt*, which had been sent by the navy from Milford Haven to assist, and followed the warship back north as her searchlight probed every crevice of the coast. An hour later they found the *Green Ranger* and the lifeboat went alongside, but failed to attract the attention of the seven-man steaming crew aboard, who were below decks at the time. It was an extremely hazardous position for the lifeboat, in danger of being either smashed against the wreck or on the rocks with

137

every wave, yet Coxswain Cann held his boat in this position for 15 minutes, hanging on to the wreck with a grappling hook, their searchlight shining on her superstructure. Cann rightly received the Silver Medal of the RNLI for the rescue, while the Hartland LSA crew were awarded the Ministry of Transport's shield for the most distinguished rescue of 1962-3, having clambered down the cliff face in appalling conditions in order to get within 80 metres of the wreck. The *Green Ranger* later broke in two amidships and soon after was lost.

One of the last wrecks in this chapter had much in common with earlier incidents, since the first knowledge of the disaster was the appearance of two French seamen on the doorstep of Elmscott farm, at 7 am on 16 March 1969. Much the same scene was being enacted at South Hole farm, one mile away, where two more survivors were calling a Mr Gifford from his bed. It transpired they were four of the five survivors out of a crew of seven from the L'Orient trawler *Goliath*, which lay on her starboard side a short distance from the foot of the 152 metre high cliffs at Sandor, less than half a mile from where the *Green Ranger* had been wrecked. Her helmsman was steering the ordered course of 165 degrees when she struck, but in the dark the crew had no idea as to where they were. The four men who had appeared at the two farms had, in fact, scaled almost sheer cliffs in bare feet, scrambling over razor sharp granite outcrops and thick brambles to reach the top.

After the trawler had gone ashore, her crew of six left in the ship's inflatable liferaft, but the sea threw them out, two men drowning in their attempt to reach the rocks. Only 24 hours after going ashore, the trawler's stern broke off and she very soon went completely to pieces, but even the steep cliffs did not deter people from clambering down to the site to recover a souvenir or take photographs. Her captain, who stayed aboard when the rest of the crew left, was later rescued by Mr Gifford and his sons.

The *Eva V* (ex-*Rika*)(ex-*Adele*), was under tow of the *Carlo*, her engine having been removed, when she broke adrift, and stranded under Green cliff, Abbotsham, where the wreck was plundered and set on fire on 18 March 1981. It was New Year's Eve 1982 when Hartland Point claimed the Panamanian registered *Johanna*, a 960 tons gross motor vessel carrying wheat to Barry. Four crew were rescued by helicopter from RAF Chivenor, her three officers by the Clovelly lifeboat. The next day the narrow roads leading to the point were jammed solid with cars, bringing people from all over the south-west, with an estimated 150 people aboard

The Panama registered motor vessel Johanna, *lies broken on the rocks less than 400 yards from Hartland Point lighthouse, after going ashore with a cargo of wheat on New Year's Eve, 1982.*

at any one time, stripping the wreck of anything of value, either as souvenirs, or to sell.

To date the *Rose-in-June*, a Fowey registered motorised fishing vessel based at Bideford, was the last victim of this coast. She commenced to take in water 32 miles off Hartland on 16 March 1992. Her distress call brought the *Charleen* alongside which took her in tow to the survey ship *Northern Explorer*, who put a pump on board, but shortly after the *Rose-in-June* foundered.

7

Westward Ho! to Somerset

Since time immemorial, the high cliffs that run almost unbroken from Hartland to the Somerset border have offered shelter from the prevailing wind. Vessels leaving the Severn Sea, later referred to as the North Channel and today as the Bristol Channel, found Barnstaple or Bideford Bay a safe and welcome anchorage, and in consequence brought about the growth of these ports. Eventually, silting of the rivers and creeks restricted the size of vessels using the ports after which Appledore came into its own with coasting traffic, handling vast quantities of culm and limestone.

There are few early references to shipwreck in this area, though there is evidence of its extent and, inevitably, the volume of shipping in and out of such a treacherous estuary must have led to losses. A Customs collector at Bideford in 1852, at a time when the port required 26 such officials to conduct its business, listed 75 ships which had been wrecked locally over a period of 40 years, and in 1858 an Appledore man stated that, '62 wrecks had taken place locally in the previous 59 years'. The earliest recorded wreck in the vicinity dates back to the time of Gytha, wife of Earl Godwin and mother of King Harold. She attributed her husband's delivery from shipwreck near Hartland to the agency of St Nectan, and as a mark of appreciation founded a collegiate church at Stoke. Another example was a vessel from Flushing, which was driven ashore and wrecked at Appledore early in 1627. Of English origin, ship and crew had been captured by the Spanish some six months before remaining in the service of the French, the seamen then making their escape and getting back to England. The squire took possession of the goods cast ashore from the wreck hereabouts as reported on 6 January 1627: 'Sir John Drake taking examination and has possession of the goods cast ashore from the wreck.' 1668 saw an unidentified vessel carrying hides and tallow lost on Braunton Sands, another carrying muskets and ammunition on the bar in 1689, and the first named wreck, the *Johannan & Mary*, carrying wool, tallow and linen on 28 November 1735.

Detailed information about wrecks can often be found in Custom

House deposition books, and typically, that for the wreck of the *Sally* of Bristol, on 15 September 1769 states:

> 'At two of the clock next morning, it came cloudy and thick and squally weather for some time. Soon afterwards, there was so little wind the master could not have command of the ship, and he imagined further to the eastward than he really was, on which he sounded six or seven fathoms of water, and let go his best bower. She still driving till at last she struck aft, and came abroad side to, upon which this deponent and the rest of the crew took to their boat to save their lives, and got on shore at a place called Burroughs, in the parish of Northam.'

There followed, on 12 December 1770, the wreck of the snow *Juba*, another Bristol-owned vessel. She quickly went to pieces and her crew drowned, leaving, to quote the Customs record book, 'a cask of palm oil, with a few elephant's teeth, taken up and put under the care of the Riding Officer'. One year later, in October, there were two wrecks on the same day, the brigantine *Diana*, from Boston with timber, lost on Pickwell Sands, and the Barnstaple-owned *Cato*, also carrying wood, on Saunton Sands. It was about this time that a large Dutch East Indiaman went ashore at Westward Ho! and was wrecked. At irregular intervals, the timbers of a ship uncover on the beach there so that the complete outline of the vessel can be traced, in much the same manner as the *Amsterdam* at Bexhill, near Hastings, but the vessel as yet remains unidentified.

Until it was demolished in 1952, an interesting structure connected with wreck was the stone tower known as Chanter's Folly. It was erected in 1800 by a Bideford merchant named Chanter to afford a vantage point from which to watch for the return of the various ships in which he had a financial interest. On the very first occasion he used it, he saw his son's ship wrecked on the bar. In his anguish, he ordered that the tower was never to be used again, and it subsequently fell into ruin.

Despite an obvious need for a lifeboat at Appledore, by the early 1800s the only assistance available from the shore in the event of shipwreck was the Manby rocket apparatus. Then, on 2 October 1821, the Fowey-registered schooner *Bee* fell victim to the estuary, the remains of another vessel, still unidentified, were found ashore on Saunton Sands, and Appledore got its first lifeboat. This was the one ton, four-oared *Volunteer*, which arrived towards the end of February 1825 and was installed in a barn near the old King's Watch House. She performed no

LONDON II 1941

STAR OF GHENT 1890
ZEPHYR 1889
LARCHWOOD 1916
PAZ 1912
WILLIAM 1883

ANTWERPEN 1941
NORA 1907
STAN WOOLAWAY 1967
ISLANDER 1891
PELTON 1881
T.G.V 1889
UTILITY 1874
CORNIST 1872
COLLIER 1914
ANN 1850
Bull Point
DULCE NOMBRE DE JESUS 1861
GIPSEY 1862
MARQUIS OF LORNE 1883
PERI 1863
ODIN 1878
Rockham Bay
THOMAS CRISP 1850
Morte Stone
A.C.L.1894
Morte Point
SARAH KING 1873
NEWTOWN 1916
Mortehoe
JOHN & HENRY 1870
PERI 1863
HANNAH 1850
I'LL TRY 1859
PRINCESS ROYAL 1848
POLACCA BRIG 1850
ANN 1859
Morte
ROSE 1859
Bay
CHARFIELD 1719
HANNAH 1859
TRIDENT 1858
CLARA 1859
THISTLE 1859
MATTHEW THOMPSON 1859
ANNE 1858
AYRORE 1889
WILLIAM & JANE 1850
ROCKAWAY 1867
Baggy Leap
OCEAN SPRAY 1947
LEE BAY 1935
CERES 1936
HARFORD 1829
MARKET
HMS WEAZLE 1799
MAID 1854
Baggy Point
CATHERINE 1890
THREE BROTHERS 1879
HAABET 1895
Croyde
Asp Rock
ARAB 1879
Bay

Woolacombe Sands

WESTWARD HO
TO
SOMERSET(1)
—Chapter Seven—

Georgeham

Braunton

ST. LOUIS 1886
Barnstaple
VOLANT 1918
CHALCIOPE 1884
JONATHON WEIR 1884
or
JANE AND MARY 1880
WARDEN 1857
HENRY PATTERSON 1864
Bideford Bay
LITTLE TEST 1843
UNIDENTIFIED 1859
ERATO 1636
MARY 1867
LOUISA 1863
OLD HEAD 1917
PACE 1868
UNIDENTIFIED
ROSSEKOP II 1972
TINTO 1872
Braunton
1823
SURPRISE 1917
MARYANN 1873
DELABOLE 1833
Burrows
ANNE BROOKES 1873
JUBA 1770
WILLIAM WOOLAWAY
CATO 1771
1973
EXPRESS 1873
BEE 1821
RELIANCE 1869
HENRIETTA 1836
FELICITY 1858
SECRET 1854
HOPE 1880
SUPREME
MARQUIS 1854
CAROLINE 1959
SAGESSE
DASHER 1850
Bar
1852
JOHN AND LILLY 1843
ALBION 1845
TORRIDGE 1853
JOHANNAH & MARY 1735
PRINCE ALBERT 1850
ELIZABETH 1854
GANGES 1843
DANIEL 1829
HARMONY 1867
GEM 1890
BETSY 1831
ANN 1878
HEROINE 1878
JOHN AND MARY 1845
NORTHESK 1859
CLIFTON 1858
LYDNEY TRADER 1875
GRATITUDE 1882
ELIZA 1870
TRIAL 1873
MUSE 1877
River Taw
MY DIANE 1976
ANDREE 1908
PAUL 1852
ROSSEKOP II
1972
UNIDENTIFIED 1627
UNITY 1922
NESS 1845
DIANA 1771
ELIZABETH 1833
SALLY 1769
Appledore
SALISBURY 1749
Northam
MARY ANN 1833
Burrows
R.Torridge
Westward Ho
©R.Larn. 1996

useful service until 11 September 1829, when she made two trips to the south tail of the bar in appalling conditions during a north-westerly gale to save all twelve crew and passengers from the Bristol packet sloop *Daniel*. The fact that the Royal National Institute for the Preservation of Life from Shipwreck rewarded three of the lifeboatmen with silver medals, and the others with money, speaks for itself. But even the *Volunteer* was unable to save the lives of the three local men aboard the sloop *Betsey*, which capsized on the bar on 3 March 1831.

As a direct result of this tragedy, the local businessmen formed themselves into the North Devon Humane Society, which set about the provision of another lifeboat and a larger boathouse nearer the sea. As a result, a second lifeboat, the *Assistance*, arrived on 27 December 1831 and was not idle for long, being called out on 6 March 1833 to save the lives of nine men who had been working on the hull of the schooner *Delabole*, blown ashore and wrecked at Saunton Sands on 20 February that same year. This wreck had been sold to two Braunton men who had engaged labourers to discharge her coal cargo and it was they who were in danger when a northerly gale sprang up.

Some seven months later the *Assistance* was out again, this time to investigate a report that a brig had foundered off Northam on 24 November. She proved to be the *Mary Ann* of Exeter, whose crew had drowned long before the lifeboat arrived, so that it returned empty-handed. Some hours later, when movements in the brig's rigging suggested that someone had managed to get back on board, the lifeboat went out for a second time, manned by a fresh crew. The movements seen from the shore proved, however, to be a piece of flapping canvas, and it was while this was being examined at close quarters that a huge wave caught the coxswain unawares and the *Assistance* capsized. All but three of her crew swam clear, these three, rather foolishly perhaps, had lashed themselves to their thwarts and two drowned; the third man managed to keep his head above water in the upturned boat and, providentially, was still alive when the boat washed ashore. Less than a month later both boats were out again, this time to the Liverpool ship *Elizabeth*, from Calcutta, which stranded near Westward Ho! on 17 December.

For the next two years things went very quiet, then in 1836 three incidents took place, one of which nearly brought about a second lifeboat disaster. The sloop *Lovely Peggy* of Cardigan got on the bar on 16 January, her crew being saved by the *Volunteer*, after which the same lifeboat rescued eight men from the Irish brig *Erato* on the 30th. It was the

Plymouth schooner *Henrietta* that rolled right over on top of the lifeboat, after it had gone to her assistance on 29 November. Miraculously both vessels righted themselves, the lifeboat suffering only a few broken oars, and all eleven aboard the schooner were rescued.

A long series of gales, which reached a climax between 14-16 January 1843, brought about another series of wreck incidents. A barque with the regal name of *Albert Edward Prince of Wales*, carrying soap, candles, and other general cargo, had already been stranded on Northam Burrows and well looted on 15 January 1843, the same night that the West African trading vessel *John & Lilley*, of Liverpool, was wrecked near Saunton, at the northern end of Braunton Burrows. For eleven days her crew had battled against the elements, being blown from the north coast of Cornwall across the Bristol Channel to south Wales, then back to Devon, where finally they lost their rudder and went ashore. Capt Towns and his crew of 25, the majority of whom were very drunk, were saved, but the same cannot be said of her valuable cargo. Bound for Africa, the *John & Lilley* carried cotton goods, domestic pots and pans, muskets, gunpowder, foodstuffs, and other luxuries which the locals were not slow to appreciate.

On 14 February 1845 the Bideford-owned *John & Mary* was wrecked, and two days before Christmas of the same year the barque *Ness*, carrying rum for her home port of Bristol, also the Dartmouth schooner *Albion* were lost on the coast. The latter went to pieces on North Tail before either lifeboat could reach her, and six seamen drowned as a result. This particular incident, all too familiar at the time, made it perfectly obvious that the existing position of the lifeboats, as well as the boats themselves, were inadequate to meet the ever growing number of shipwrecks. Arrangements were therefore made for the old six-oared *Assistance* to be moved to a new site on the north bank of the estuary, but a new boathouse was not completed until the summer of 1848, the *Assistance*, strangely enough, never being used from this site, and replaced by the *Dolphin* in 1857.

Earlier that year, yet a third lifeboat, the *Petrel*, was added to the growing fleet, stationed on the south bank, near Appledore. On 29 February 1848, called out on her first service, to help the schooner *Bideford*, she became swamped and was forced to return empty-handed. Although it must have been obvious that there was something drastically wrong with the new boat, she was put back in her boathouse without any sort of trial or investigation to evaluate her seaworthiness and remained there for two years before being called out again. This time it was to assist the crew of the brigantine *Dasher* of St Ives, which stranded on the bar on 23 March 1850 during a north-westerly gale. Predictably, the *Petrel* filled with water before she was half way to the wreck, and had it not been for the timely intervention of the *Volunteer* all five of the brigantine's crew might have been lost; as it was, only John Ninnes, the cabin boy, drowned.

By 1856, with the original *Volunteer* replaced by a newer boat named *Mermaid*, the area was well prepared for a forthcoming spate of wrecks, despite the fact that the useless *Petrel* was retained until 1861. On 8 October 1857 the American ship *Warden* was stranded and broken up in the vicinity of Baggy Point, seven of her crew losing their lives; the *Felicity* of Milford was wrecked on the bar on 18 December 1858, to be followed by the Fowey-owned schooner *Caroline* on 11 March 1859 and another schooner, the *Clifton*, the following day. A night rescue by Appledore men in the two lifeboats saved six lives from among the crew of the brig *North Eske* on 2 November 1859, but they were unable to reach the *Meridian* of Fowey on 15 November 1864 and she was lost with all hands. While no two wreck incidents are ever alike, most that followed during the 1860s and 1870s were almost a repetition of those already described.

In ballast for Newport, the Bideford-owned *Mary* was running up Channel at night on 5 January 1876 when another vessel was sighted dead ahead. Capt Glover called out to her, 'Port your helm!' and did the same himself, but the other vessel went to starboard and the two ships collided. Locked together by a fouled anchor, they drifted for over a mile, during which time Glover clambered aboard the other vessel to ascertain her name, but the crew refused to tell him. After being ordered back aboard his sinking smack, the Bideford men were abandoned to their fate but, fortunately, were taken in tow by the schooner *Polacco* and managed to reach Saunton Sands, where the *Mary* went to pieces.

Typical of the many shipwrecks which do not appear in lifeboat records was that of the 84 ton, wooden brigantine *Muse*. Carrying pitch from Gloucester to St Nazaire, with a crew of five, she got into the bay on 20 February 1877 and was unable to beat clear. At 4.30 am, with the wind blowing a full gale from the north-west, she went ashore and within three hours nothing remained but a few planks. There was only one survivor, Charles Le Croix, who got ashore on a piece of wreckage. During 1880, a similar incident concerned the Barnstaple schooner *Hope*, Vaggers master, which went onto Braunton Sands on 24 November and deserves special mention since she was an incredible 102 years old when wrecked.

Surprisingly, there had been no steamship incidents until 1881, when two occurred within ten months. The first was the British collier *Ranee*, stranded on Saunton Sands on 7 October during hazy weather. Less than nine months old at the time, the 617 ton ship was refloated and saved, whereas the second was completely destroyed by fire. This was the 14 ton, wooden-hulled paddle steamer *Gratitude*, which was lying alongside Westacott's shipbuilding yard, close to Barnstaple bridge. Sergeant Eddy of the local police first spotted the fire and roused her crew during the early hours of 2 July 1882. Every effort was made to extinguish the flames, but she was completely gutted and sank after burning to the waterline.

A great many of the sailing vessels which met with disaster on this stretch of coast had, in fact, reached the open Atlantic outward bound, only to encounter accident or unfavourable winds forcing them to turn back. Typical of these was the brigantine *Jonathon Weir* of Monckton NB which left Newport for Cuba with coal and ran into a series of gales off the Scillies on 23 January 1884. Several huge seas broke over her deck, parting the backstays of both her fore and main masts, so that all sail had to be furled. Drifting helpless before the wind, she was blown into the bay, then onto Saunton Sands near Down End, and was finally wrecked. Fortunately her crew of eight, plus one passenger and a stowaway, remained aboard until low water, when they scrambled to safety.

A marked decline in the number of wreck incidents is apparent for the period 1885 to 1900, with only four vessels lost in the vicinity. Of these, the schooner *St Louis*, stranded on 12 December 1886 with five of her crew drowned, was the only wreck close to Appledore. A Norwegian brig showing distress signals was sighted off Clovelly on 4 October 1895 and the lifeboat put out and rescued her crew of ten, but the ship herself, the *Haabet*, drifted right across to Croyde Bay before stranding on the beach.

Since then, this particular part of Bideford Bay has seen less than a dozen ships lost, which include the brigantine *Charles P. Knight*, at Westward Ho! on 11 September 1903, and the 18 year old French ketch *Andree*, near the bar on 21 April 1908. Carrying coal, the *Andree* struck submerged wreckage two miles south of the bell buoy, and had to be run ashore, in what proved a vain attempt to save her. Two schooners, the *Surprise* and the *Volant* were victims of the bar during the First World War, and the obsolete coastal destroyer HMS *Sandfly* got on Pebble Ridge, at Westward Ho! on 7 October 1920, whilst being towed to a breaker's yard at Milford Haven. Two years later the *Unity*, a steam trawler, foundered about 450 metres offshore and the wreck had to be

The coastal destroyer HMS Sandfly, *renumbered TB-4, lies wrecked near Westward Ho! on 7 October 1920, whilst on its way to a breaker's yard.*

dispersed by explosives when it proved a navigational hazard.

There then followed the disgraceful business of the *Elsa Kuehlke*, which revived old wrecking instincts locally. It was Sunday, 24 October 1926, when this German schooner appeared off Westward Ho! with a bad leak whilst carrying clay from Fremmington. Her captain decided to beach her, but badly holed in the attempt she became a total loss. Hundreds of scavengers invaded the wreck, taking anything of value, and a West Country newspaper reported: 'They behaved in the most disgraceful manner, pillaging all they could lay their hands on, even personal photographs.' Eventually someone set fire to her remains, which put an end to any further theft, but pieces of her still remain beneath the cliffs on the Cornborough side of the beach.

The last wrecks here to date included the 114 ton motor fishing vessel *Rossekop II*, which went to pieces on Airy Point at 9.45 pm on 4 November 1972, all the clothing and belongings of the captain, his wife and three children being stolen. The following year the suction dredger *William Woolaway*, of Southampton, sister ship to the *Stan Woolaway*, lost off Bull Point in 1967, stranded in the Taw opposite Anchor Woods

The German auxiliary three-masted schooner Fimmo, *of Geestemunde, stranded off Braunton, North Devon, 1 May 1923, after a chain in her steering gear parted and she went out of control. She was later refloated and repaired at Appledore.*

on 23 March 1973, but was subsequently refloated, whilst *My Diane*, a motor fishing vessel, capsized one mile south-east of Bideford Fairway buoy on 8 October 1976 and broke up whilst attempting to enter the estuary in rough weather. In 1977, on 7 April, a sand-laden barge was reported as having sunk in the river, her crew being rescued by helicopter.

At the north-east corner of Barnstaple Bay two prominent headlands, Baggy Point and Morte Point, along with the infamous Morte, or Death Stone, form the pincers of a giant trap. In the days of sail it was feared by shipmasters even more than Hartland Point, and vessels at anchor in the bay maintained a constant watch in case the wind changed, for this stretch of coast is particularly vulnerable to gales which sweep in from the west or north. Without question, dozens of 16th and 17th century wrecks took place here, but only details of the snow *Charfield*, stranded on Woolacombe Sands in June 1719, have passed down to the present day. The only 18th century wreck recorded in detail was, in fact, the most tragic on the entire north Devon coast. The vessel was the British naval sloop o'war *Weazle*, which sank near Baggy Point on 12 February 1799 during a furious north-northwesterly gale. It is best described by John James of Bideford, who, five days after the event, wrote in a letter to a friend:

'I heard on Wednesday last, a funeral sermon for 106 persons unfortunately lost in the *Weazle* on Sunday night. She was in the bay that afternoon, and as people went to church, the seafaring men felt some anxiety, if the wind should shift a point and blow, which it did. They made every effort to get out to sea, and in vain kept firing signals of distress. It is supposed she got round Baggy Point and struck upon Morte rocks; that fine ship perished and as yet only one body has been taken up, but many are watching from opposite the beach, both yesterday and today, and are fishing up fragments of the wreck. We have since heard the wreck is visible at low water, this side of Baggy Point. A sloop that was in distress in the bay on Monday or Tuesday has also gone down, her fate is uncertain. It is expected many bodies will float and be driven on shore the coming spring.'

There was one woman among the 106 dead, a memorial to whom exists at Northam church; a great many were laid to rest at Braunton, and a gravestone to William Kidman, one of the victims, survives at Georgham. In recent years, the *Weazle*'s remaining iron cannon and other items on the seabed were located by a local diving club, whose members landed one of the guns.

A notable feature of shipwrecks in this corner of Devon was the unusually heavy loss of life. Few ships went ashore here with survivors, and by far the greater number were lost with all hands. The Swansea brigantine *Harford*, loaded with copper ore for south Wales, was one of the unlucky vessels to strike Baggy Point to be lost with all six crew on 26 August 1829, but some were more fortunate and the *Princess Royal* of London, wrecked off Baggy Point on the last day of March 1848, lost no one. She is worth a mention, since her cargo of sugar from Mauritius attracted a great many wreckers to Barricane cove, where she was stripped bare before the authorities could intervene.

The Morte Stone claimed the next victim, the Bristol schooner *Thomas Crisp*, on 18 January 1850, after leaving Bristol for Barbados with a general cargo. Fog and gale-force winds in the Channel caused her master, Francis Farr, to put about for Penarth roads, but with the lookouts unable to see beyond their own jib-boom, she went ashore on the Devon coast. The jollyboat was prepared for launching, but a huge wave washed boat and crew overboard, all but her captain, who drowned, managing to get back aboard. Bailing furiously with their seaboots and sou'westers, they managed to remain afloat until rescued by the packet paddle-steamer *Brilliant*, which landed them at Hayle.

The 1850s saw a total of 15 wrecks here, the most tragic period being 24-26 October 1859, known as the *Royal Charter* gale, the worst storm on record in the British Isles. During its first day, 195 wrecks occurred around the country, but it was the third day, the 26th, that saw seven vessels lost in Morte Bay. The first to go down was a 40 year old schooner, *Ann*, lost with all seven crew; she was followed shortly afterwards by the *Rose*, another schooner, with only one survivor; the *Hannah*, again with only one saved, and the pilot cutter *I'll Try*, from which only two were saved.

Rockham Bay, to the north of Morte Point, has been the grave for many a fine ship, and it was here that the brig *Dulce Nombre de Jesus* met her end on New Year's Day 1861, with five crew members drowned. The brigantine *Gipsey* followed, on the Slipper rock in 1862; the *Peri*, a two-masted schooner in 1863; the barque *Janvrin* in 1864; the barque *Rockway* in 1867; the *Dart* in 1869; and the *Mary Matthews* on 17 March 1870. Storm and fog brought about the majority of these losses, but fire and collision continued to take its annual toll, with incidents such as the *Sarah King*. Late in the evening of 25 January 1873, the deck officer of the Hayle packet steamer *Bride* sighted a green light on his starboard bow, which appeared to follow him round when he made a change of course. Four minutes later the packet sliced into the side of the brigantine *Sarah King* of London, when close to Morte Point. So quickly did the sailing vessel fill and sink that the 14 crew and three passengers aboard had no alternative but to leap overboard, but all were rescued and landed at Ilfracombe.

It was the 1880s before the first steamship was lost hereabouts, this being the *Pelton* on 26 March 1881. Then, as if to confirm the superstition that such events always happen in threes, the *Uzzia* went ashore in 1882, and the *Lynx* the following year. The *Pelton*, a Newcastle-registered ship of 816 tons gross, laden with coal for Havre, foundered near Bull Point with the loss of all but one of her 17 crew, a particularly tragic outcome fortunately not repeated in either of the following steamship incidents. Thomas Hogg, a seaman, was the sole survivor from the *Pelton*, and stated in his deposition that all had gone well until they were off the Scillies. A severe gale then caused her cargo to shift and she took a list to port. When water commenced to enter her forward hold, seven of the crew elected to leave the ship in a lifeboat, Hogg among them. They got clear in the starboard boat and watched the steamer founder shortly after. For five hours they rowed around, bailing continually, and in this short period five of their number died from exposure, one man with his arms around Hogg's neck. The schooner *Ureah* then sighted them and went to their assistance but, in getting close alongside, caused the lifeboat to capsize. The two remaining survivors were thrown into the sea, only Hogg escaping alive from beneath the upturned boat.

Although the lifeboat *Grace Woodbury*, previously named the *Jack-a-Jack*, had been installed at Woolacombe in 1871 as a secondary boat for the Ilfracombe station, whose principal boat could not always get round Bull Point to Morte Bay in bad weather, she was only launched to perform a service twice in 29 years on station! One of these occasions was to the steamer *Lynx*, on 6 March 1883. Carrying coal for Portreath, in Cornwall, the *Lynx* sprang a leak and had to be run ashore at Woolacombe to prevent her foundering. Although the lifeboat was launched, the steamer had been driven so far up the beach that the *Grace Woodbury* was unable to get alongside without going aground herself. At low water the leak was repaired but attempts to winch her off using kedge anchors failed. Worsening weather conditions opened up additional leaks and it began to look as if the *Lynx* was finished, until the lifeboatmen set to work, refloated her, and got her safely into Appledore.

Of the many ships stranded at Baggy Point, the largest and certainly the most welcome so far as the locals were concerned, since it took place in the depths of a particularly hard winter, was the iron, full-rigged ship *Penthesilea* on 19 January 1890. She went ashore during a west-southwesterly hurricane, leaving what one inhabitant described as 'a prodigious amount of coal on the beach, free for the asking', which naturally provided fuel for many a local hearth.

Two years later hopes ran high that a cargo of pitprops was also in the offing, since the *Maria* of Gloucester, on passage from Cork to Llanelly, went ashore at midnight on 22 April 1892. Her crew reached Ilfracombe in their own boat, but on returning to the Morte area overland next day in the hope of salvaging personal effects, found that the vessel had refloated herself and drifted out to sea, never to be heard of again. From then on the majority of wrecks, as one would expect, were steamships, starting with the *Paz*, of Montevideo, which collided with another Uruguay-registered steamer, the *Olavarria*, seven miles west of Bull Point on 25 May 1912. The *Paz*, built by Priestman of Sunderland as the *Sir Richard Grenville*, foundered as a result, but without loss of life.

Although the remains of wreck are not usually visible for long on the coast of Devon and Cornwall, the boiler and some iron frames of the Bristol-owned steamer *Collier* are still visible despite the fact she stranded and broke up on 28 January 1914. One of the smallest steamers to be lost on the Devon coast, the 114 ton net *Collier*, had a remarkable career which began at the shipyard of J. Reid, Port Glasgow, in 1849, and ended with her being the oldest steamship classed with Lloyd's Register when she was lost.

She was on her way to Hayle in ballast and was steaming in dense fog with both captain and mate on deck when they saw the red sector light of Bull Point, which indicated they were 'standing into danger'. Before they could take avoiding action, the ship went ashore on Rockham beach at dead low water and, as the tide turned, she washed higher up the beach until she became wedged between two rocks. Capt Dyer of the Morthoe rocket brigade assembled his team and apparatus on the clifftop, but the *Collier* was too far away for them to be of any assistance. In any case their efforts were wasted, since the steamer's crew had already got away in the ship's punt. The Ilfracombe lifeboat then appeared on the scene under tow from the steamer *Devonia* and took aboard Capt Wright, Mate Jefferies, Engineer Thompson, two firemen, three able seamen, a dog, a cat, and a pet goldfinch in a cage.

During the First World War the only casualty due to enemy action close

Perched high and dry on a rock between Barricane beach and Harris's cove, near Woolacombe, North Devon, the s.s. Newtown, *of London, was carrying pitprops for Newport when she drove ashore on 7 January 1916 to become a total loss.*

enough inshore to be classed as a Devon wreck was the Liverpool steamer *Bengrove*, torpedoed and sunk on 7 March 1915, but strandings and collisions continued to take their toll.

Without question, the most spectacular wreck photograph taken on this part of the coast was of the wooden ketch *Dido C* of Barnstaple, as she lay perched high and dry on the Morte Stone on 16 September 1936. After stranding in hazy weather, her three-man crew were taken off by the Ilfracombe lifeboat *Rosabella*, since it was feared she would break her back, but at high water, still intact, she was refloated and towed clear.

Another interesting wreck took place in 1936, that of the motorised sailing ketch *Ceres*, the oldest vessel classed with Lloyd's. Built at Salcombe in 1811, four years before the battle of Waterloo, she served as a munitions carrier throughout the Napoleonic wars. In 1936, with a cargo of slag and a two man crew, she was on passage from Swansea to her home port of Bude, where she was owned by Messrs Petherick & Sons. Off

154

Whilst seemingly in an impossible position to be saved, the Barnstaple ketch Dido C was successfully refloated undamaged, after going ashore on the Morte Stone, off Morte Point, on 16 September 1936.

Baggy Point, she sprang a leak on 25 November and finally sank 450 metres offshore, leaving her topmasts showing above the surface until, soon after, she went to pieces. The last foundering here was that of the 278 ton sand dredger *Stan Woolaway* of Southampton, which sank a mile offshore on 13 March 1967. She was returning to Barnstaple, full laden, when she developed a list and foundered. Three years later, from amongst the wreckage on the bottom, members of the Ilfracombe and North Devon Sub-Aqua Club recovered the ship's bell, which was returned to its original owners. In appreciation, they, in turn, granted sole ownership and salvage rights of the wreck to the divers.

From Bull Point, east to Glenthorne, which marks the border with Somerset, lie 23 miles of the highest and most formidable cliffs in the whole of Devon. Its general inaccessibility, sparse population, and open countryside, made this stretch of coast popular with the smuggling fraternity and history records a great many 17th and 18th century 'goings on' connected with this activity. Chambercombe Farm, inland from Ilfracombe, has, however, a more sinister connection with gentlemen of 'the other trade', the wreckers, if legend is to be believed. It is said that here, many years ago, a small, sealed room was discovered, in which was found the skeleton of a young woman lying on a bed, and everything covered in thick cobwebs. Thought to be the body of a Spanish girl who had survived the wreck of some ship lured ashore by the infamous wreckers of Hele Bay, it was thought she had been immured after being stripped of valuable jewellery; but it is not in character for wreckers of this coast to go to so much trouble when another corpse on the beach was neither here nor there, unless perhaps a ransom was intended.

Punctuated with dozens of small headlands and inlets, the coast here abounds with hazards and represents a formidable obstacle to shipping, with no haven other than at Ilfracombe. The earliest recorded wreck at Ilfracombe appears to have occurred in 1635, since in the parish church there is a tomb marked 31 October of that year, bearing the inscription: 'Bryant Tooker and two Frenchmen, parte of a shipps companie called ye *John*, were drowned at our harbour mouth.'

At some time during the following century, a rich Spanish ship came ashore during a gale in a cove once outside of the harbour but now enclosed by the breakwater. Gold and silver coins are found there from time to time, and a contemporary report suggests that this wreck was: 'A big ship, ashore in 1782, said to have been one of Rodney's prizes, but by others that she was a Bristol slaver.' Yet another source states: '. . a vessel, returning from the West Indies with black prisoners, was driven ashore at Ilfracombe early in the 19th century, and that for years coins, both gold and silver, along with jewels, were found at low water, in the shingle. The vessel was ballasted with yellow shingle and this can still be seen.' Perhaps these reports refer to the transport *London*, carrying British troops and French prisoners of war, lost in Rapparee cove on 9 October 1796. Thirty people were drowned in this wreck, 16 of whom were local men who had attempted to swim out to her from ashore. Since the dates of wreck incidents are often grossly distorted, it should not be overlooked that the incident bears a resemblance to the loss of the *Arms of Bristol* on 26 March 1675. This particular wreck is well documented and described as: 'A very fine ship of 350 tons, armed with 26 guns, from Bristol to Barbadoes, in the West Indies, cast away near Ilfracombe, but 40 got to land, some in ship's boats and some driven in on wreck, 16 persons being drowned. Very little of her cargo has been saved, and very little likelihood of saving much more.'

Unfortunately, no further authenticated incidents of wreck are known till 1780 when, on 2 October, the *Nostra Seignora de Bon Successo* of Lisbon stranded at the harbour mouth and went to pieces. It has been suggested that another vessel, with an almost identical name was lost on the Morte Stone the same year, but if this is so, the coincidence is remarkable, unless she stranded but got off, only to be lost at Ilfracombe.

Although it is maintained at Ilfracombe that the town's first lifeboat, provided by private subscription, was stationed there from 1828, there is no record of its service, therefore it must be assumed that local boatmen rescued the crews of the schooner *Compact* in 1833, the brig *Alice*, near Bull Point in 1834, and the schooner *Ringdove* in January 1843. It was a particularly fierce gale, eventually reaching hurricane force, which wrecked the 54 ton smack *William* of Fowey on 5 January 1850 and, later the same day, the Padstow schooner *Amelia*. Carrying a cargo of iron and coal valued at £130, the *Amelia*'s master, Thomas Avery, attempted to enter the harbour at night in fog, but she struck a rock and sank. Avery was severely reprimanded at the Board of Trade enquiry for not having gone up channel and anchored in Penarth Roads to await daybreak. Although a great many similar incidents followed, listed in the wreck index, the majority were of little or no present-day significance.

It was 1889 when the steamer *Lymington* was lost near Ilfracombe with no survivors, the one and only steamship to be stranded near the port. A public enquiry into the loss opened at Ilfracombe town hall on 8 February, the first witness being William Robins, caretaker of the auxiliary lifeboat at Morthoe. He stated that just before 2 am on Saturday, 2 February, he heard that distress signals had been fired in the vicinity of Bull Point. He informed the coastguards, who set off with their rocket apparatus while he rode to Ilfracombe to tell the lifeboat secretary. On arrival, he found the lifeboat crew already assembled, dressed, and preparing to launch, having been summoned at least an hour previously by maroons fired from Lantern Hill, the news having reached there from Lee, the scene of the wreck.

A messenger arrived at the lifeboat station shortly after Mr Robins' appearance to say that the lifeboat would be useless, and that it was the rocket apparatus that was required. The entire crew had then set off on foot, pushing the heavy rocket cart to the Castle coffee shop, where horses were waiting. Unfortunately, it was 3 am before they reached the village of

The Gloucester registered ketch Arabella, *ashore near the entrance to Ilfracombe harbour, sitting high and dry on Britton rock on 2 October 1895. All four crew and two local men were drowned in the wreck.*

Lee, and another hour passed before they were on the clifftop overlooking the wreck site, by which time the *Lymington* had gone to pieces and all her crew drowned. The stern of the wreck was later found near the bathing cove, half a mile from Lee, and the bow section was seen drifting around offshore.

Few wreck incidents have taken place east of Ilfracombe, where Lynmouth is the last remaining haven in Devon. Although of no size, Lynmouth housed a lifeboat from 1869 to 1944, performing on average one service every three years, which indicates the frequency of incidents. An iron schooner, the *Monte Moro* of South Shields, was said to have struck a rock some two miles offshore and had to be beached in Combemartin Bay on 4 August 1876, but the obstruction was more likely to have been floating wreckage. A similar incident caused the Swansea smack *Edith* to founder in a position two miles north-east of Hangman Point in 1877, while the Barnstaple polacca *Henrietta* became a total loss after stranding near Higher Hangman on 2 October 1880.

Although the sailing ship *Forrest Hall* was subsequently saved and hence not classified as wreck, no record such as this would be complete without reference to what was a quite remarkable and arduous service, unique in the history of the RNLI. It began on 12 January 1899, when the lifeboat secretary at Lynmouth, Tom Bevan, received a telegram from the Anchor Hotel, at Porlock Weir, stating that a large sailing ship was in distress in the bay and flying signals requesting assistance.

Normally, the Lynmouth lifeboat would have been launched and gone east along the coast, but with a full north-westerly gale blowing, seas were breaking clean over the esplanade and the approach roads were flooded to a depth of a metre, far too dangerous and rough to risk the boat and its crew. No one had ever contemplated taking the heavy boat and carriage by road to Porlock before but, with no alternative, it was unanimously agreed they would attempt to get the ten-oared *Louisa* over Countisbury Hill. Unless one has traversed this route, the significance of this decision cannot be fully appreciated. It represented a journey of twelve miles from sea level up to 1,400 feet and back to sea level again, at night in the pouring rain, with a full gale blowing, and only oil lamps for illumination. Even today, with every possible mechanical aid, it would be considered a remarkable achievement.

It was an operation that required the utmost co-operation from everyone in the village and before the lifeboat and carriage, weighing some eight tons, could set off at 7 pm, a gang of men and horses went ahead, measuring the width of the road, demolishing obstructions, and tearing down any banks that might impede the boat's progress. Twenty horses were harnessed together and, assisted by every able-bodied man, woman and child, they set off up the fearful slope. Their first mishap occurred, fortunately, after they had reached the top of Countisbury, when a wheel fell off the carriage. By the time this had been refitted and everything was ready to proceed, everyone was soaked to the skin and enthusiasm for the task had begun to wane.

More than half of the helpers declined to go any further and turned back to Lynmouth, leaving about 20 men to complete the journey. Not long afterwards, they met up with the advance gang who had completely removed a long length of stone wall on the Lynmouth side of Glenthorn White Gate, only to find that the carriage could not get down Ashton

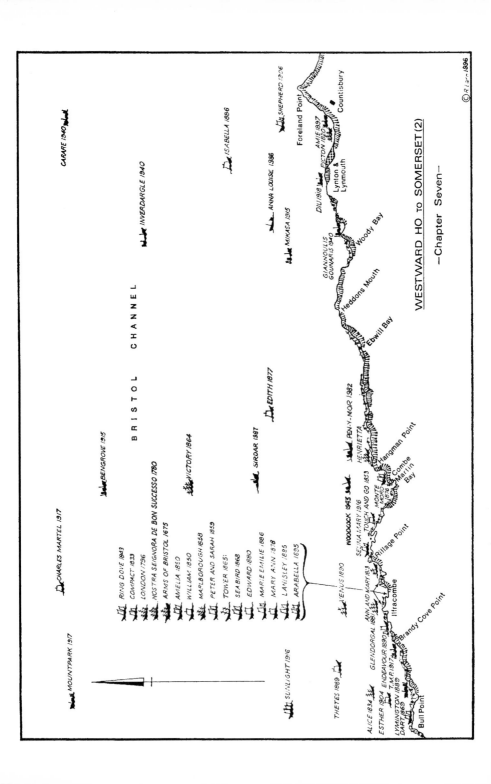

MOUNTPARK 1917

CHARLES MARTEL 1917

CARARE 1940

BENGROVE 1915

RING DOVE 1843
COMPACT 1833
LONDON 1796
NOSTRA SEIGNORA DE BON SUCCESSO 1780
ARMS OF BRISTOL 1675
AMELIA 1850
WILLIAM 1850
MARLBOROUGH 1858
PETER AND SARAH 1859
TOWER 1865
SEABIRD 1868
EDWARD 1880
MARIE EMILIE 1886
MARY ANN 1878
LANISLEY 1895
ARABELLA 1685

INVERDARGLE 1940

ISABELLA 1886

B   R   I   S   T   O   L   C   H   A   N   N   E   L

ANNA LOUISE 1936

VICTORY 1864

MIKASA 1915

SIRDAR 1987

EDITH 1877

SHEPHERD 1206

Foreland Point

DIU 1918
PICTON 1820
AMIE 1897
Countisbury
Lynton &
Lynmouth

GIANNOULIS
GOUNARIS 1940

Woody Bay

Heddons Mouth

Ebwill Bay

WOODCOCK 1915
SELINA MARY 1916
TOUCH AND GO 1853
PEN-Y-MOR 1982
HENRIETTA
Hangman Point
MONTE
MORO
1976
Combe
Martin
Bay

SUNLIGHT 1916

VENUS 1890

Rillage Point

ANN AND MARY 1813
GLENDORGAL 1881
Ilfracombe

THETES 1889

ALICE 1834
ESTHER 1904 ENDEAVOUR 1890
T.M.P. 1917
LYMINGTON 1889
DART 1865
Brandy Cove Point
Bull Point

© R.... 1896

WESTWARD HO to SOMERSET (2)

—Chapter Seven—

Lane. Without hesitation they removed the boat from its carriage and took it through the narrow section of road on skids, moving it forward two metres at a time. Meanwhile, the bulky carriage was taken through a side gate, across several fields, and back on to the main road further ahead, where it awaited the lifeboat's arrival. From this point on, everything was downhill, but it was necessary to employ almost all the men on the drag ropes, or in checking the wheels with giant wedges, as they slipped and skidded down a gradient of one in four.

In Porlock itself, finding a cottage was in the way, they knocked down a corner of the building, much to the indignation of the old lady who lived there. She had never seen a lifeboat before but when told of the ship in distress, she readily helped to remove granite blocks from her own home. With the sea so close, the men hoped that all the obstacles had been overcome, only to find that the seawall at Porlock Weir had been washed away and the road was impassable. Back they all went with the *Louisa*, along the higher road, where a fallen tree blocked their path, and had to be cut up before they could proceed.

Eventually, at 6am they reached the beach, exhausted and utterly soaked. With the *Forrest Hall* still in the bay, her anchors dragging, the vessel creeping closer to the shore by the minute, they had no alternative but to launch the boat immediately and go to her assistance. They reached the ship, but found there was nothing they could do until daybreak, by which time it was hoped that the tug which had been towing the *Forrest Hall* when she broke adrift, would reappear. At 7am the tug, the *Jane Jolliffe* of Liverpool, entered the bay, reconnected her towing hawser, and took the ship to Barry none the worse for the experience. The Lynmouth men, though in an advanced state of exhaustion and in worse condition than the ship's crew, insisted on going with them and arrived in Barry on the 13th, having neither slept nor eaten for well over 24 hours. After a well-earned meal and a rest, they returned to Porlock, from where the lifeboat was towed back to Lynmouth by sea. Ten years later, the *Forrest Hall* was wrecked and lost near Auckland, New Zealand, on 27 February 1909.

The losses up until 1996 in this area include the steam yacht, *Pen-Y-Mor*, which sank in 43 metres depth after striking an underwater object on 25 August 1982; the motorised fishing vessel *Anna Louise* two miles north-east of Highveer Point on 8 September 1986 and the *Sirdar*, a steam tug which foundered in 30 metres depth in heavy weather on 10 September 1987.

8
Lundy Island

In the year 1786 the merchants of Bristol, claiming that Lundy took such a 'great toll of shipping', offered to build, equip and maintain a lighthouse on the island entirely at their own expense. In retrospect, this reference to a great many wrecks was undoubtedly an exaggeration, since even during the second half of the 19th century, the peak years for shipping losses around the United Kingdom, an average of less than one vessel a year was lost on Lundy and it is most unlikely that the toll would have been any greater in the late 1700s.

Situated twelve miles north-west of Hartland Point and the north Devon coast, this lonely, three mile long granite platform of volcanic origin lies at the entrance to the Bristol Channel, directly in the path of what was once a major shipping route to the coal ports of south Wales and, of course, Bristol itself. Considering the vast numbers of ships that have passed this way during the last two centuries alone, it is remarkable that so few losses have occurred on the island.

Like the Isles of Scilly, its Cornish counterpart, Lundy has never had its own newspaper, so that apart from the logbooks of the Trinity House lighthouse keepers, known to have been started in 1819 but unfortunately no longer in existence, no complete record of wreck was ever officially maintained on the island. For a short time during the late 1800s, there was a Receiver of Wreck on Lundy, but apart from one incomplete volume covering the period 1868-85, even these depositions and letter books have been lost. With no lifeboat and a population seldom greater than three dozen, information concerning losses on Lundy have, in general, been passed on by word of mouth. In all probability shipwrecks during the 1700s never reached the ears of those on the mainland at all, and in support of this it is worth noting that issues of Lloyd's List between 1742 and 1756 make not one mention of a ship being lost on Lundy.

The earliest reference to wreck here is that of the *Marie*, a collier, which was lost on Lundy on 19 September 1757, after which it was September 1768 before news was received on the mainland that a large brigantine, the

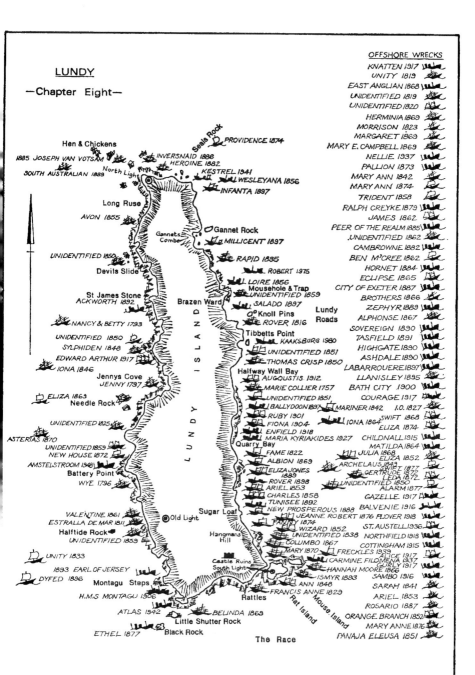

LUNDY

—Chapter Eight—

Susanna, Captain Wallis, had been found abandoned, foundered three miles north of Lundy. In February 1793 the *Nancy & Betty*, St Ives to Swansea, sank close inshore, followed by a Chepstow vessel, the *Wye*, which is said to have been wrecked and lost with all hands in December 1796, and the Bristol ship *Jenny* on 20 February the following year. Homeward bound from West Africa with ivory and gold dust, she was lost on the west side of the island at a spot known to this day as Jenny's Cove. Much has been made of this incident and one source insists that the *Jenny* was a British frigate, lost on 28 December 1809 with $1,000,000 of gold specie, but in point of fact there has not been a single Royal Navy warship that bore that name.

Seventeen other sailing vessels were lost in the first half of the 19th century, only the brig *Anne*, built at Mevagissey in 1794, having left any sort of story in her wake. St Ives to Cardiff in ballast to load coal, this schooner became a total wreck at 2 am on 2 February when she hit the western side of Lundy in fog. Three of her crew got into the ship's boat which was swept out to sea, leaving Captain Richards, the cabin boy and a passenger stranded on board. The captain and the boy then jumped overboard and attempted to swim ashore but presumably drowned, since neither were ever seen again. The passenger, a young man from Bridgwater remained in the rigging for 13 hours until discovered by local fishermen, who took him into their boat and landed him on the island.

Whilst north Devon newspapers sometimes printed detailed accounts of Lundy shipwrecks, for the majority only the bare details were recorded, or there was no mention at all, only Lloyd's List offering any detail, reported through one of their shipping agents. The St Ives registered brig *Valient* was typical of the many collisions off Lundy. Carrying copper ore from Portreath to Swansea with a crew of seven, she was rammed amidships by the brig *Maid of Errin*, of Truro, in thick, rough conditions on 2 February 1849. The latter reached St Ives with much damage, unaware of the identity of the vessel she had sunk with all hands. It was only when a capsized boat was picked up near the island bearing the name *Valient*, that the wreck was identified, whose master and mate left two widows and eleven orphans between them. A similar incident the following year saw the *Glenlyon* in collision on 29 April nine miles west of Lundy. It was only when a desk, containing the ship's logbook, with accounts, journal and other documents were picked up floating, along with a medicine chest the same day, that the victim was revealed to be the *Countess of Bective*, on passage from Cuba to Swansea. Her crew were later saved from their own boat.

Fire-damp is a potential hazard for any vessel carrying wet coal, and the Elsfleth registered brigantine *Ariel* was completely wrecked by a heavy explosion on 30 April 1853, 18 miles west of Lundy, when the accumulated coal gas ignited. The ship's boy had been sent into the hold with a lighted candle which he dropped accidentally, causing the accident. One seaman was blown to pieces, the mate suffered a shattered leg and the boy received serious burns. Although some five miles away, it was fortunate that the Hayle schooner *Auspicious* heard the explosion, going to their assistance and saving the crew, landing them at Hayle.

Many a drowned seaman was laid to rest in a grave on the island, Captain Chellew, Mate Wallace, Able Seaman Mattria and William Garvey, a ship's boy, all from the St Ives schooner *James*, which sank off Lundy on 19 March 1862 after developing a serious leak, being just one example. In this case there was one survivor out of the crew of five, William Turner, who was able to identity the bodies, otherwise they would have been buried simply as 'Unidentified seaman, found drowned'.

The very first steamship wreck off Lundy island took place on 2 January 1864, when the paddle-steamer *Iona II*, built as a fast ferry for service on the Clyde in 1863 at Govan, was wrecked on the east side. She had been bought in secret by an American living in Virginia, allegedly to run contraband guns and supplies for the Confederate army in the American Civil War. The wreck was relocated by John Shaw in 1976, who was running a London based Lundy sport-diving holiday venture. Artefacts from the wreck have since been deposited with the Greenock Museum, the site being designated under the Protection of Wrecks Act 1973 as No 2 of 1989.

Two large barques were lost within a month of each other in 1871, the Liverpool registered *Brenda*, carrying railway lines from Newport to New Orleans on 14 February, and the Swansea registered *Cornwall*, on 19 March. The former left Cardiff on the 13th, being towed across the Bristol Channel until off Lundy. After the tug cast-off, all sail was set including the topgallants, but due to a course error she drove between the Knoll Pins rocks and Gunn Point at 3.35 am. They managed to get her off but seconds later she struck again, remaining fast, to become a total loss. The *Cornwall* was carrying a cargo of guano from Sombrero to Gloucester when she was in collision with the steamship *Himalaya*, carrying railway lines from Newport to Revel. Both vessels were showing their full navigation lights, both had lookouts posted forward and a pilot on board when they struck each other in fog. Five of the barque's crew managed to scramble on board the bow of the steamer, and the pilot was later rescued from the sea, but she took ten crew and one passenger to the bottom with her.

The next steamship loss was the *Pallion*, of London, which foundered seven miles west of Lundy on 5 November 1873 when her propeller shaft broke, causing a severe leak, followed by the steamship *Ethel* on the Outer Shutter Rocks on 6 February 1877 with a cargo of iron-ore brought from Spain. She sank within minutes of striking, mate John Laurence being the sole survivor out of a crew of 20.

The Knoll Pins rocks, which claimed the barque *Brenda* in 1871, was also the resting place of the steamer *Peer of the Realm*, Cardiff to Bombay with coal, when she struck in fog on 12 February 1885. Built by Doxfords at Sunderland in 1876, the wreck was purchased by a marine engineer named Common. He set about dumping her cargo with a view to refloating the vessel, but she was a total loss eventually. Over the next 15 years, four full-rigged ships were lost in these waters, in addition to seven steamships.

The 21 crew of the steamship *Tunisie*, stranded on the Sugar Loaf rock, Lundy, on 19 February 1892, owed their lives to the ingenuity of John McCarthy, keeper of the Old Lighthouse, who rigged a home-made breeches buoy out of an explosive fog signal, a length of iron pipe, lengths of old codline and a canvas coal bag, a rescue which took seven hours to complete in a blinding snowstorm. This improvisation was necessary since the island had no rocket apparatus of its own at the time.

The largest shipwreck ever on Lundy was a Royal Navy battleship. During the afternoon of Tuesday, 29 May 1906, the relatively new *Montagu* anchored off Lundy in the course of fleet exercises. She attempted to communicate with the Isles of Scilly by means of the recently installed 'wireless telegraphic signalling apparatus', but found the distance too great. These early radio trials were of considerable importance to the navy, and had it not been for the dense fog which quickly enveloped her, the *Montagu* would have slowly reduced the distance until communication was achieved. At anchor, the risk of collision with a merchant vessel was high, and her captain decided to move closer to Lundy. Soundings were taken at regular intervals and the lookouts warned to listen for the Lundy fog signals as the ship closed on the island. At 2 pm on 30 May, a depth of 17 fathoms was reported, but twelve minutes later, when the navigating officer thought they were at least four miles offshore, the warship shuddered to a halt, having run ashore on the Shutter rock on the south-west corner of

The Royal Navy battleship Montagu, *14,000 tons, which was wrecked on Shutter rock, Lundy, in fog, on 30 May 1906. Every effort was made to refloat her but failed, despite the full assistance of the Pembroke Naval Dockyard and thousands of men.*

Lundy. Attempts were made to get her off using her engines, alternately at full ahead and astern, but she remained fast and leaked so badly that a landing party was detailed to scale the cliffs and report to the authorities.

On reaching the clifftops, the lieutenant in charge found a footpath, the north-south track which follows the western coastline. Unaware that less than half a mile to their right lay both the settlement and south lighthouse, the party turned north and walked the entire length of Lundy until they reached the north lighthouse at the opposite end. At first, the keeper was unable to understand what it was they wanted, until it dawned on him that his unexpected callers imagined themselves on the mainland, and that this was the Hartland light. The lieutenant was emphatic in his belief that the *Montagu* was stranded on the north Devon coast, and after some heated words on the subject the keeper turned his back on them with the irrefutable remark, 'Do you imagine I don't know which bloody light I'm keeping?'

With her lower compartments flooded and the hull working heavily on the rocks, lacking any salvage equipment of its own, the navy called upon the assistance of the Liverpool Salvage Company and one of its most experienced salvage officers, Capt Young. This brought the famous

Following the stranding of HMS Montagu *an aerial walkway was constructed from the cliff top giving safe access to the wreck, from which the guns, ammunition and naval stores were recovered, before the ship was broken up where she lay.*

salvage steamer *Ranger* to the scene, but instead of making the best use of Capt Young's experience by putting him in charge of the work he was seconded in an advisory capacity only to Admiral Sir A.K. Wilson RN, commander of the Channel Fleet, a brilliant naval officer full of ideas, but totally inexperienced when dealing with a wrecked ship. A fleet of vessels were ordered to the scene, battleships, cruisers and destroyers, with picket boats buzzing about between them like wasps. Working parties of seamen, hundreds strong, appeared on board the *Montagu* and succeeded in doing little else but get in each other's way. The final straw came when the admiral seriously suggested to Capt Young that they fill the entire ship with sheets of cork and let the rising tide float her clear!

By now it was obvious that the *Montagu* was lost and Capt Young suggested that they could salvage the barrels of the twelve-inch guns, which were the very latest wire-wound Mk 10, weighing 48 tons each and costing £9,040. Apart from their value, the nation's reserve stock of such guns was then very low, following the need to replace defective ordnance in the *Majestic* and *Canopus* class warships. Overnight the fleet and its glittering staff of navy 'brass' disappeared, leaving the cloth-capped, overalled experts to complete the task in peace.

For technical reasons, it was necessary to blow out a portion of the ship's side, alongside the forward and after turrets, to allow the massive gun barrels to drop down in the hull, from where they were lifted clear of the barbettes. It was here that Tommy Hyland, the foreman, and his Liverpool riggers came into their own, erecting 18 metre high sheerlegs to which were attached 100 ton lifting blocks. These blocks, dug out from some half-forgotten hiding place, had last been used to lift the boilers out of Brunel's *Great Eastern*. Massive four-fold purchases were rigged with 25 cm manilla, and with only the assistance of a donkey engine on the upper deck, clear of the waves, the first of the forward guns was lifted clear, placed in a waiting lighter, and taken to Pembroke Dock. Three days later a second barrel was on its way to Wales, and to celebrate the successful salvaging of two guns in 21 days a concert was held aboard the wreck. Alf Gloyne, the chief diver, amazed everyone by giving a very creditable tap dance routine; Kearney, the fireman, played the concertina and Capt Young sang 'Blow the man down', by which time everyone was too drunk to appreciate fully the 40 verse poem specially written by him for the occasion which began: 'Midst the cheers of the spectators, the *Ranger* left the town . . .' Within days, both after guns were safely on their way to the dockyard and the salvage crew still aboard were joined by the Western Marine Salvage Co of Penzance. Between them, they stripped the *Montagu* of her

The Greek steamship Maria Kyriakides *aground on Lundy Island after running ashore in dense fog at the Quarries, on the eastern side of the island on 24 March 1929.*

many condensers, pumps and tons of non-ferrous metals.

A naval court-martial was ordered to be held aboard Nelson's flagship, HMS *Victory*, at Portsmouth, at which Capt Adair and his chief navigating officer, Lt Dathan, were jointly charged with 'having by negligence or default, did hazard, strand or lose HMS *Montagu*'. The arguments for the defence hinged on an unpredictable tidal set, which put the battleship out of its estimated position, and the fact that the Lundy fog signals were not heard, either before they went ashore, whilst on the rocks, or when the landing party reached the top of the cliffs. Certainly, had the signals been audible the landing party would not have walked the length of the island, away from the sound, and it is perhaps significant that Trinity House later sent a vessel to the island to steam round at varying distances to establish the effectiveness of the fog signals. The court found the charges against both officers proven, Capt

This remarkable aerial photograph showing the whole of Lundy from the south-east side, includes the wrecked Italian steamship Carmine Filomena, *of Genoa, which became a total wreck on Mouse Island on 1 July 1937.*

Adair being severely reprimanded and dismissed his ship, Lt Dathan receiving an identical punishment, plus the loss of two years seniority in rank. Six months after the incident the salvage men left the wreck to the sea and, weakened by explosives and dismantling, the remains were reduced by the first winter gales to a heap of rusting pieces, scarcely visible at high tide.

Since 1906 some 15 steamships have met their end in these waters, plus twelve sailing vessels and more recently, since 1942, a total of five motor vessels, the last actual wreck on Lundy Island being the *Kaaksburg*, lost on Tibbets Point on 6 November 1980. Registered at Itzehoe, Germany, this 486 tons gross vessel in ballast, was on passage from Sharpness to Kiel when she was caught in wind conditions north-east force 8-9. Her plight was reported by the *Padberg*, who sent out a Mayday distress signal which was picked up by the Mumbles coastguard station in South Wales, who alerted the rescue services. Both the Croyde Bay lifeboat and an RAF Seaking helicopter went to their rescue, but in the meantime the seven man crew of the wreck had abandoned ship, climbed up a shallow cliff and were huddled under the lee of a rock from where they were winched to safety, being landed at RAF Chivenor.

Acknowledgements

Appreciation and thanks are extended particularly to John Behenna of Slapton, Devon, for allowing the reproduction of many photographs from his extensive collection of Devon shipwrecks, also for his contribution in reading the original manuscript and offering suggestions and information whereby the content was greatly improved. Also to John Davies of Truro, Cornwall, who is a mine of information regarding West Country-built ships and shipwrecks, by whom any query – no matter how small – is always answered promptly and with reassuring accuracy; also to Clive Carter, who shares an equal interest in West Country shipwrecks; to all three friends, my sincere thanks. Other contributors include the late Eric Collins of Penzance, G.E. Mills of Redruth and Frank Strike of Porthleven.

To Alec Reynolds, of MOD(N) Hydrographic Office, Taunton, who drew the wreck maps, and K. V. Burns, retired librarian of the naval and Devon reference library collection, Plymouth, who offered so much advice and assistance. To the curator and staff of the Royal Institute of Cornwall; the archivist and staff of HM Customs & Excise Library, London; and the superintendents, librarians and staff of the St Austell, Redruth, Falmouth, Exeter City and Torquay public libraries (reference sections). Also the British Library (BM Reading Room and Colindale Newspaper Library), National Maritime Museum, Guildhall Library, Public Records Office at Kew and Chancery Lane, Historic Manuscripts Commission and Lloyd's Register of Shipping.

For additional photographs, I thank F. E. Gibson (Isles of Scilly); National Maritime Museum; Imperial War Museum; R. Rossiter (Paignton); A. R. Tucker (Dartmouth); B. Salmon (Wembury); L. Carlile Davis (Plymouth); G. Dunn (Torquay); J. Horsley (Brixham); R. L. Knight (Barnstaple) and the *Western Morning News* (Plymouth). To John Farmer, Cornwall County Librarian and Arts Officer, who so strongly supported our plea, successfully I should add, to the British

Library that a lending copy microfilm should be made available of Lloyd's List, from 1827 to the end of the First World War.

To Mary Richards of Gorran Haven, Cornwall, our shipwreck secretary, who keyboarded the manuscript and ship index etc and as ever, shows great patience and tolerance, and to Nicholas Battle of Countryside Books, for the opportunity to update and republish this volume after a 20 year absence from bookshops, my thanks and appreciation. Last but not least, to Bridget, my wife and constant companion, who has made a considerable contribution to this and many other books by way of research, my sincere thanks for all her encouragement and support. Regarding shipwreck enthusiasts, she learnt a long time ago – 'if you can't beat them, join them!'

Bibliography

Baring-Gould, S. *Book of the West*, vols 1 & 2 (1899)

Barlow, V. & Etherton, P.T. *Tempestuous Isle* (1950)

Behenna, J. *Westcountry Shipwrecks* (1974)

Boquet, M. *Lundy Shipwrecks*, 18th Report of the Lundy Field Society (1967)

Bowring, W.D. *Ilfracombe Throughout the Ages* (1931)

Boyle, V.C. & Payne, A. *Devon Harbours* (1952)

Burton, S.H. *The North Devon Coast* (1954)

Burton, S.H. *The South Devon Coast* (1954)

Campbell, A. *Armada Cannon* (1899)

Chanter, J.R. *Lundy Island* (1924)

Clamp, A.L. *Shipwrecks around Bigbury Bay* (1970)

Clamp, A.L. *The Loss of the Herzogin Cecilie* (1971)

Colledge, J.J. *Ships of the Royal Navy*, vols 1 & 2 (1969)

Dawson, A.J. *Britain's Lifeboats* (1923)

Delderfield, E.R. *Torbay Story* (1951)

Ellis, A.C. *An Historical Survey of Torquay* (1898)

Erikkson, P. *The Duchess* (1958)

Farr, G. *Wreck & Rescue in the Bristol Channel*, Truro (1966)

Farr, G. *Wreck & Rescue on the Coast of Devon*, Truro (1968)

Garbett, G. & Skelton, I. *The Wreck of the Metta Catharina*

Gardiner, W.F. *Barnstaple* (1897)

Grant, R.M. *U-Boats Destroyed* (1964)

Greenhill, B. *The Merchant Schooners*, vols 1 & 2 (1968)

Hepper, D.J. *British Warship Losses in the Age of Sail* (1994)

Hocking, C.A. *A Dictionary of Disasters at Sea*, vols 1 & 2 (1969)

Jameson, W. *The Most Formidable Thing* (1965)

Jewitt, L. *A History of Plymouth* (1873)

Langham, A. & M. *Lundy, Bristol Channel* (1960)

Langham, A. & M. *Lundy* (1970)

Larn, R. *Devon Shipwrecks* (1974)

Larn, R. *Shipwrecks of Great Britain & Ireland* (1981)
Larn, R. & B. *Shipwreck Index of the British Isles*, vol 1 (1995)
Lewis, R.W. *Lundy, Its History, & Natural History* (1925)
Lyson. *Magna Britannia, History of Devonshire* (1822)
Majdalany, F. *The Red Rocks of Eddystone* (1959)
McDonald, K. *Dive South Devon – a Diver Guide* (1996)
Mitchell, P. *The Wreckers Guide to South West Devon*, Part 1 (1986)
Mitchell, P. *The Wreckers Guide to South West Devon*, Part 2 (1992)
Mitchell, P. & Roseveare, R. *Shipwrecks Around Plymouth Sound*
Murch, D. & Fairweather, L. *Wreck & Rescue on the South Hams Coast* (1980)
Oppenheim, M.M. *The Maritime History of Devon* (1908)
Page, W. *Victoria County History of Devon*, vols 1 & 2
Page, W.J. *The Coasts of Devon and Lundy Island* (1875)
Pearse, Chope, R. *Early Tours in Devon & Cornwall* (1969)
Pearse, Chope, R. *The Book of Hartland* (1940)
Presland, J. *Torquay* (1920)
Rogers, I. *Ships & Shipyards of Bideford* (1947)
Russell, P. *Dartmouth* (1950)
Steinman, S.G. *Some Account of the Island of Lundy*
Tennent, A.J. *British Merchant Ships sunk by U-Boats in the 1914-1918 War* (1990)
Worth, R.N. *History of Plymouth* (1890)

Index of ships

This Index includes every incident and ship mentioned in the text, but is not intended to represent a definitive index of Devon shipwrecks, since such a list would be impossible and even a near definitive list would occupy many more pages than this publication could allow. Abbreviations used to denote ship types:

SS	steamship	Tr	transport	
Mv	motor vessel	Pt	privateer	
Mfv	motor fishing vessel	Sn	snow	
S	sailing ship	Tg	tug	
Frs	full-rigged ship	HMS/1	HM ship of 1st rate	
Bq	barque	HMS/2	HM ship of 2nd rate	
Bqn	barquentine	HMS/3	HM ship of 3rd rate	
Br	brig	HMS/4	HM ship of 4th rate	
Brn	brigantine	HMS/5	HM ship of 5th rate	
Kt	ketch	HMS/6	HM ship of 6th rate	
Yl	yawl	HMS/B	HM battleship	
Sk	smack	HMS/S	HM submarine	
Sl	sloop	HMS/T	HM trawler	
Sc	schooner			

Name	Type	Date	Location
Amphion	HMS/5	22.09.1796	Plymouth
Amphitrite	S	04.01.1909	Berry Head
Amulet	Br	28.10.1852	Seaton
Amy	Sc	08.11.1883	Salcombe
Amy	Sl	17.09.1924	Torbay
Angelina	S	27.12.1852	Torbay
Anglo-American	S	05.11.1915	Torbay
Ann	Brn	30.04.1811	Bigbury Bay
Ann	Sl	00.00.1839	Plymouth
Ann	Kt	28.05.1863	Dartmouth
Ann	S	10.01.1866	Torbay
Anna Elise	Kt	10.11.1852	Dartmouth
Anna Maria	Sc	23.07.1862	Bolt Head
Anna Rebecca	S	06.04.1852	Off Start Point
Annie	S	14.10.1877	Teignmouth
Annie	Bgn	16.02.1879	Salcombe
Ann & Maria	Sc	21.01.1862	Off Start Point
Antelope	S	13.01.1786	Slapton Sands
Arrowhead	Mv	02.02.1956	Exmouth
Assegai	Sc	29.08.1886	Salcombe
Asturias	SS	20.03.1917	Off Bolt Head
Atlanta	Sc	03.01.1854	Exmouth
Augusta	S	31.08.1872	Plymouth
Auguste	Br	25.02.1882	Rame Head
Augustine	Br	20.02.1861	Plymouth
Augustus	HMS/Br	07.07.1801	Plymouth
Aurora	Sl	03.11.1881	Teignmouth
Avon	Kt	01.11.1882	Plymouth
Bamba	Yt	23.09.1946	Brixham
Barbara	Br	00.00.1838	Bigbury Bay
Baroda	Kt	10.12.1890	Plymouth
Baron	S	08.09.1886	Plymouth
Baron Van Pallandt	Bq	27.11.1881	Plymouth
Bayawanna	Barge	31.12.1896	Off Torbay
Bee	S	05.01.1891	Berry Head
Belle	S	10.01.1866	Torbay
Belle	Sk	18.12.1874	Bigbury Bay
Bellona	Pt	05.09.1779	Teignmouth
Bellona	S	00.09.1807	Bolt Head
Benin	SS	12.03.1881	Off Start Point
Benmohr	SS	25.02.1932	Salcombe
Berar	Bq	07.10.1896	Sidmouth
Berry Castle	SS	08.08.1888	River Dart
Betsey	Tr	11.01.1816	Bigbury Bay
Betsey Anna	SS	17.08.1926	Prawle Point
Betty R	Mv	00.05.1971	Torbay
Bia	Sl	05.01.1888	Teignmouth
Bidart	SS	30.08.1918	Start Bay
Biscay	S	23.02.1795	Torbay
Biscay	Frs	22.12.1795	Torbay
Bishop	S	17.11.1766	Nr Sidmouth
Bleamoor	SS	27.11.1917	Off Berry Head
Blesk	SS	01.12.1896	Bolt Tail
Blue Jacket	Sc	10.01.1866	Torbay
Bonito	Bq	24.03.1854	Off Start Point
Bon Ordre	Pt	11.02.1799	Plymouth
Bon Pasteur	Kt	26.01.1884	Plymouth
Borderdene	SS	13.01.1942	Off Start Point
Bosphorus	SS	12.08.1888	Eddystone
Boy Aubrey	Kt	00.00.1930	Off Start Point
Boy Dennis	Kt	26.04.1917	Off Start Point
Bretagne	SS	10.08.1918	Off Exmouth
Bretton Hall	SS	06.12.1885	Berry Head
Britannia	S	10.01.1866	Torbay
British Queen	Sc	01.02.1860	Off Start Point
British Tar	S	20.01.1804	Plymouth
Briton	S	10.01.1866	Torbay
Briton	Kt	16.04.1913	Plymouth
Broadmayne	SS	02.01.1921	Dartmouth
Brothers	S	16.11.1812	Exmouth
Brothers	Sc	27.12.1852	Plymouth
Brothers	Sl	11.04.1854	Yealm
Brothers	Sl	29.03.1881	Salcombe
Busston	SS	09.04.1941	Off Berry Head
Cabot	Bq	28.12.1868	Plymouth
Caledonia	S	23.11.1824	Plymouth
Cambria	S	10.01.1866	Torbay
Cantabria	SS	13.12.1932	Bolt Head
Canterbury Bell	Kt	05.10.1904	Teignmouth
Cape Coast	Tr	27.02.1745	Torbay
Captain	HMS/3	22.03.1813	Plymouth
Cariad	Kt	08.06.1917	Off Start Point
Caroline	S	20.12.1851	Bigbury Bay
Caroline	Sl	00.00.1853	Plymouth
Catalune	SS	15.11.1857	Off Start Point
Catherine	S	03.01.1786	Plymouth
Catherine Allen	Mfv	28.10.1973	Brixham
Cato	Tr	12.01.1828	Plymouth
Cato	S	03.01.1847	Torbay
Cecilia	Kt	15.10.1880	Off Start Point
Centurian	HMS/5	22.12.1689	Plymouth
Cerbere	Br	19.02.1804	Berry Head
Ceres	S	18.08.1864	Eddystone
Chantiloupe	S	00.00.1772	Bigbury Bay
Charles & Henry	HMS/6	29.11.1689	Plymouth
Charlwood	Bq	26.10.1891	Eddystone
Charming Molly	S	12.12.1763	Nr Teignmouth
Charter	SS	07.01.1933	Salcombe
Cheapside	SS	18.06.1910	Start Point
Cheshire Witch	S	10.01.1866	Torbay
Chinaman	S	00.03.1873	Prawle Point
Chittagong	Bqr	30.01.1883	Salcombe
Christiana	Sc	14.01.1865	Plymouth
Christina	Sc	10.01.1866	Torbay
City of Antwerp	SS	16.10.1866	Eddystone
City of Exeter	S	09.02.1846	Brixham
City of Hamburg	SS	07.08.1888	Bolt Head

Name	Type	Date	Location
City of Rochester	S	23.11.1824	Plymouth
City of Swansea	SS	25.09.1917	Exmouth
Clan Stuart	SS	11.03.1940	Off Start Point
Claude Marie	Mv	25.11.1955	Start Point
Claverly	SS	20.08.1917	Eddystone
Clyde	SS	14.10.1917	Sidmouth
Colchester	HMS/5	16.01.1704	Plymouth
Colonist	S	23.11.1824	Plymouth
Colonel Buller	Sk	10.01.1866	Torbay
Colosie	Br	04.12.1838	Plymouth
Colpoys	HMS/6	09.01.1806	Plymouth
Come On	S	08.12.1886	Teignmouth
Comet	Sc	09.11.1878	Dartmouth
Commerce	Sc	05.12.1838	Plymouth
Commerce de Paris	Br	15.12.1869	Bigbury Bay
Commerzieweathin Haupt	Br	25.11.1865	Plymouth
Commodore	Sc	16.09.1882	Eddystone
Concord	Kt	30.11.1916	Off Start Point
Concordia	Kt	23.11.1824	Plymouth
Conqueror	HMS/3	26.10.1760	Plymouth
Constance	S	20.09.1862	Plymouth
Constance	SS	21.01.1888	Plymouth
Constantia	SS	16.10.1882	Eddystone
Constantine	Sl	15.03.1866	Plymouth
Coquette	S	18.12.1890	Eddystone
Coquille	HMS/4	18.12.1789	Plymouth
Coromandel	S	23.11.1824	Plymouth
Coronation	HMS/2	03.09.1691	Off Rame Head
Cosmopolite	Pr	25.12.1803	Plymouth
Cosray 10	Barge	07.12.1959	Torbay
Cossack	HMS/B	28.10.1854	Plymouth
Courier	Br	10.01.1866	Torbay
Courser	Sc	13.02.1870	Dartmouth
Coventry	S	18.10.1812	Plymouth
Crane	HMS/Sc	26.10.1808	Plymouth
Crocodile	HMS/5	09.05.1784	Start Point
Crocodile	Br	03.09.1866	Salcombe
Crossowen	Br	08.05.1908	Bigbury Bay
Crown Prize	HMS/6	09.02.1692	Dartmouth
Crystal Palace	S	09.03.1862	Plymouth
Curacao Packet	Sc	08.12.1872	Plymouth
Cuthbert	S	20.05.1883	Salcombe
Czardwitz	Br	15.10.1877	Plymouth
Dahlia	Kt	24.11.1900	Plymouth
Daisy	S	09.12.1912	Dartmouth
Daphne	S	03.01.1792	Bigbury Bay
Daphne	Sc	07.08.1862	Off Start Point
Daring	Sl	16.06.1863	Eddystone
Dart	S	19.02.1833	Plymouth
Dartmeet	SS	30.11.1918	Eddystone
Dawn	S	20.09.1890	Plymouth
Dazzle	Sl	03.03.1891	Start Point
Dazzler	S	10.11.1866	Plymouth
Deborah	Br	10.01.1866	Torbay
Delight	S	17.01.1788	Off Dartmouth
Derwent	SS	23.01.1862	Off Start Point
Deventia	SS	12.02.1929	Bolt Tail
De Vrouw Eopke	S	00.12.1814	Dartmouth
Diana	S	06.01.1797	Bigbury Bay
Die Fraumetta Catharina Von			Drake's Island
Flensburg	S	10.12.1785	Plymouth
Dolphin	Sk	06.08.1881	Start Point
Don Lorenzo	SS	17.11.1927	Brixham
Dorothea	Mfv	17.02.72	Newf'd Cove
Dove	S	03.01.1872	Off Beer Head
Dove	S	16.05.1881	Salcombe
Dragon	S	23.08.1757	Bolt Head
Dragon	Sl	06.11.1798	Bigbury Bay
Dryad	Frs	10.03.1891	Start Point
Dryan	Br	10.01.1866	Torbay
Duchess of Devonshire	SS	27.08.1934	Sidmouth
Dudley Rose	SS	09.04.1941	Off Torbay
Duke of Marlborough	Br	11.10.1836	Torquay
Dulce Nombre de Jesus	Br	01.01.1861	Rockham Bay
Dunwich	HMS/6	00.00.1714	Plymouth
Dutch ship	Br	20.12.1748	Off Berry Head
Dutton	S	26.01.1796	Plymouth
Eastern Prince	SS	30.08.1917	Off Eddystone
Ebenezer	Sc	24.02.1798	Plymouth
Echo	HMS/6	16.02.1781	Plymouth
Eclipse	S	19.10.1812	Plymouth
Eden	S	15.10.1846	Nr Yealm
Edward Triplett	Sk	06.02.1850	Torbay
Eider	SS	02.03.1922	Berry Head
Ellen Rickmers	Bq	29.11.1882	Plymouth
Elise	Bq	01.09.1883	Plymouth
Eliza	S	00.00.1828	Torquay
Eliza	Sl	13.11.1852	Plymouth
Eliza	Sc	12.02.1863	Plymouth
Eliza	Br	08.12.1872	Plymouth
Eliza & Ann	Sc	14.11.1860	Plymouth
Elizabeth	S	22.02.1767	Bigbury Bay
Elizabeth	Sc	01.11.1859	Plymouth
Elizabeth	Kt	20.03.1871	Off Start Point
Elizabeth	Kt	07.07.1890	Plymouth
Elizabeth Lass	Brn	10.01.1866	Dartmouth
Elizabeth Lewis	Br	10.01.1866	Torbay
Elizabeth Maria	S	31.10.1851	Topsham
Elizabeth Mary Ann	Sc	11.01.1887	Sidmouth
Elk	SS		Plymouth
Ellen Edwards	S	10.01.1866	Torbay

Elise	Kt	27.02.1900	Eddystone
Emile	Br	10.03.1891	Berry Head
Emilie	Bq	29.05.1870	Prawle Point
Emilie & Charles	Brn	10.01.1866	Torbay
Emily	Kt	14.01.1881	Eddystone
Emma	S	22.11.1889	Plymouth
Emmanuel	Br	00.01.1863	Plymouth
Emmeline	Bq	31.12.1872	Sidmouth
Empire Alfred	Tg	17.12.1944	Torbay
Empire Harry	Tg	06.06.1945	Bolt Tail
Encourage	Mv	05.10.1940	Plymouth
Encouragement	Sk	14.03.1862	Start Bay
Endeavour	S	18.12.1798	Plymouth
English Trader	SS	23.01.1937	Dartmouth
Ensign	Sc	30.01.1915	Salcombe
Erin	S	05.03.1850	Teignmouth
Erin	Br	00.03.1833	Plymouth
Erna	Sc	21.02.1914	Plymouth
Ernest	Kt	10.01.1866	Torbay
Esperance	Sc	18.09.1879	Off Start Point
Espoir	Br	22.11.1865	Plymouth
Ethiope	SS	28.05.1915	Off Start Point
Eureka	Br	06.02.1870	Dartmouth
Exeter	HMS/3	12.09.1691	Plymouth
Expeditious	S	27.02.1745	Torbay
Fair City	Sc	08.01.1919	Plymouth
Faith	Sc	06.09.1851	Eddystone
Faith	S	11.01.1887	Plymouth
Falcon	Kt	01.02.1971	Plymouth
Favourite	Bq	29.04.1854	Off Start Point
Favourite	Kt	26.02.1886	Off Start Point
Favourite	Kt	09.09.1916	Off Start Point
Fearful	Br	08.12.1872	Plymouth
Fearless	HMS/6	22.01.1804	Plymouth
Fear Not	Sk	24.01.1854	Plymouth
Fernwood	HMS	18.09.1942	Dartmouth
Ferret	Sc	28.01.1851	Off Start Point
Ferry Boat		10.07.1952	Dartmouth
Florence	Kt	30.11.1905	Off Start Point
Florence May	Kt	01.01.1886	Plymouth
Florence Nightingale	S	10.01.1866	Torbay
Florinda	Kt	30.07.1890	Prawle Point
Flying Fish	Sk	00.12.1870	Torquay
Forerunner	Kt	10.01.1866	Torbay
Forget-me-not	S	07.05.1891	Plymouth
Formidable	HMS/Bs	01.01.1915	Off Start Point
Fortitude	Sc	10.01.1866	Torbay
Fortuna	Sc	28.10.1880	Plymouth
Four Brothers	Sk	21.01.1880	Off Bolt Head
Fratelli Borghino	Br	08.12.1872	Plymouth
Frederick Julins	S	10.11.1799	Bigbury Bay
Frederick William	Br	05.09.1872	Sidmouth
Freedom	S	00.11.1809	Start Bay
Friends	S	30.05.1852	Yealm
Friends	Sc	03.01.1854	Dawlish
Fylrix	Mv	22.11.1984	Jennycliff Bay
Galicia	SS	12.05.1917	Teignmouth
Gannet	Kt	01.12.1950	Exmouth
Gascoyne	S	19.10.1812	Plymouth
Gatinais	Mv	03.12.1942	Off Start Point
Gazelle	Kt	03.03.1864	Eddystone
Gefion	SS	25.10.1917	Teignmouth
General Gates	S	18.10.1812	Plymouth
General Lee	Sk	00.00.1867	Plymouth
General Leman	Kt	29.01.1918	Off Berry Head
George	S	12.01.1786	Salcombe
George	Br	11.05.1860	Rame Head
George 4th	S	20.01.1830	Scabacombe Sands
George & Ann	S	23.10.1808	Bigbury Bay
George Canning	S	23.11.1824	Plymouth
George Green	S	00.01.1877	Bigbury Bay
George Thomas	Sc	06.02.1869	Eddystone
Glad Tidings	S	15.12.1882	Salcombe
Glenrose	SS	10.01.1921	Plymouth
Glen Strathallan	SS	27.04.1970	Plymouth
Glocliffe	SS	19.08.1917	Teignmouth
Glory	S	18.02.1785	Nr Plymouth
Gomer	Sc	03.09.1881	Prawle Point
Gossamer	Frs	10.12.1868	Prawle Point
Goyaz	SS	25.12.1912	Plymouth
Grace	S	10.01.1866	Torbay
Grampus	S	10.01.1786	Bigbury Bay
Greatham	SS	22.01.1918	Dartmouth
Greleen	SS	22.09.1917	Off Berry Head
Gronsund	Sc	04.01.1894	Exmouth
Guild Mayor	Sc	25.12.1912	Plymouth
Gwen Jones	Sc	05.11.1888	Torbay
HM (TB) 99	HMS	00.00.1907	Off Berry Head
H.29	HMS/Sm	09.08.1926	Plymouth
Haabert Anker	Bq	29.11.1853	River Exe
Hafod	Sc	24.02.1879	Off Dartmouth
Halloween	Frs	17.01.1887	Nr Bolt Head
Hanover	Br	10.01.1866	Torbay
Happy Return	S	19.02.1743	Bigbury Bay
Harewood	Sc	16.06.1852	Beer Head
Harlequin	Sk	08.07.1852	Plymouth
Harmony	S	27.02.1862	Off Plymouth
Harriet Preston	Sc	30.01.1862	Torbay
Harriet Thompson	Sc	27.05.1915	Plymouth
Harwich	HMS/3	03.09.1691	Plymouth
Havering	S	30.03.1860	Plymouth
Hawthorn	Bq	07.03.1881	Off Start Point
Haydon	Tr	12.01.1828	Plymouth
Hayle	Brn	19.02.1878	Off Start Point
Hazard	Brn	01.12.1877	Off Start Point

180

Name	Type	Date	Location
Heir Apparent	Sc	08.08.1880	Off Start Point
Helen	Kt	10.01.1866	Torbay
Henrietta	HMS/3	25.12.1689	Plymouth
Henrietta	Sc	16.12.1939	Off Start Point
Herald	Bq	15.01.1853	Off Start Point
Hero	S	11.10.1864	Teignmouth
Herzogin Cecilie	Bq	25.04.1936	Salcombe
Hiawartha	S	21.02.1861	Plymouth
Hibernia	Br	23.11.1824	Plymouth
Hibernia	Sc	25.01.1853	Plymouth
Hilkelina	S	10.01.1866	Torbay
Hiogo	SS	01.10.1867	Eddystone
Honor	Brn	10.01.1866	Torbay
Hope	Sl	29.12.1852	Berry Head
Hope	S	14.10.1877	Teignmouth
Hopper barge No 42	SS	12.09.1913	Plymouth
Horace	S	18.10.1812	Plymouth
Hoy	S	08.10.1857	Bigbury Bay
Ida	S	19.08.1889	Plymouth
Imogene	HMS/6	10.10.1840	Plymouth
Indian Trader	Tr	13.01.1828	Plymouth
Industry	Sk	16.01.1851	Plymouth
Industry	S	20.10.1862	Salcombe
Integrity	S	28.01.1852	Teignmouth
Intrepede	HMS	10.01.1942	Salcombe
Ira	Sk	24.01.1878	Off Start Point
Irex	Kt	17.05.1899	Plymouth
Irmagermaine	SS	03.10.1943	Off Berry Head
Iron Crown	Bq	20.10.1881	Teignmouth
Isabella	Sk	06.02.1850	Brixham
Jacobe	Br	10.01.1866	Torbay
James	S	12.04.1801	Torbay
James	S	00.00.1833	Plymouth
James	Sc	10.01.1866	Torbay
James Hattie	Kt	00.00.1866	Plymouth
James McGee	SS	20.06.1940	Off Start Point
James Otis	SS	07.02.1945	Off Start Point
Jane	S	20.01.1804	Plymouth
Jane	S	09.03.1891	Plymouth
Jane Burrow	Sk	28.04.1852	Off Start Point
Jane Eliza	Sc	15.01.1851	Sidmouth
Jane Rowe	SS	28.02.1914	Bolt Tail
Jasper	HMS/6	21.01.1817	Plymouth
Jean Baptiste	Sc	30.12.1921	Brixham
Jean Celeste	Brn	24.11.1874	Torbay
Jeau Ceres	S	02.03.1881	Bolt Tail
Jebba	SS	18.03.1907	Bolt Tail
Jed	HMS/Dty	29.07.1920	Dartmouth
Jeku	S		Salcombe
Jellicoe Rose	Kt	26.11.1938	Plymouth
Jessie	S	10.01.1866	Torbay
Jessie	S	30.06.1881	Dartmouth
Jessie Lawson	Tr	13.01.1828	Plymouth
Jeune Adelle	S	13.12.1814	Plymouth
Joffre	SS/Tg	27.05.1925	Bolt Tail
Johann 2nd	Br	22.11.1865	Plymouth
John	S	00.00.1573	Exmouth
John	S	00.11.1824	Yealm
John	Sl	18.11.1862	Teignmouth
John & Hannah	S	20.03.1752	Plymouth
John & Martha	S	25.12.1798	Plymouth
John & Robert	Tr	13.01.1828	Plymouth
John Bailey	S	08.01.1867	Bolt Tail
John Boyle	SS	04.04.1876	Off Start
John Hermann	S	19.12.1847	Berry Head
John Johnasson	SS	10.10.1907	Torquay
John May	Br	28.10.1880	Plymouth
John Munro	Sc	23.03.1866	Plymouth
Johnny Toole	Kt	26.12.1912	Plymouth
John Paley	Sc	04.02.1852	Torbay
John Pardew	S	10.11.1878	Plymouth
John Parley	Sc	04.02.1852	Torquay
Jong Backe	S	20.01.1804	Plymouth
Josephine Andis	S	01.02.1874	Plymouth
J.P.R.	Sc	30.11.1873	Plymouth
J.S.T.	S	22.12.1882	Plymouth
Julia	Brn	05.01.1867	Exmouth
Julia	S	09.03.1891	Plymouth
Julianna	S	18.11.1755	Dartmouth
Jupiter	S	15.01.1828	Plymouth
K.32	Tr	27.01.1795	Plymouth
Karel	S	24.01.1852	Plymouth
Kate	Bqn	23.03.1887	Plymouth
Kathleen	Sl	26.04.1887	Eddystone
Katie	Kt	09.03.1891	Plymouth
Kentish Coast	SS	16.11.1928	Plymouth
Kendall Castle	SS	15.09.1918	Off Berry Head
King Crispin	S	31.03.1876	Plymouth
Kingfisher	S	28.01.1869	Off Teignmouth
Kingston Alalite	HMS	10.11.1940	Plymouth
LC-18	HMS	04.12.1943	Start Bay
Lab	SS	19.11.1942	Eddystone
La Coquille	Prize	14.12.1798	Plymouth
Lady Alice	Sc	10.10.1875	Off Start Point
Lady Elizabeth	Kt	20.01.1899	Plymouth
Lady Hayter	Sl	12.01.1899	Exmouth
Lady of Avenel	S	15.10.1877	Plymouth
Lady of the Lake	Sk	10.01.1866	Torbay
Lady of the Lake	Sk	29.03.1878	Sidmouth
Lady Shelborne	S	15.10.1877	Plymouth
Lady Young	Bq	27.10.1880	Bantham
Laertes	SS	01.08.1917	Off Prawle
Lalla Rookh	Bq	03.03.1873	Prawle Point
L'Amiable Maria	Br	00.12.1786	Plymouth
Landing Craft 332		00.00.1942	Off Salcombe
Landing Craft 362		00.00.1942	Off Salcombe
Larina	S	14.01.1828	Bolt Tail

Lark	S	14.12.1827	Off Dartmouth
Langport	HMS/3	25.12.1689	Plymouth
Lark	Sc	00.01.1855	Paignton
Latona	Kt	14.01.1902	Off Start Point
Laurel	Sl	01.01.1904	Dawlish
Laurel	Brn	23.11.1872	Plymouth
La Victore	Br	23.03.1799	Plymouth
Lavinia	Sk	21.01.1887	Eddystone
Lavinia	HMS/5	00.00.1868	Plymouth
Leander	Brn	12.04.1801	Torbay
Le Colosse	Br	00.00.1839	Plymouth
L'Effronteur	Pt	20.01.1804	Plymouth
Le Jeune	S	19.12.1814	Plymouth
Les Deux Amis	S	25.12.1803	Plymouth
Les Deux Amis	S	26.01.1828	Off Plymouth
Les Trois Anges	S	08.12.1872	Plymouth
Liberta	SS	15.02.1926	Bolt Head
Liberty	Sk	08.12.1838	Plymouth
Lighter			
(un-named)		07.09.1813	Plymouth
Lillie	SS	15.12.1894	Eddystone
Lindbergh	Mfv	19.02.1943	Off Berry Head
Lion	Kt	16.09.1859	Off Berry Head
Little Florie	Brn	26.01.1864	Eddystone
Lively	S	10.01.1866	Torbay
Livonia	SS	03.12.1917	Off Start Point
Lizzie Ellen	Sc	10.03.1891	Start Bay
Lochwood	SS	02.04.1915	Off Start Point
London	S	00.12.1778	Torbay
Lord Inchcape	SS/Tr	25.10.1940	Plymouth
Lord Nelson	HMS/Sc	31.01.1805	Dartmouth
Lord Nelson	S	26.11.1810	Off Start Point
Lorenz	Br	08.12.1872	Plymouth
Louisa	Sl	01.03.1859	Guia Cove
Louisa	S	14.10.1854	Plymouth
Louisa	S	00.03.1859	Salcombe
Louise	S	31.12.1829	Start Point
Louise	Br	08.02.1865	Seaton
Louis Sheid	SS	08.12.1939	Bigbury Bay
Lovely	S	26.11.1757	Plymouth
Lovely Lady	Sc	25.05.1863	Off Start Point
Lovie	S	06.06.1888	Plymouth
Loyal Comfort	S	20.09.1749	Plymouth
Loyalty	Br	23.11.1824	Plymouth
Lucy	SS/Tg	30.04.1890	Plymouth
Lucy Ann	Sl	26.01.1853	Exmouth
Lunesdale	Sc	10.03.1891	Start Bay
Lydia	Sc	17.03.1853	Seaton
Lyra	Sl	27.09.1904	Off Start Point
Maid of Alicant	S	06.12.1848	Plymouth
Main	Kt	27.07.1892	Plymouth
Maine	SS	23.03.1917	Salcombe
Marana	SS	09.03.1891	Start Point
Margaret	S	17.11.1767	Nr Salcombe
Margaret Ann	S	10.01.1866	Torbay
Marian	S	30.11.1868	Torbay
Marie Adele	Sc	27.03.1973	Plymouth
Marie Blanche	S	16.09.1886	Plymouth
Marie Elizabeth	Sl	25.02.1874	Exmouth
Marie Louise	S	08.01.1867	Salcombe
Marie Theresa	Br	04.12.1872	Prawle Point
Marjolene	Mv	22.12.1956	Off Start Point
Markum	Kt	17.04.1917	Off Start Point
Mary	S	04.02.1755	Seaton
Mary	Br	11.11.1795	Plymouth
Mary	Sc	05.01.1850	Exmouth
Mary	Sc	05.01.1851	Exmouth
Mary	S	06.12.1920	Plymouth
Mary Ann	S	17.01.1828	Plymouth
Mary Ann	S	24.11.1854	Plymouth
Mary Ann	Br	10.01.1866	Torbay
Mary Laing	Bq	30.04.1851	Eddystone
Mater Dei	Kt	09.12.1891	Exmouth
Matilda	Sl	29.09.1812	Torbay
Medina	SS	28.04.1917	Off Start Point
Madoc	SS	26.11.1940	Eddystone
Meirion	Frs	07.09.1879	Prawle Point
Melbury	Sk	19.11.1867	Exmouth
Memory	S	17.02.1877	Plymouth
Merc Enterprise		early 1970s	Eddystone
Merchant	Sl	11.07.1852	Plymouth
Mermaid	HMS/6	25.02.1693	Plymouth
Mermaid	HMS/5	05.01.1699	Plymouth
Merry Lass	Sl	29.03.1889	Dartmouth
Meteor	S	20.12.1873	Plymouth
M.I	HMS/Sm	12.11.1825	Off Start Point
Minesweeper			
No 382	HMS	07.05.1945	Off Berry Head
Minnie	S	01.12.1882	Berry Head
Mischief	Sc	22.11.1865	Plymouth
Miura	Sl	02.01.1867	Plymouth
Mizpah	S	04.02.1899	Plymouth
ML. 160	HMS	06.05.1942	Brixham
Monarch	Kt	22.02.1917	Eddystone
Monda	Brn	10.01.1866	Torbay
Moon	S	20.02.1817	Exmouth
Moor	HMS/4	07.03.1716	Plymouth
Morning Star	Kt	14.10.1910	Dartmouth
Moulin	Frs	07.08.1862	Off Start Point
Myra	S	08.09.1866	Plymouth
Mystery	S	09.03.1891	Plymouth
Nahant	S	18.03.1846	Berry Head
Nancy	S	22.01.1861	Start Bay
Naphtalie	Sc	22.11.1886	Eddystone
Native	Sc	00.00.1841	Torquay
Nebraska	Sk	01.02.1895	Plymouth
Neches	SS	15.05.1918	Off Start Point
Nellie Bywater	Mfv	28.12.1951	Bolt Tail

182

Nelly	Br	30.11.1804	Berry Head	Primrose	S/Aux	27.07.1923	Exmouth
Nelly	Sk	27.07.1852	Bolt Head	Princess Beatrice	S	10.01.1866	Torbay
Nepaul	SS	10.12.1890	Plymouth	Princess Mary	S	19.01.1817	Plymouth
Neptune	S	31.01.1881	Salcombe	Princess of Thule	Sc	05.11.1916	Dartmouth
Nera	S	00.12.1885	Eddystone	Prinses			
Newholm	SS	08.09.1917	Start Point	Whilhelmina	Mv	05.11.1972	Teignmouth
Nimble	HMS	20.02.1847	Off Berry Head	Prius Senior	S	27.02.1878	Off Start Point
Nimble	Kt	06.01.1888	Off Start Point	Prometheus	Sc	29.11.1853	Seaton
Nora Roas	Sc	10.05.1883	Plymouth	Providence	S	16.12.1785	Plymouth
Norbiton	SS	13.08.1887	Off Start Point	Providence	S	13.01.1786	Plymouth
Nordstern	SS	13.01.1888	Off Start Point	Providence	S	21.12.1798	Plymouth
Nordzee		15.01.1979	Jennycliff Bay	Providence	Tr	19.11.1808	Bolt Head
Norman	Sc	17.10.1843	Plymouth	Providence	S	18.10.1812	Plymouth
Northwind	Mv	22.12.1864	Torbay	Providence	S	12.12.1814	Plymouth
Nosted V	SS	02.11.1917	Prawle	Providence	S	10.01.1828	Plymouth
Notre Dame de				Providence	S	10.01.1866	Torbay
Bogoyne	S	20.11.1763	Nr Dartmouth	Pursue	Kt	28.04.1917	Eddystone
Nymph	S	10.03.1891	Start Point Point	Pyrame	S	10.01.1866	Torbay
Ocean	Sl	02.02.1853	Plymouth	Queen Victoria	SS	05.01.1861	Plymouth
Ocean Queen	Br	26.12.1852	Plymouth	Quiver	S	10.03.1891	Torbay
Ocean's Pride	Kt	08.06.1917	Off Start Point	Ramillies	HMS/2	15.02.1760	Bolt Head
Oceanus	Bq	17.09.1854	Off Start Point	Randolph	Bq	01.10.1869	Eddystone
Olive Branch	Sk	17.01.1856	Start Point Point	Ranger	S	29.04.1865	Off Dawlish
Onward	Kt	08.06.1917	Off Start Point	Rebecca	Sl	00.00.1836	Torquay
Orb	S	26.09.1851	Bolt Tail	Record Reign	Aux/Kt	08.02.1935	Sidmouth
Orderly	S	25.09.1861	Dartmouth	Recovery	Sc	08.09.1868	Beer Head
Oregon	Bq	18.12.1890	Off Bolt Head	Red Cross Knight	Kt	18.01.1881	Torbay
Orion	Brn	19.12.1887	Plymouth	Redness	S	18.10.1812	Plymouth
Orlock Head	SS	11.03.1940	Off Start Point	Reformation	Kt	26.03.1883	Off Start Point
Ottowa	Sc	26.12.1912	Plymouth	Resolution	S	13.12.1806	Salcombe
Owner's Delight	S	00.01.1817	Dartmouth	Retrencia	Br	23.11.1824	Plymouth
Pallas	HMS/5	04.07.1810	Plymouth	Reward	S	12.04.1801	Torbay
Palmyra	Sc	08.01.1867	Plymouth	R.H. Jones	Bq	14.10.1877	Plymouth
Patria	Bq	22.03.1886	Salcombe	Ricardo	Br	26.12.1869	Salcombe
Patriot	S	00.00.1895	Plymouth	Richard	S	14.10.1877	Teignmouth
Pauline	Brn	31.10.1817	Salcombe	Rion	Kt	01.12.1917	Off Start Point
Paulsgrove	S	16.11.1637	Plymouth	River Lagen	SS	08.01.1924	Torbay
Paulus Heinkes	Sc	00.06.1880	Eddystone	Riversdale	SS	18.12.1917	Off Prawle
Peronne	SS	01.09.1917	Torbay	Robert	Kt	07.12.1904	Off Start Point
Persian Monarch	SS	24.03.1888	Slapton Sands	Robin John	Mfv	06.06.1972	Off Eddystone
Persier	SS	11.02.1945	Bigbury Bay	Rochefort	SS	08.04.1910	Plymouth
Petrinick	S	23.11.1824	Plymouth	Roelfuia	S	19.12.1850	Berry Head
Picton Castle	HMS	19.02.1917	Dartmouth	Rofe	Br	27.12.1798	Bigbury Bay
Pierre des Celiers	HMS	13.08.1942	Salcombe	Rosa	S	18.06.1887	Dartmouth
Pilot	Br	03.04.1892	Plymouth	Rose	S	30.11.1798	Bigbury Bay
Pinedene	SS	17.01.1901	Prawle Point	Rosamond	S	02.01.1786	Plymouth
Pioneer	Kt	21.12.1877	Torbay	Rothesay	SS	14.10.1877	Plymouth
Pioneer	SS/Tg	24.08.1889	Teignmouth	Rotorua	SS	22.03.1917	Off Start Point
Plover	S	21.01.1868	Off Start Point	Rover	Tr	12.12.1804	Yealm Point
Plympton	S	12.01.1828	Plymouth	Ruperra	SS	27.01.1881	Bolt Head
Polly	S	29.11.1890	Plymouth	Sabina	Kt	30.11.1868	Torbay
Postilion	S	00.00.1732	Start Bay	Salem	Kt	10.01.1866	Torbay
Premier	Kt	27.11.1917	Off Start Point	Sally	Br	00.07.1822	Exmouth
Pride	Sc	07.03.1882	Plymouth	Sally	S	08.02.1785	Plymouth

Name	Type	Date	Location	Name	Type	Date	Location
Sally	S	21.10.1850	Eddystone	St Domingo	S	10.01.1748	Bigbury Bay
Salvage Craft		04.12.1943	Start Bay	Steadfast		05.11.1963	Torbay
Samson	Sc	28.02.1868	Off Start Point	Star de Zee	SS	12.10.1942	Off Berry Head
Sandsend	SS	00.04.1891	Start Point	St Leonards	Tr	17.09.1883	Off Start Point
San Pedro Mayor	S	28.10.1588	Bolt Head	St Louis	Sc	12.12.1886	Saunton Sands
Sarah	S	11.03.1758	Plymouth	St Patrick	SS	26.11.1912	Off Start Point
Sarah	Sc	15.10.1877	Sidmouth	St Pierre	Brn	09.12.1897	Plymouth
Satanicle		30.12.1935	Lyme Bay	Stryn	SS	10.06.1918	Off Berry Head
Saudadoes	HMS/5	00.00.1712	Plymouth	Sultan	Sc	26.12.1852	Plymouth
Savage	HMS/6	00.02.1762	Torbay	Surprise	S	10.02.1872	Eddystone
Sceptre	Br	23.11.1824	Plymouth	Susie Patui	Kt	03.03.1891	Off Start Point
Scotia	S	23.11.1824	Plymouth	Swanston	Sc	08.03.1922	Plymouth
Scythian	S	10.01.1866	Torbay	Swift	Sl	28.03.1875	Torbay
Seagull	Sl	17.09.1798	Plymouth	Talavera	HMS/3	27.09.1840	Plymouth
Seahorse	HMS/6	26.12.1711	Dartmouth	Tamar	S	07.04.1798	Plymouth
Sebastian	SS	06.12.1929	Torbay	Tanrogan	Mv	00.01.1972	Torbay
Selim	Bq	01.12.1882	Off Start Point	Tarascon	MFV	22.03.1938	Steeple Cove
Selina	Tr	21.11.1808	Bigbury Bay	Tasmania	Sc	04.11.1918	Thurlestone
Sevilla	SS	25.04.1918	Off Teignmouth	Tavy	Kt	22.06.1902	Plymouth
Shamrock	SS	11.11.1851	Torquay	Tavy &			
Shannon	HMS	21.08.1887	Plymouth	Tees Packet	Sc	09.09.1886	Off Start Point
Shepherdess	S	00.12.1849	Plymouth	TB No 3	HMS	21.10.1920	Off Plymouth
Silver Lining	Kt	03.12.1909	Dawlish	Teaser	S	06.03.1863	Beer
Sincerity	S	17.01.1797	Plymouth	Teaser	Sc	08.01.1867	Plymouth
Sir George				Tehwija	Sc	10.10.1907	Exmouth
Seymour	S	11.12.1876	Off Start Point	Teesdale	SS	15.06.1917	Salcombe
Sky	S	10.01.1866	Torbay	Telegram	S	10.01.1866	Torbay
Sloman	Frs	09.12.1861	Torbay	Telegraph	HMS/5	18.01.1817	Plymouth
Sly Boots	Kt	04.01.1881	Off Start Point	Tellus	S	10.08.1887	Eddystone
Sophia	S	13.02.1852		Temperance	S	20.12.1873	Plymouth
Sophia	S	05.02.1858	Plymouth	Ternefjell	SS	24.05.1953	Off Start Point
Sophia Jane	Br	24.06.1876	Off Start Point	Test	Kt	14.03.1918	Eddystone
Soudan	SS	27.06.1887	Salcombe	Test	Aux/S	15.08.1932	Dartmouth
Southampton	S	08.02.1757	Dartmouth	Theador	Br	14.02.1874	Bolt Head
South Coaster	SS	13.12.1943	Exmouth	The Galliot	S	16.01.1753	Bigbury Bay
Sparkling Wine	Kt	04.05.1900	Off Start Point	Thekla	Bq	08.05.1981	Off Prawle Point
Speculator	Br	12.01.1828	Plymouth	The Maria	S	20.06.1774	Plymouth
Speedwell	S	03.01.1786	Plymouth	Theadora & Sarah	Bq	17.12.1851	Eddystone
Speedwell	Sc	30.12.1860	Plymouth	Thetis	S	00.00.1838	Plymouth
Speedy	Sc	10.07.1864	Plymouth	Thetis	Sc	28.10.1880	Plymouth
Spennymoor	SS	28.05.1915	Off Start Point	Thistle	Kt	11.06.1913	Plymouth
Spirit of the				Thomas & Mary	Sc	10.01.1866	Torbay
Ocean	Bq	23.03.1866	Prawle Point	Thomas & Nancy	Sc	22.02.1853	Eddystone
Staghound	HMS	27.03.1942	Torquay	Thornborough	Pr	02.11.1806	Exmouth
St Antonio Boa				Thought	Sl	18.02.1859	Plymouth
Viagen	S	03.01.1786	Plymouth	Three Brothers	S	20.07.1879	Saunton Sands
St Anthony	S	06.02.1757	Plymouth	Three Crowns	S	28.12.1755	Bigbury Bay
St Domingo	S	10.01.1748	Bigbury Bay	Tiger	Tr	27.02.1745	Berry Head
Star	Br	23.11.1824	Plymouth	Torbay Lass	Kt	08.06.1917	Off Start Point
Star	S	18.12.1847	Salcombe	Totness Castle	SS	09.11.1967	Bigbury Bay
Star	Kt	05.01.1869	Teignmouth	Touquet	SS	11.04.1934	Prawle Point
Stately	Bq	10.01.1866	Torbay	Trito	SS	00.02.1934	Start Bay
Stephen Knight	S	15.01.1828	Plymouth	Tweegesultas	S	30.12.1785	Plymouth
St Catherine	S	05.08.1753	Salcombe	Two Brothers	Sl	12.01.1784	Berry Head

184

Two Brothers	S	15.08.1852	Off Start
Two Brothers	Sl	17.06.1869	Dartmouth
Two Sisters	S	13.04.1880	Teignmouth
UC-51		17.11.1917	Start Bay
UC-65		03.11.1917	Off Dartmouth
Umberleigh	SS	20.09.1930	Plymouth
Uncle Jack	Kt	25.11.1868	Plymouth
Unicorn	SS	08.04.1923	Off Plymouth
Union	S	26.01.1828	Off Plymouth
Unity	Br	00.12.1830	Exmouth
Unique	Kt	21.01.1879	Exmouth
Untiring	HMS/Sm	25.07.1957	Off Start Point
Useful	Br	10.01.1866	Torbay
Utility	Sc	31.01.1879	Off Prawle Point
Valentin	Brn	12.02.1883	Plymouth
Vectis	SS	15.02.1912	Plymouth
Veghstroon		21.11.1914	Plymouth
Venerable	HMS/3	24.11.1804	Torbay
Vengeance	HMS/6	00.10.1766	Plymouth
Venus	S	09.03.1891	Plymouth
Veronica	S	15.05.1890	Plymouth
Victorie	S	00.07.1838	Dartmouth
Victorian	SS	18.11.1869	Plymouth
Vigilant	HMS	05.12.1819	Nr Torbay
Villa Nova	Brn	27.12.1879	Bigbury Bay
Vine	S	18.08.1898	Plymouth
Vixen	Kt	18.01.1912	Exmouth
Volere	Bq	06.03.1881	Salcombe
Wallace	S	06.11.1873	Torquay
Wanderer	Sc	27.12.1852	Bolt Head
Warrior	Brn	07.01.1882	Teignmouth
Warsaw	SS	20.12.1917	Off Start Point
Waterloo	S	12.02.1852	Off Start Point
Washington	S	23.10.1779	Plymouth
Wave	S	04.02.1871	Dartmouth
Wave	Sc	07.08.1877	Sidmouth
Welcome	Sl	24.03.1852	Exmouth
Wellington	Bq	28.01.1885	Plymouth
Wesley	S	21.01.1873	Plymouth
Westergate	SS	21.04.1918	Off Start Point
Western Lass	Sc	27.10.1916	Start Point
Western Star	Sc	01.01.1873	Plymouth
Westmoorland	Bq	14.07.1871	Bolt Tail
W.H. Dwyer	SS	26.08.1917	Off Berry Head
White Horse	S	20.08.1870	Torbay
Widdecombe	S	26.11.1810	Exmouth
Widgeon	SS	11.07.1871	Eddystone
Wierkelyk	S	26.01.1781	Plymouth
Wild Rose	Bq	10.01.1866	Torbay
William & Ann	S	13.12.1866	Torbay
William & Emma		27.10.1916	Salcombe
William & Jane	S	22.12.1749	Berry Head
Wolf	S	06.11.1691	Plymouth
Wonder	Barge	09.03.1875	Off Teignmouth

Yeves No 2	Sc	14.10.1877	Bigbury Bay
Young William	Br	29.09.1812	Torbay
Yvonne	Bqn	03.10.1920	Plymouth
Zeelust	S	02.01.1786	Plymouth
Zephyr	SS	10.11.1963	Start Point
Zouaz	Br	10.01.1866	Torbay

Unidentified Wrecks

Name	Date	Type	Location
Unidentified	26.12.1675	A Dutchman, with salt	Plymouth
Unidentified		A Hull ship, with wine	Plymouth
Unidentified		A Dover-Dunkirk ship	Plymouth
Unidentified	26.09.1744	A collier ashore	Plymouth
Unidentified	Early Jan 1753	A galliot, with wine	Bigbury Bay
Unidentified	06.02.1757	French privateer	Bigbury Bay
Unidentified	06.02.1857	Vessel seen to founder	Bigbury Bay
Unidentified	11.09.1767	On rocks in Cattewater, lost	Plymouth
Unidentified	12.03.1780	Many wrecks ashore	Plymouth
Unidentified	26.01.1781	Vessel London to Liverpool	Start Point
Unidentified	13.01.1876	Swedish vessel and another ashore	Plymouth
Unidentified	00.00.1787	Five ships ashore today	Plymouth
Unidentified	31.10.1789	Danish sloop o'war lost	Dartmouth
Unidentified	04.11.1800	Smuggling lugger sunk	Plymouth
Unidentified	25.12.1803	Brig, wrecked ashore	Plymouth
Unidentified	10.02.1804	Sloop carrying butter	Plymouth
Unidentified	19.01.1804	Large brig found wrecked	Wembury
Unidentified	20.01.1804	Two fishing sloops lost	Plymouth
Unidentified	23.10.1808	French privateer went down	Bigbury Bay
Unidentified	01.12.1813	A hoy has struck Shag Rock	Plymouth
Unidentified	17.01.1851	Wreck at Sidmouth	Sidmouth
Unidentified	29.11.1865	Various wrecks in Sound	Plymouth
Unidentified	12.12.1865	Wreck on	Plymouth

Name	Rig	Date	Location
Gleaner	S	17.01.1851	Ilfracombe
Glendorgal	S	10.12.1881	Ilfracombe
Goliath	Mv	16.03.1969	Hartland
Goonlaze	Sc	05.02.1901	Peppercombe
Gratitude	SS	03.07.1882	Barnstaple
Green Ranger	Mv	17.11.1962	Hartland
Gregvnog	SS	18.04.1918	Hartland
Grimsby	SS	13.08.1897	Hartland
Hannah	Sk	26.10.1859	Morte Bay
Hanna Jensen	Sc	15.11.1923	Clovelly
Henrietta	S	02.10.1880	Ilfracombe
Henry Patterson	Brn	20.10.1854	Barnstaple
Heroine	Sc	24.03.1878	Barnstaple
H.F. Bolt	Kt	07.11.1900	Clovelly
Hoche	SS	01.07.1882	Hartland Point
Hope	Sc	24.11.1880	Braunton
Huddersfield	SS	27.01.1908	Clovelly
I'll Try	S	26.10.1859	Morte Bay
Industry	Kt	30.06.1890	Braunton
Iris	Sc	17.10.1859	Hartland
Isabella	Brn	10.02.1852	Hartland
Isabella	S	16.12.1886	Lynmouth
Islander	Sc	19.03.1891	Bull Point
Itchen	SS	28.08.1888	Hartland
Jane & Mary	Sc	27.12.1880	Braunton
Jim	Sk	28.10.1870	Clovelly
Johanna	Mv	31.12.1982	Hartland
Johannah & Mary	S	28.11.1735	Barnstaple
John & Henry	Sc	12.10.1870	Morte Point
John & Lilly	S	15.01.1843	Appledore
Lanisley	Sc	02.10.1895	Ilfracombe
Larchwood	SS	14.01.1916	Off Bull Point
Little Jane	Kt	31.10.1940	Clovelly
Little Test	Sc	16.01.1843	Saunton
Lizzie Morton	Sc	18.03.1876	Ilfracombe
Llanisley	Sc	02.10.1895	Off Hartland
Lochlibo	S	27.02.1859	Hartland
Louisa	S	01.01.1863	Braunton
Lymington	SS	02.02.1889	Ilfracombe
Lynx	SS	06.03.1883	Morte Bay
Maria	S	22.04.1892	Morte Point
Marianela	SS	00.00.1921	Off Ilfracombe
Marie Emilie	Kt	18.10.1886	Ilfracombe
Market Maid	Sk	04.07.1854	Baggy Point
Marlborough	Bq	26.10.1858	Ilfracombe
Marquis	S	03.01.1854	Appledore
Marquis of Lorne	Sc	30.07.1883	Rockham Bay
Mars	Sk	03.09.1860	Hartland
Marsouin	S	06.02.1818	Hartland
Martha	S	02.03.1743	Barnstaple
Mary	S	14.12.1827	Croyde Bay
Mary	S	09.03.1828	Croyde Bay
Mary	Sk	05.01.1867	Bideford
Mary Ann	S	24.11.1833	Appledore
Mary Ann	S	29.10.1878	Ilfracombe
Matthew Thompson	Sc	26.10.1859	Bull Point
Moliere	SS	27.05.1918	Hartland
Monte Moro	Sc	04.08.1876	Ilfracombe
Mountpark	SS	21.08.1917	Off Bull Point
Mousse Le Moyec	SS	06.12.1940	Hartland
Muse	Brn	20.02.1877	Barnstaple
Nancy	Sc	18.03.1869	Hartland
Nepenthe	Bq	16.11.1863	Hartland
Nettleton	SS	11.02.1916	Hartland
Newton	SS	21.03.1886	Hartland
Newton	SS	07.01.1916	Barnstaple
Nikita	Sc	00.09.1894	Ilfracombe
Nora	S	06.10.1907	Bull Point
Nostra Seignora de Bon Successo	S	02.10.1780	Ilfracombe
Nouvelle Societe	Sk	27.12.1878	Baggy Point
Odin	Br	21.10.1878	Morte Point
Odone	Bq	12.09.1869	Clovelly
Ouse	SS	03.03.1910	Hartland
Padarn	Brn	28.01.1869	Mothecombe
Paul	Sc	24.04.1852	Appledore
Paz	SS	25.05.1912	Bull Point
Pelton	SS	26.03.1881	Nr Bull Point
Pen-y-Mor		25.08.1982	N. Devon
Penthesilea	Frs	19.01.1890	Baggy Point
Perri	Sc	00.02.1863	Morte Point
Perrosian	Sc	05.01.1923	Clovelly
Persistent	SS	03.06.1919	Off Lynmouth
Peter & Sarah	S	01.11.1859	Ilfracombe
Petrel	Sk	02.10.1895	Clovelly
Phyllis	SS	17.05.1918	Hartland
Polacco	Br	04.09.1850	Morte Bay
Pollux	Frs	09.11.1851	Clovelly
Prince Albert	S	20.11.1850	Appledore
Queen	S	31.03.1866	Hartland
Queenswood	SS	16.02.1917	Clovelly
Queen Victoria	Sc	22.08.1868	Clovelly
Ranee	SS	07.10.1881	Appledore
Reliance	Sc	12.09.1869	Appledore
Rewa	SS	04.01.1918	Hartland
Richard & Elizabeth	Sk	26.10.1859	Hartland
Rollon	SS	27.10.1916	Hartland
Rose	Sc	26.10.1859	Morte Bay
Rose	Kt	07.12.1891	Clovelly
Rose-in-June	Mfv	16.03.1992	Hartland
Rossekop II	Mfv	04.11.1972	Bideford
St. Louis	Sc	12.12.1886	Saunton Sands
Salisbury	S	00.03.1749	Appledore
Saltash	Sc	23.08.1870	Hartland
Saltburn	HMS	07.12.1946	Hartland
Sandfly	HMS	07.10.1920	Westward Ho!

Name	Type	Date	Location		Name	Type	Date	Location
Sandwich	S	11.11.1785	Barnstaple Bay		Westward	S	09.01.1898	Hartland
Sarah	Sc	24.03.1857	Hartland		William	Sk	05.01.1850	Ilfracombe
Sarah King	S	25.01.1873	Morte Point		William	Sc	06.02.1883	Off Bull Point
Sea Bird	S	14.03.1868	Ilfracombe		William & Jane	Sk	15.02.1850	Ilfracombe
Secres	Bq	18.01.1854	Appledore		William & Mary	S	15.10.1886	Clovelly
Selina Mary	Kt	16.10.1916	Ilfracombe		Wisbech	SS	14.08.1917	Hartland
Silurian	SS	02.09.1880	Hartland		Woodlands	S	15.10.1886	Clovelly
Sir R.R. Vyvian	S	08.03.1845	Hartland		Woodlark	Mv	13.12.1967	Morte Point
Sir T.D. Acland	Sc	22.07.1862	Bull Point		Woolton	S	15.02.1785	Barnstaple Bay
Sivdar		10.09.1987	N. Devon		Zephyr	SS	29.09.1889	Off Bull Point
Sjofna	SS	23.11.1944	Hartland		Zuma	Br	20.12.1871	Clovelly
Stan Woolaway	Mv	13.03.1967	Off Bull Point					
Star of Ghent	S	12.04.1890	Off Morte Point		**UNIDENTIFIED WRECKS**			
Star of Peace	Sc	18.02.1887	Hartland		Name	Date	Type	Location
St Clair	Sc	17.02.1915	Mothecombe		Unidentified	10.04.1823	A wreck	Bideford Bay
St Georges	SS	17.07.1918	Hartland		Unidentified	10.02.1852	Wreck	Hartland
St John Baptista	S	00.00.1795	Mothecombe		Unidentified	26.10.1859	Cutter lost	Appledore
St Joseph	Br	10.09.1882	Hartland		Unidentified	23.01.1860	American ship,	Hartland
Strathisla	Kt	23.09.1884	Bideford				bottom up	
Sunflower	Kt	06.02.1910	Woodcombe					
Sunlight	Sc	16.11.1916	Off Bull Point		**LUNDY**			
Superior	Sc	26.10.1886	Barnstaple Bay		Name	Type	Date	Location
Supreme Largesse	Br	16.12.1852	Bideford		Abbotsford	Bq	00.04.1836	Lundy
Surprise	Sc	04.10.1917	Bideford		Ackworth	SS	22.04.1892	Lundy
Susanna	S	02.12.1763	Nr Bideford		Alarm	Sk	12.08.1877	Off Lundy
Svint	SS	11.07.1941	Hartland		Albion	S	20.03.1869	Lundy
Talisman	SS	29.06.1906	Morte Point		Alice	Sc	20.01.1917	Off Lundy
Tamar	Sk	04.12.1859	Hartland		Alphonse	Bq	07.10.1867	Lundy
Temptress	SS		Off Bull Point		Amstelstroom	Mv	18.07.1948	Lundy
T.G.V.	Br	30.07.1889	Off Bull Point		Ann	Brn	02.02.1848	Lundy
Thames	Sc	07.10.1863	Sharpness Point		Archelaus	S	07.11.1849	Lundy
Thetes	Sk	21.08.1889	Ilfracombe		Ariel	S	30.04.1853	Lundy
Thistle	Brn	26.10.1859	Morte Bay		Ashdale	SS	10.09.1890	Off Lundy
Thistlemoor	SS	03.12.1909	Hartland		Asterias	Bq	21.05.1870	Off Lundy
Tinto	Bq	08.12.1872	Barnstaple Bay		Atlas	Mv	10.10.1942	Lundy
T.M.P.	MFV	12.02.1917	Ilfracombe		Augoustis	S	30.11.1912	Off Lundy
Tonton Pierre	S	25.04.1853	Bideford		Auricula	SS	01.05.1908	Lundy
Torridge	Sc	13.09.1853	Appledore		Avon	Bq	26.02.1855	Lundy
Touch & Go	S	15.11.1953	Ilfracombe		Ballydoon	SS	01.11.1897	Lundy
Tower	S	14.10.1865	Ilfracombe		Balvenie	SS	24.07.1916	Off Lundy
Trial	Brn	02.01.1873	Bideford		Bath City	SS	24.02.1900	Off Lundy
Try On	S	15.10.1886	Clovelly		Belinda	Br	06.04.1869	Off Lundy
Unity	SS	00.05.1922	Bideford Bay		Ben M'Cree	S	03.11.1862	Off Lundy
Uppingham	SS	23.12.1890	Hartland		Bosweden	Sc	15.10.1886	Off Lundy
Uzzia	SS	26.03.1882	Bull Point		Brenda	Bq	14.02.1871	Lundy
Venus	Brn	27.09.1890	Ilfracombe		Brothers	S	27.11.1866	Off Lundy
Victory	Bq	02.01.1864	Ilfracombe		Burnswark	Bq	13.12.1882	Lundy
Ville de Bayonne	SS	16.02.1917	Clovelly		Cambronne	SS	26.11.1882	Off Lundy
Volant	Sc	28.03.1918	Braunton Sands		Canterbury Bell	SS	05.01.1922	Off Lundy
Warden	Bq	08.10.1857	Braunton Sands		Caroline	Sm	18.02.1868	Lundy
War Tabard	SS	07.12.1929	Off Hartland		Charles	Sc	13.03.1858	Lundy
Waterwitch	SS	06.03.1850	Appledore		Chesapeake	Sc	28.06.1862	Off Lundy
Weazle	HMS/5	12.01.1799	Baggy Point		Chidwall	SS	01.04.1915	Off Lundy
Welbury	SS	24.04.1900	Hartland		Choice	Sc	20.04.1856	Off Lundy

Name	Type	Date	Location
City of Exeter	SS	11.03.1887	Off Lundy
Colombo	Bq	27.10.1867	Lundy
Cottingham	SS	26.12.1915	Off Lundy
Courage	SS	30.11.1917	Lundy
Dyfed	S	22.01.1896	Lundy
Earl of Jersey	SS/Tg	28.11.1898	Off Lundy
East Anglian	SS	14.01.1868	Lundy
Eclipse	S	05.04.1865	Lundy
Edward Arthur	Sc	02.01.1916	Lundy
Electric	Tg	08.05.1888	Lundy
Eliza	Br	14.01.1852	Lundy
Eliza	Sk	30.12.1869	Off Lundy
Eliza	S	23.03.1873	Off Lundy
Eliza Jones	Sc	16.12.1889	Lundy
Elsie	SS	30.01.1888	Lundy
Escort	Kt	21.04.1899	Off Lundy
Estrella de Mar	Sc	00.00.1811	Lundy
Ethel	SS	03.02.1877	Off Lundy
Fame	S	07.02.1822	Lundy
Fanny	Sk	05.10.1874	Lundy
Fiona	Kt	06.05.1904	Lundy
Francis Anne	Bqn	21.03.1829	Lundy
Frederick	Sk	04.11.1857	Lundy
Gazelle	SS	30.11.1917	Lundy
Gertrude	Br	07.05.1872	Lundy
Gurly	SS	26.11.1917	Off Lundy
Hannah More	Frs	18.03.1866	Lundy
Hector	SS	28.03.1865	Lundy
Hermina	Br	30.01.1869	Off Lundy
Heroine	Bqn	13.12.1882	Lundy
Highgate	SS	19.02.1890	Off Lundy
Hornet	SS	27.01.1884	Off Lundy
Infanta	S	19.05.1897	Lundy
Inversnaid	Frs	16.10.1886	Lundy
I.O.	Sc	23.04.1827	Lundy
Iona	SS	02.01.1864	Off Lundy
Ismyr	Brn	01.12.1893	Lundy
James	Sc	19.03.1862	Off Lundy
Janet	S	17.12.1851	Off Lundy
Jean & Robert	Sc	15.01.1876	Lundy
Jenny	S	20.02.1797	Lundy
Joseph F. Votsam	S	14.05.1855	Lundy
Julia	Sc	01.11.1868	Off Lundy
Kaaksburg	Mv	06.11.1980	Lundy
Knatten	SS	20.08.1917	Off Lundy
Labarrouere	SS	25.11.1897	Off Lundy
Lamb (?)	Sc	20.01.1820	Lundy
Leda	Sc	28.02.1872	Off Lundy
Leonard Pearce	SS	11.01.1940	Off Lundy
Lewis Charles	Sc	09.02.1861	Lundy
Loire	SS	12.08.1855	Lundy
London II	SS	22.03.1941	Off Lundy
Madby Ann	SS	17.06.1928	Off Lundy
Margaret	Br	22.04.1869	Off Lundy
Marie	S	19.09.1757	Lundy
Mariner	Sk	19.03.1842	Lundy
Mary	Brn	16.12.1870	Lundy
Mary Ann	S	27.04.1873	Off Lundy
Mary Ann	Bqn	02.02.1842	Off Lundy
Mary Ann	Brn	13.08.1876	Off Lundy
Matilda	SS	04.04.1864	Off Lundy
Millicent	Kt	01.04.1897	Off Lundy
Montagu	HMS/B	29.05.1906	Lundy
Morrison	Brn	00.00.1823	Off Lundy
Nancy & Betty	S	00.02.1793	Off Lundy
Nellie	Mv	13.07.1937	Off Lundy
Newhouse	S	05.09.1872	Lundy
New Prosperous	S	14.02.1888	Lundy
Northfield	SS	03.03.1918	Lundy
Orange Branch	Sc	23.07.1852	Lundy
Pallion	SS	05.11.1873	Off Lundy
Panaja Eleusa	S	22.10.1851	Off Lundy
Peace	Sk	02.11.1859	Lundy
Peer of the Realm	SS	12.02.1885	Lundy
Plover	SS	11.05.1918	Off Lundy
Plymouth	Sc	29.08.1859	Off Lundy
Providence	Sk	07.06.1874	Off Lundy
Radnor	SS	09.05.1888	Lundy
Ralph Creyke	SS	20.02.1879	Off Lundy
Rapid	S	21.08.1835	Lundy
Rosario	Brn	04.03.1887	Off Lundy
Rover	Sl	17.11.1816	Lundy
Rover	Barge	31.08.1898	Lundy
Ruby	S	24.04.1901	Off Lundy
Salado	SS	21.03.1897	Lundy
Sambo	SS	26.03.1916	Lundy
South Australian	SS	14.02.1889	Off Lundy
Sovereign	S	19.02.1890	Off Lundy
Speculation	c	14.02.1890	Nr Lundy
Swift	Sc	08.10.1868	Off Lundy
Swift	S	17.10.1877	Off Lundy
Sylphiden	Bq	12.02.1848	Lundy
Tasfield	SS	22.11.1891	Off Lundy
Taxiarchis	SS	28.03.1931	Lundy
Teneriefa	Mv	26.02.1940	Off Lundy
Thomas Crisp	Br	18.01.1850	Lundy
Trident	Sk	15.04.1858	Lundy
Tunisee	SS	19.02.1892	Lundy
Unity	Sl	01.05.1819	Off Lundy
Unity	Sk	12.01.1833	Off Lundy
Valentine	Brn	23.05.1861	Lundy
Wesleyana	Sc	18.01.1856	Lundy
Wizard	Sc	13.01.1852	Lundy
Wye	S	00.12.1796	Lundy

General Index